With lots of love + prayers as you celebrate your First Communion.

Lisa + Stephen

Easter 2011

Explore the Bible

Religious and Moral Education Press
A division of SCM-Canterbury Press Ltd
A wholly owned subsidiary of Hymns Ancient & Modern Ltd
St Mary's Works, St Mary's Plain
Norwich, Norfolk NR3 3BH

Original Italian Edition *Navigare nella Bibbia*
Copyright © 2001 Claudiana editrice
Copyright © Editrice ELLEDICE 2001

English translation copyright © 2002 Heather Savini

All rights reserved. No part of this publication may be reproduced, stored in a retrieval system, or transmitted, in any form or by any means, electronic, electrostatic, magnetic tape, mechanical, photocopying, recording or otherwise, without permission in writing from the publishers.

This edition first published 2002

ISBN 1-85175-276-5

Italian edition created and edited by **Silvana Colombu, Silvia Gastaldi, Manuel Kromer, Claire Musatti**

Illustrated by **Silvia Gastaldi, Massimiliano Cambellotti, Elisa Corsani**

Entries contributed by **Giovanni Carrari, Fulvio Ferrario, Maria Giradet, Liddia Maggi, Claire Musatti, Eric Noffke, Thomas Soggiri**

Consultants: **Eugenio Bernardini, Yann Redalie, J. Alberto Soggin**

The original Italian edition was produced in collaboration with Servizio Istruzione ed Educazione della Federazione delle Chiese evangeliche in Italia.

Scriptures in this edition quoted from the *Good News Bible* published by The Bible Societies/HarperCollins Publishers Ltd UK © American Bible Society, 1966, 1971, 1976, 1992.

Printed in Italy by Arti Grafiche, Pomezia for SCM-Canterbury Press Ltd, Norwich.

Explore the Bible

A Study Guidebook

Edited by Silvana Colombu, Silvia Gastaldi, Manuel Kromer and Claire Musatti

English translation by Heather Savini

RMEP

RELIGIOUS AND MORAL EDUCATION PRESS

CONTENTS

Setting Off: how to use this book	6
The Red Route	8
Themes to Explore	10
When: a Bible time-line	12
Where: the ancient world and Palestine at the time of Jesus	14
Abraham	16
Acts of the Apostles	18
Amos	20
Assyria	22
Babel	24
Babylonia	26
Bible	28
Canaan	34
Church	36
Commandments	38
Covenant	40
Creation	42
Daniel	46
David	48
Desert	52
Diaspora	54
Disciples	56
Easter	58
Egypt	60
Elijah	62
Elisha	64
Exile	66
Exodus	68
Faith	70
God	72
Gospels	76
Holy Spirit	78
Idolatry	80
Isaac	82
Isaiah	84
Jacob	86
Jeremiah	88

Jerusalem	90
Jesus	92
Jesus' birth	96
Job	98
John the Baptist	100
Jonah	102
Joseph	104
Joshua	106
Josiah	108
Judah	110
Judges	112
Law and justice	114
Letters	116
Lot	118
Mary	120
Moses	122
Noah	126
Parables	128
Passion	130
Paul	134
Paul's journeys	136
Peace	138
Pentecost	140
Peter	142
Prayer	144
Prophecy	148
Psalms	150
Religious life	152
Resurrection appearances	156
Return and rebuilding	158
Revelation	160
Rome	162
Ruth	164
Sabbath	166
Samuel	170
Sarah	172
Saul	174
Sin, repentance and forgiveness	176
Solomon	178
Synagogue	180
Temple	182
Women in the Bible	184
Index	188

SETTING OFF: HOW TO USE THIS BOOK

What it is

This book presents lots of information about the Bible and the events, ideas and people it contains. At the same time, it aims to stimulate curiosity about the Bible. It is a reference book, but it is also more than that: it invites readers to explore and get to know the Bible without the need for other resources – except a copy of the Bible itself.

In addition

This is an interactive resource in which cross-referencing throughout enables readers to follow a 'red route' (see pages 8-9) which visits all the entries in a logical order.

What's more

Readers can explore themes that occur in different parts of the Bible by visiting the entries in the book suggested in the short thematic 'tours' on pages 10-11.

Finally

The coloured illustrations add richness to the text. The text speaks to the mind or intellect, but the illustrations will stimulate the imagination. The combination of these two elements will broaden the horizons of your journey of exploration.

Every new letter of the alphabet is large in size and brightly coloured. In the entries that follow, the letter reappears in a smaller form, on the coloured strip down the side of each left-hand page. It's difficult to lose your way in the course of your journey!

ABRAHAM
A man on the move

Abraham came from Ur and lived at Haran, surrounded by his father's tribe and his own family. One day Abraham heard a voice. God said to him: 'Leave your country, your relatives, and your father's home, and go to a land that I am going to show you. I will give you many descendants, and they will become a great nation. I will bless you ... And through you I will bless all the nations.' *(Genesis 12:1-3)*

The departure

A small caravan set out. Where were they going? They didn't know. What guarantee did they have that they should be going? None. God's words echoed in Abraham's mind: 'I will give you many descendants.' What a strange promise! Abraham and his wife Sarah were childless and no longer young. Yet, after the farewells and the goodbyes from rather puzzled friends, the journey towards Canaan had begun....

The arrival

The Promised Land was, in fact, inhabited. The Canaanites lived there. Still trusting God, Abraham crossed the length and breadth of the country, built altars to his God and pitched camp in a mountainous and arid area.

The colours of the strips down the side of left-hand pages indicate the general topic to which the entry relates:
Blue = people; purple = the biblical world; green = faith and religion; brown = history and background
These colours will help those exploring or researching by topic.

abc In addition to the main heading, every entry has a subheading that gets straight into the heart of the subject and aims to engage the feelings and interest of the reader.

The windows in each entry give background information or show you how to explore further.

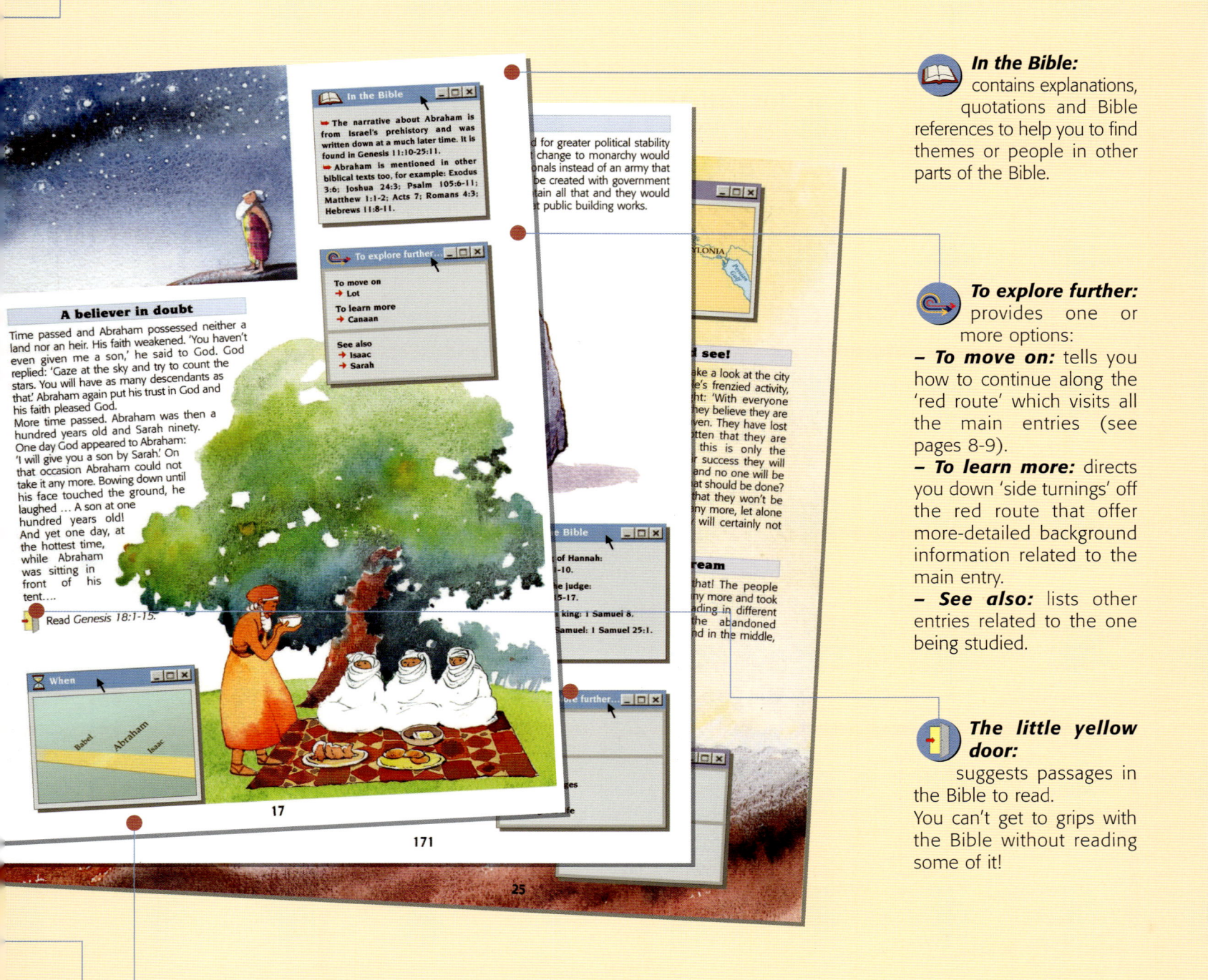

In the Bible:
contains explanations, quotations and Bible references to help you to find themes or people in other parts of the Bible.

To explore further:
provides one or more options:
– **To move on:** tells you how to continue along the 'red route' which visits all the main entries (see pages 8-9).
– **To learn more:** directs you down 'side turnings' off the red route that offer more-detailed background information related to the main entry.
– **See also:** lists other entries related to the one being studied.

The little yellow door:
suggests passages in the Bible to read.
You can't get to grips with the Bible without reading some of it!

Where and **When:** show relevant sections of the maps on pages 14-15 and the time-line on pages 12-13.

A believer in doubt
Time passed and Abraham possessed neither a land nor an heir. His faith weakened. 'You haven't even given me a son,' he said to God. God replied: 'Gaze at the sky and try to count the stars. You will have as many descendants as that.' Abraham again put his trust in God and his faith pleased God.
More time passed. Abraham was then a hundred years old and Sarah ninety. One day God appeared to Abraham: 'I will give you a son by Sarah.' On that occasion Abraham could not take it any more. Bowing down until his face touched the ground, he laughed … A son at one hundred years old! And yet one day, at the hottest time, while Abraham was sitting in front of his tent….

Read *Genesis 18:1-15*.

In the Bible
- The narrative about Abraham is from Israel's prehistory and was written down at a much later time. It is found in Genesis 11:10-25:11.
- Abraham is mentioned in other biblical texts too, for example: Exodus 3:6; Joshua 24:3; Psalm 105:6-11; Matthew 1:1-2; Acts 7; Romans 4:3; Hebrews 11:8-11.

To explore further…
To move on
→ Lot
To learn more
→ Canaan

See also
→ Isaac
→ Sarah

7

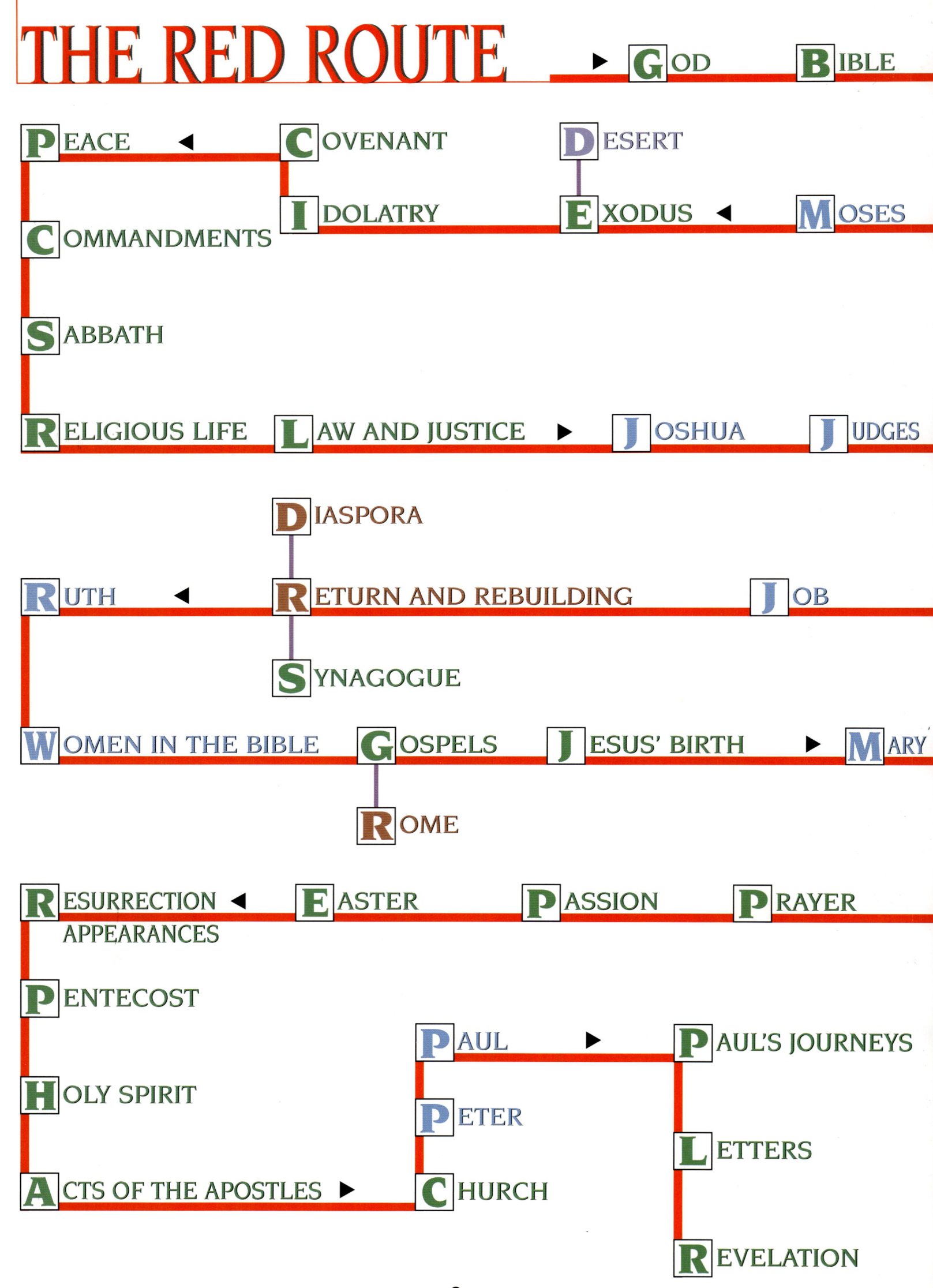

THE RED ROUTE

▶ **G**od **B**ible

Peace ◀ **C**ovenant **D**esert

Idolatry **E**xodus ◀ **M**oses

Commandments

Sabbath

Religious life **L**aw and justice ▶ **J**oshua **J**udges

Diaspora

Ruth ◀ **R**eturn and rebuilding **J**ob

Synagogue

Women in the bible **G**ospels **J**esus' birth ▶ **M**ary

Rome

Resurrection ◀ **E**aster **P**assion **P**rayer
appearances

Pentecost

Paul ▶ **P**aul's journeys

Holy spirit **P**eter

Letters

Acts of the apostles ▶ **C**hurch

Revelation

Red Route Map

CREATION — **C**ANAAN

EGYPT — **N**OAH ▶ **B**ABEL — **A**BRAHAM

JOSEPH ◀ **J**ACOB — **I**SAAC — **S**ARAH — **L**OT

SAUL ▶ **D**AVID — **J**ERUSALEM

SAMUEL — **A**SSYRIA

PROPHECY — **S**OLOMON — **T**EMPLE ▶ **A**MOS

JUDAH — **E**LIJAH — **E**LISHA — **I**SAIAH

PSALMS

JONAH — **D**ANIEL ◀ **E**XILE — **J**EREMIAH — **J**OSIAH

BABYLONIA

JOHN THE BAPTIST

JESUS ▶ **F**AITH — **S**IN, REPENTANCE AND FORGIVENESS

PARABLES ◀ **D**ISCIPLES

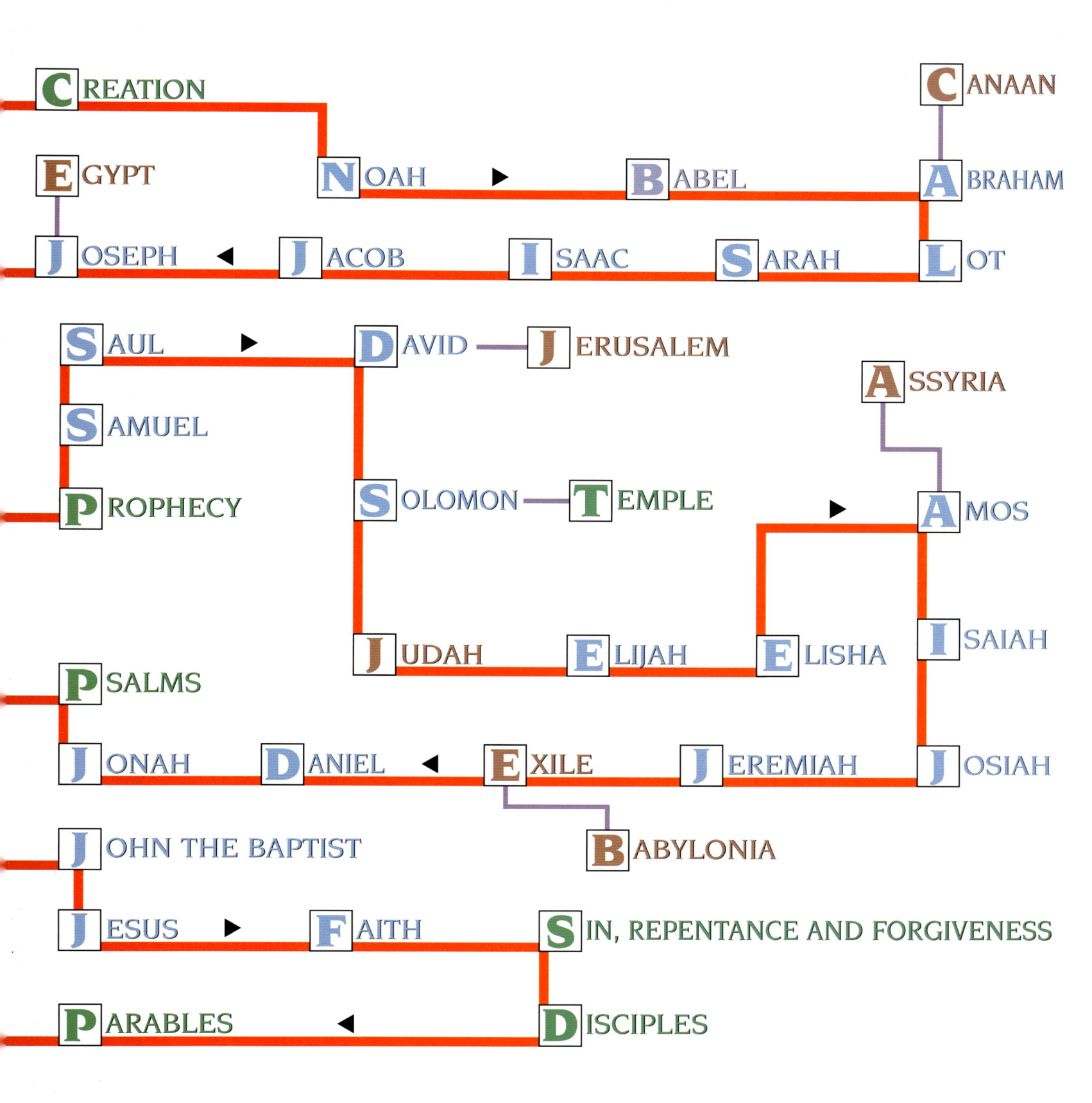

Using the Red Route

This book is a dictionary of entries in alphabetical order but it can be read as a story if you follow the red route shown here. To begin at the beginning of the story, start with the entry *God* on page 72 then use the *To explore further* window in each entry to continue your journey. In this window, the heading *To move on* will lead you along the main, red route. The heading *To learn more* directs you down the purple 'side roads' on the chart. If you decide to investigate a side road, the *To explore further* window there will show you how to move on to the next stop on the main, red route.

9

THEMES TO EXPLORE

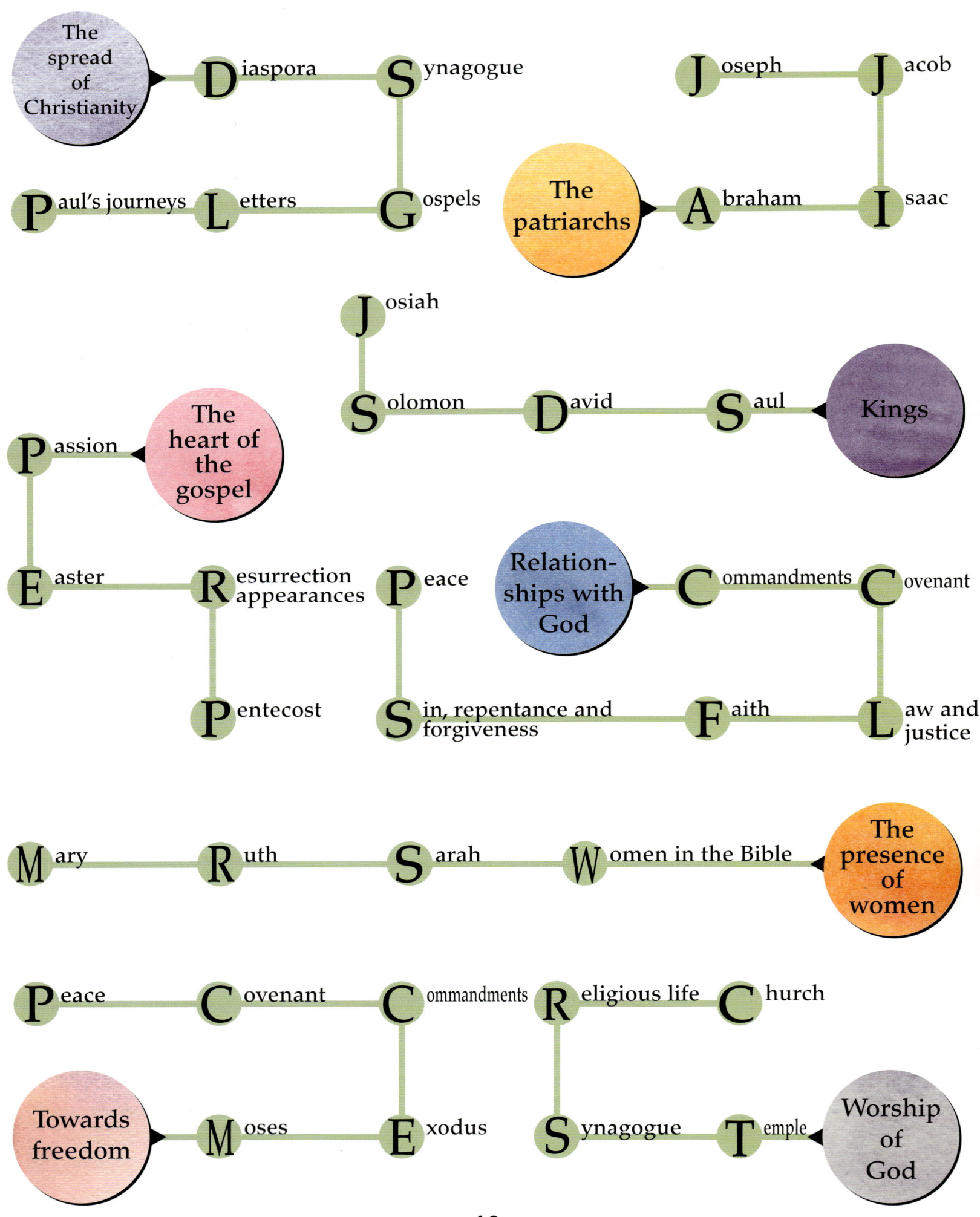

- The spread of Christianity ◄ **D**iaspora — **S**ynagogue
- **J**oseph — **J**acob
- **P**aul's journeys — **L**etters — **G**ospels
- The patriarchs ◄ **A**braham — **I**saac

- **J**osiah
- **S**olomon — **D**avid — **S**aul ► Kings
- **P**assion ◄ The heart of the gospel
- **E**aster — **R**esurrection appearances — **P**eace — Relationships with God ◄ **C**ommandments — **C**ovenant
- **P**entecost — **S**in, repentance and forgiveness — **F**aith — **L**aw and justice

- **M**ary — **R**uth — **S**arah — **W**omen in the Bible ► The presence of women

- **P**eace — **C**ovenant — **C**ommandments — **R**eligious life — **C**hurch
- Towards freedom ◄ **M**oses — **E**xodus — **S**ynagogue — **T**emple — Worship of God

10

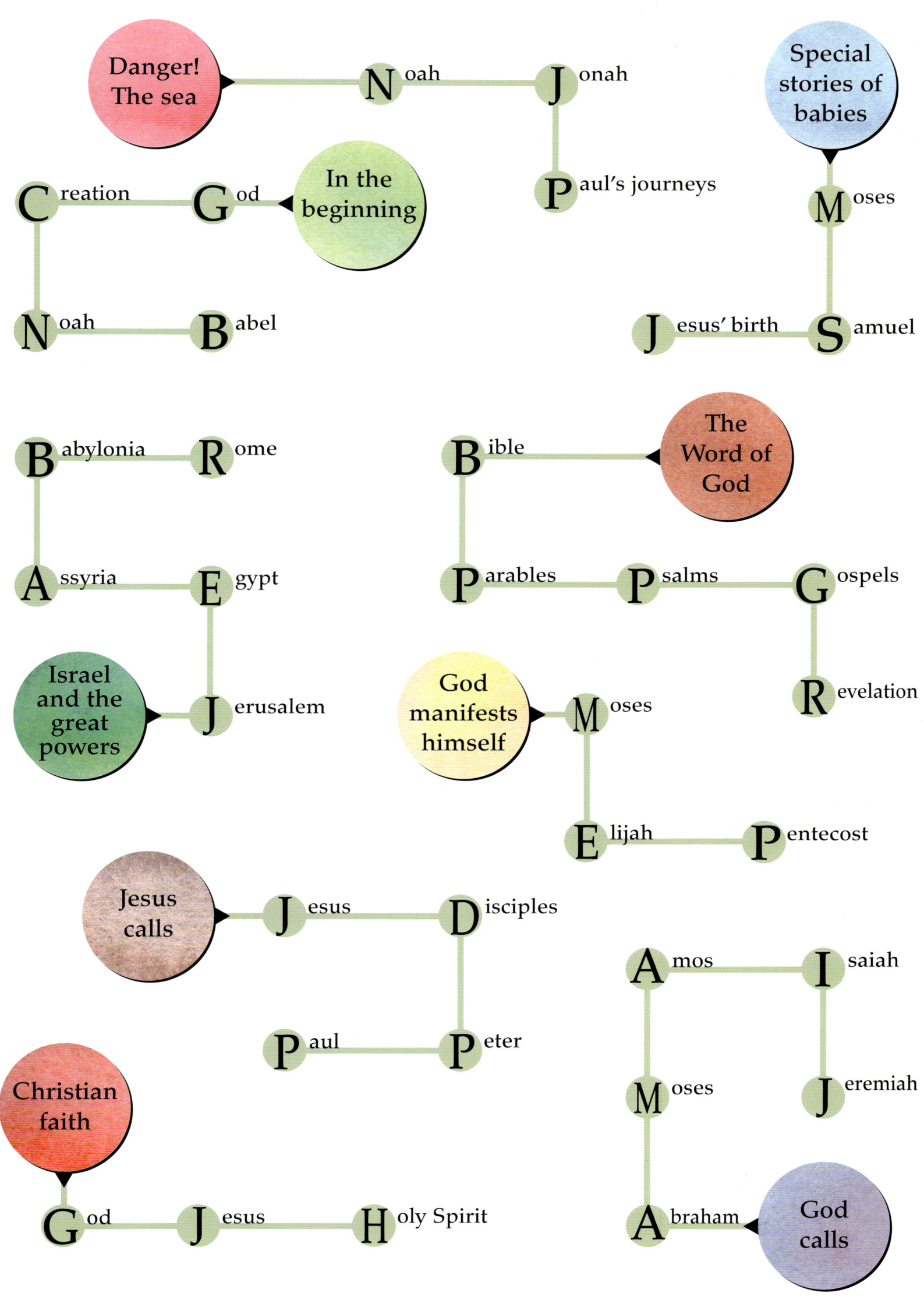

- **Danger! The sea** → Noah — Jonah
  - Jonah — Paul's journeys
- Creation — God → **In the beginning**
- Creation — Noah — Babel
- **Special stories of babies** → Moses
  - Moses — Samuel — Jesus' birth

- Babylonia — Rome
- Babylonia — Assyria — Egypt
- Egypt — Jerusalem ← **Israel and the great powers**

- Bible → **The Word of God**
- Bible — Parables — Psalms — Gospels — Revelation

- **God manifests himself** → Moses
- Moses — Elijah — Pentecost

- **Jesus calls** → Jesus — Disciples
- Paul — Peter — Disciples

- Amos — Isaiah
- Amos — Moses — Abraham
- Isaiah — Jeremiah
- Abraham → **God calls**

- **Christian faith** → God — Jesus — Holy Spirit

11

WHEN
A BIBLE TIME-LINE

Creation · Noah · Babel · Abraham · Isaac · Jacob · Joseph · Moses · Joshua · Judges · Samuel · Saul · David · Solomon

Arrival in Egypt · Exodus · Arrival in Canaan · Beginning of the monarchy · Building of the Temple · Division of the Kingdom

Northern Kingdom Israel · Elijah · Elisha

Southern Kingdom: Judah · Amos · Isaiah · Jeremiah

Destruction of Jerusalem and the Temple

700 600 500

This time-line shows the main events and people in the Bible included in this book. Sections of the time-line also appear in the *When* windows in various entries in the book, to help readers see quickly what came before and after events and people referred to there.
The yellow stripe symbolises the passing of time. At the beginning it is thinner and lighter to indicate distant times, becoming wider as it reaches events nearer to our own time. The time-line divides into two to represent the division of Solomon's kingdom then is diverted to recall the Babylonian exile before returning, like the exiles, to its original path.
When the history of Israel and Judah can be linked to the history of the great powers of the ancient world, it is possible to give some dates. In dates in this book, the abbreviations BCE (Before the Common Era) and CE (Common Era) are used to denote years before and after the birth of Jesus.

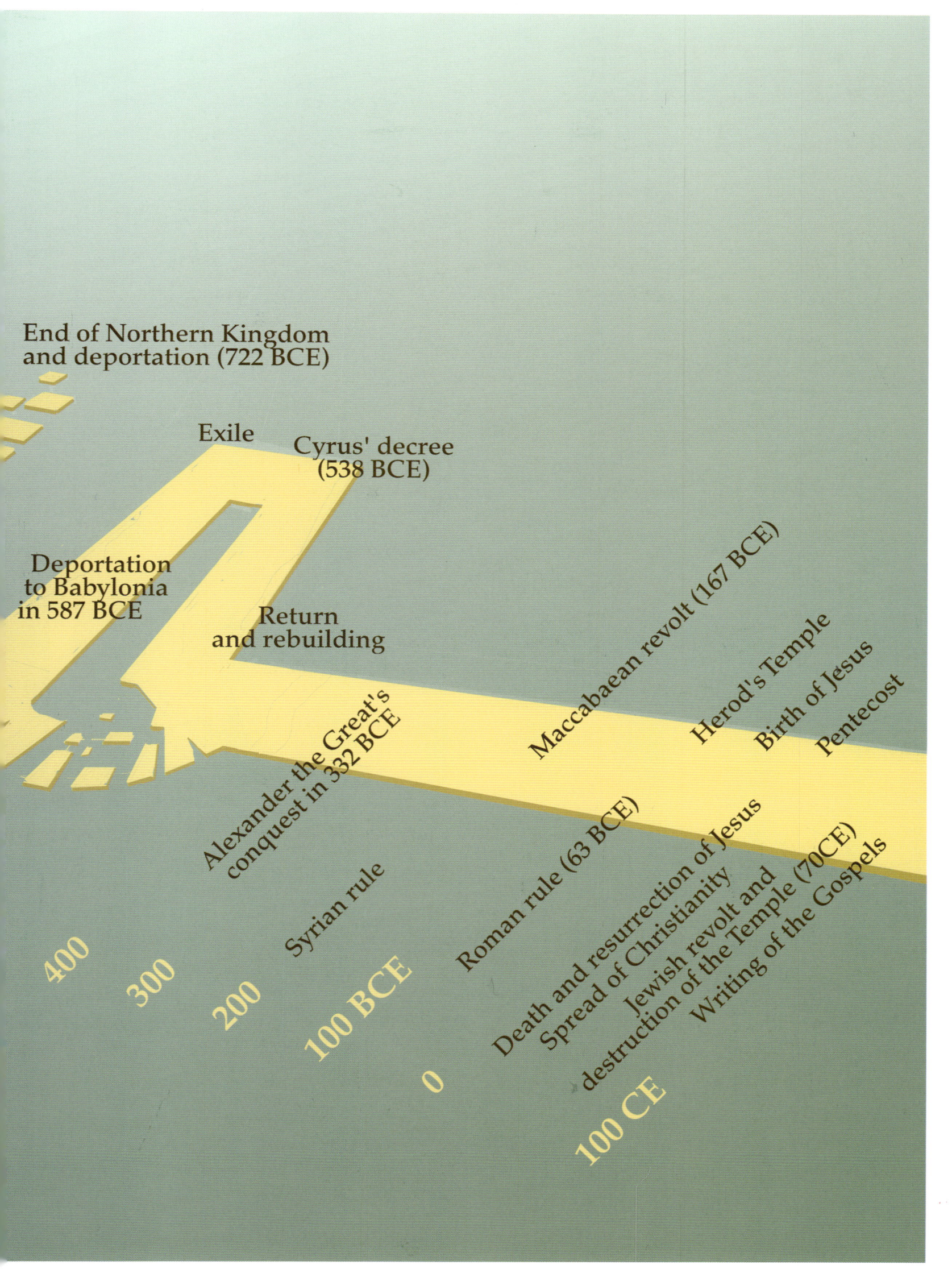

End of Northern Kingdom and deportation (722 BCE)

Exile

Cyrus' decree (538 BCE)

Deportation to Babylonia in 587 BCE

Return and rebuilding

Alexander the Great's conquest in 332 BCE

Syrian rule

Maccabaean revolt (167 BCE)

Roman rule (63 BCE)

Herod's Temple

Birth of Jesus

Pentecost

Death and resurrection of Jesus

Spread of Christianity

Jewish revolt and destruction of the Temple (70CE)

Writing of the Gospels

400 300 200 100 BCE 0 100 CE

WHERE

THE ANCIENT WORLD

PALESTINE AT THE TIME OF JESUS

- Mediterranean Sea
- Sidon
- Zarathath
- Tyre
- PHOENICIA
- SYRIA
- Damascus
- Mount Hermon
- Caesarea Philippi
- Lake Huleh
- GALILEE
- Chorazim
- Capernaum
- Bethsaida
- Yarmuk
- Sea of Galilee
- Mount Carmel
- Cana
- Nazareth
- Tiberias
- Mount Tabor
- Nain
- Gadara
- Caesarea
- DECAPOLIS
- SAMARIA
- Samaria
- Gerasa
- Mount Gerizim
- Jabbok
- Joppa
- Arimathaea
- Jordan
- PERAEA
- Ephraim
- Jericho
- JUDAEA
- Qumran
- Emmaus
- Jerusalem
- Bethany beyond Jordan
- Bethany
- Ashkelon
- Hebron
- Dead Sea
- Gaza
- Arnon
- NABATAEA
- IDUMAEA

ABRAHAM
A man on the move

Abraham came from Ur and lived at Haran, surrounded by his father's tribe and his own family. One day Abraham heard a voice. God said to him: 'Leave your country, your relatives, and your father's home, and go to a land that I am going to show you. I will give you many descendants, and they will become a great nation. I will bless you … And through you I will bless all the nations.' *(Genesis 12:1-3)*

The departure

A small caravan set out. Where were they going? They didn't know. What guarantee did they have that they should be going? None. God's words echoed in Abraham's mind: 'I will give you many descendants.' What a strange promise! Abraham and his wife Sarah were childless and no longer young. Yet, after the farewells and the goodbyes from rather puzzled friends, the journey towards Canaan had begun….

The arrival

The Promised Land was, in fact, inhabited. The Canaanites lived there. Still trusting God, Abraham crossed the length and breadth of the country, built altars to his God and pitched camp in a mountainous and arid area.

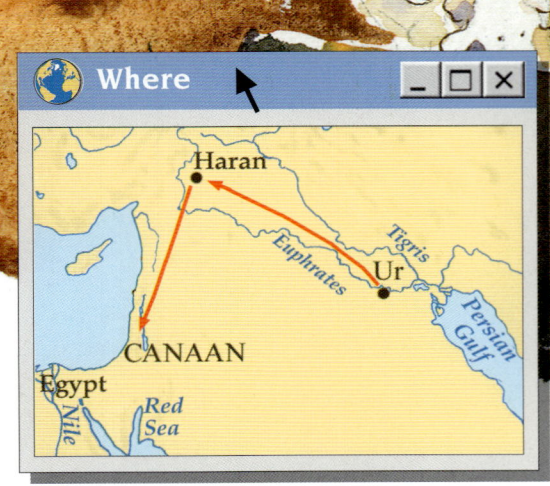

🌍 Where

In the Bible

➡ The narrative about Abraham is from Israel's prehistory and was written down at a much later time. It is found in Genesis 11:10-25:11.

➡ Abraham is mentioned in other biblical texts too, for example: Exodus 3:6; Joshua 24:3; Psalm 105:6-11; Matthew 1:1-2; Acts 7; Romans 4:3; Hebrews 11:8-11.

To explore further...

To move on
➡ Lot

To learn more
➡ Canaan

See also
➡ Isaac
➡ Sarah

A believer in doubt

Time passed and Abraham possessed neither a land nor an heir. His faith weakened. 'You haven't even given me a son,' he said to God. God replied: 'Gaze at the sky and try to count the stars. You will have as many descendants as that.' Abraham again put his trust in God and his faith pleased God.

More time passed. Abraham was then a hundred years old and Sarah ninety. One day God appeared to Abraham: 'I will give you a son by Sarah.' On that occasion Abraham could not take it any more. Bowing down until his face touched the ground, he laughed … A son at one hundred years old! And yet one day, at the hottest time, while Abraham was sitting in front of his tent….

➡ Read *Genesis 18:1-15*.

When

Babel — Abraham — Isaac

ACTS OF THE APOSTLES
The fifth Gospel

The author calls the Gospel of Luke 'my first book' *(Acts 1:1)*. The Acts of the Apostles, dedicated to the same sponsor, Theophilus, was his second one. The book tells how the early Christian communities came into being and describes their relationships with the Jewish and Roman authorities. It can be divided into two parts according to its two main characters: Peter (chapters 1-8; 10) and Paul (chapters 9; 11-28). The book of Acts has been called the fifth Gospel because it declares that, after his resurrection and ascension, Jesus continued to guide believers according to his plan. So, Jesus ordered the believers to wait for the gift of the Spirit *(Acts 1:4-5)*. That gift founded the Church on the day of Pentecost *(Acts 1:8; 2:1-13)*. The gospel would be spread from Jerusalem to Judaea and Samaria, as far as Rome and beyond.

External difficulties

From the beginning, the Church in Jerusalem had to face internal as well as external difficulties. The problems coming from outside affected the most active apostles. They were shut up in prison and brought before the Sanhedrin, the Jewish religious court. But the sound judgement of Gamaliel, a respected teacher, resulted in the apostles' being freed *(Acts 5:34-40)*.

Internal difficulties

The first Christians also had a serious internal problem. From the beginning, the Christian Church was made up of two groups: Jews from a Palestinian background and those from the Greek culture. The Greek-speaking Jews from the Diaspora (Jews who had settled abroad, from the Greek word meaning 'dispersion') thought they were discriminated against because their widows were not supported like those from Palestine. So, the apostles arranged for seven responsible men to be selected by a meeting of the Greek group in order to settle the dispute. Later they were known as deacons. Quite soon, the Greek Christians proved to be more courageous and dynamic than the Palestinian group.

Witnessing and Evangelising

From that time new problems arose from outside the Christian community. Stephen, one of the seven deacons, after a brief trial was stoned and killed in a cruel lynching. He was the first martyr. The persecution forced the Greek-speaking Christians to flee from Jerusalem *(Acts 6:8-8:3)*. However, a young man, Saul from Tarsus, (also called Paul), who had been one of the most active in the persecution, was confronted with a great personal crisis and converted to Christianity. After several years of reflection, Paul would be called to Antioch in Syria, where new and unforeseen events would happen among the Gentiles.

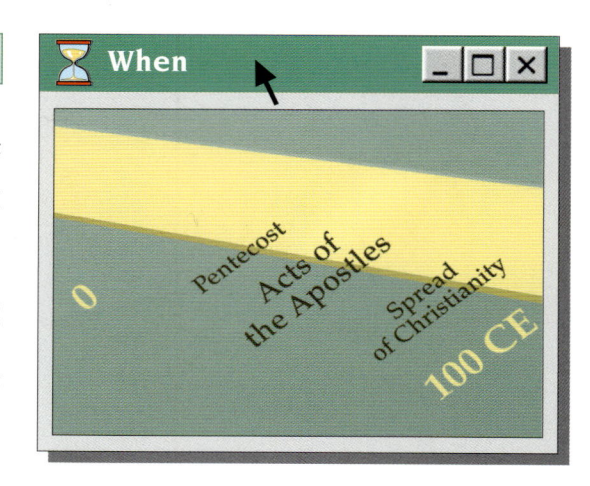

Read *Acts 11:19-26*.

The book ends abruptly. The apostle Paul was in Rome (60 CE) under house arrest waiting to be tried, but free to witness to the Jews and Gentiles. And there the narrative ends *(Acts 28:30-31)*.

When

0 — Pentecost — Acts of the Apostles — Spread of Christianity — 100 CE

To explore further…

To move on
→ Church

See also
→ Paul
→ Peter
→ Paul's journeys

AMOS
A foreign prophet

Amos spoke to the people of the Northern Kingdom in the sanctuary of Bethel, but he was not a subject of that kingdom. He had been persuaded to speak out in the name of God but he did this as a foreigner.

Amos came from Tekoa in Judah, not far from Jerusalem, in the Southern Kingdom. He had owned a herd of cattle in Tekoa and had been financially independent. He used to obtain fodder for his animals from the big leaves of the huge sycamores, which were common trees in Palestine in ancient times.

Amos went to Bethel about 760 BCE. He did not belong to any prophetic school and no one paid him for his work as a prophet.

Announcing judgement

Amos revealed God's words of judgement to the people: 'People of Israel, listen to this message which the Lord has spoken about you, the entire nation that he brought out of Egypt: "Of all the nations on earth, you are the only one I have known and cared for. That is what makes your sins so terrible, and that is why I must punish you for them."' *(Amos 3:1-2)*

Amos condemned the current situation in Israel, both from the point of view of the state and from the religious viewpoint. This resulted in a message of judgement on the whole of Israel.

When

Northern Kingdom: Israel

Amos

Isaiah

Southern Kingdom: Judah

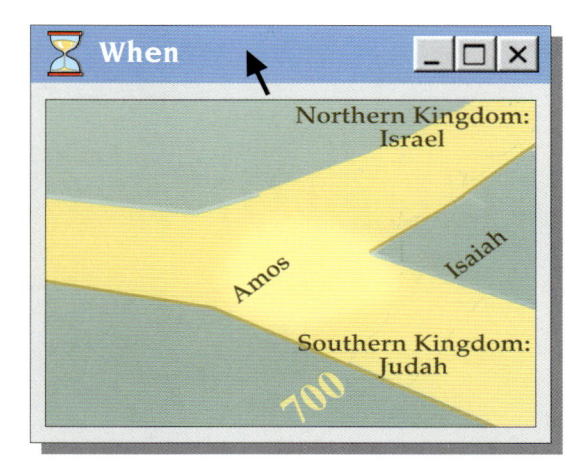

700

The people had been incapable of achieving a moral lifestyle in their country, which corresponded to the freedom God had given them. Rights and justice were trampled on in the law courts. The honest judge, and witnesses who told the truth, were hated and persecuted. Basic morality was ignored.

The rights of the poor and weak were not protected and they fell into the hands of the moneylenders. Consequently, having betrayed God's calling, the country had opted for destruction and there was no going back on that.

Amos was challenged

Amaziah, the priest at the sanctuary of Bethel, did not like these prophecies. He saw them as a threatening, political plot against the king, Jeroboam II (787-747 BCE). Amaziah warned the king and had the prophet turned out of the dining area of the sanctuary and the sanctuary itself. Then he had him expelled from the Northern Kingdom to return to his homeland in the South. But the prophet warned Amaziah that God indeed had sent him and nothing could stop God's judgement.

Read *2 Kings 17:1-8*.

In the Bible

→ A few decades later, the capital, Samaria, was destroyed and the population deported to Assyria in 722 BCE (2 Kings 17:1-6).

→ Calling: Amos 1:1; preaching: Amos 3:1-2; 2:6-7; argument with Amaziah: Amos 7:10-17.

To explore further...

To follow on
→ Isaiah

To learn more
→ Assyria

A word of hope

Nevertheless the prophet called for the people of Israel to change their ways and pleaded with God on their behalf. The book ends with hope in the salvation that God, in spite of their failure and the judgement of condemnation, would deliver when Israel gave up her false security and followed God, who alone could look after her.

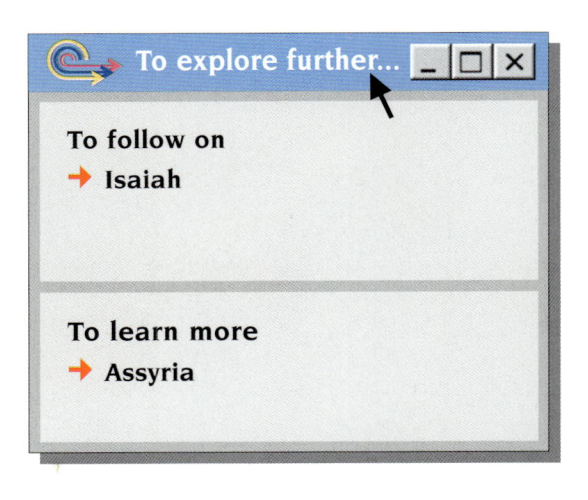

21

ASSYRIA
The land of cruel conquerors

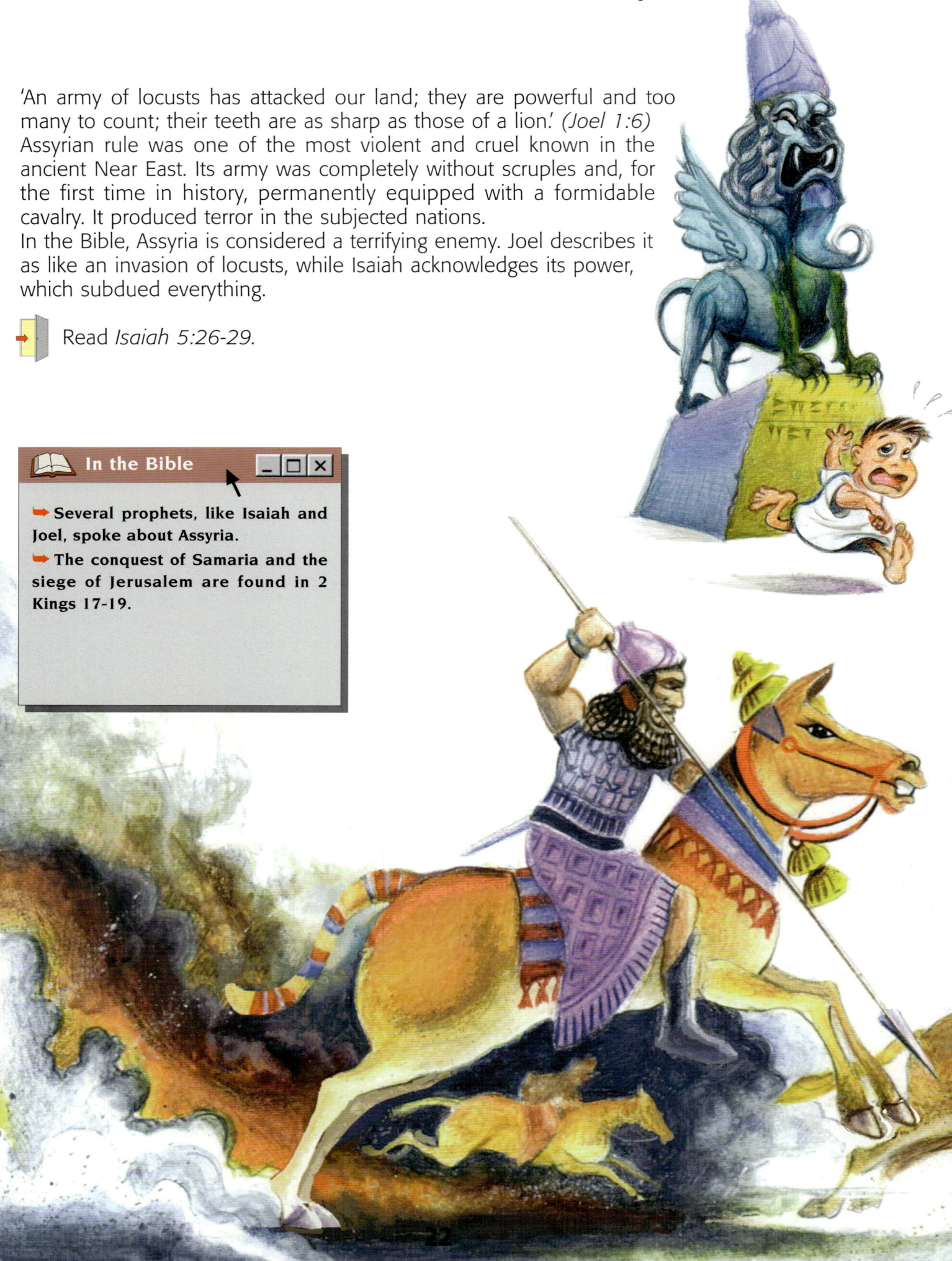

'An army of locusts has attacked our land; they are powerful and too many to count; their teeth are as sharp as those of a lion.' *(Joel 1:6)*
Assyrian rule was one of the most violent and cruel known in the ancient Near East. Its army was completely without scruples and, for the first time in history, permanently equipped with a formidable cavalry. It produced terror in the subjected nations.
In the Bible, Assyria is considered a terrifying enemy. Joel describes it as like an invasion of locusts, while Isaiah acknowledges its power, which subdued everything.

Read *Isaiah 5:26-29*.

In the Bible

➡ Several prophets, like Isaiah and Joel, spoke about Assyria.

➡ The conquest of Samaria and the siege of Jerusalem are found in 2 Kings 17-19.

The stages of their conquests

The Assyrians' imperial power was achieved in various stages. Their plans were, however, flexible depending on the situation they met along the way.

The people conquered in war were made into vassals, which meant they were not permitted to have their own foreign policy and had to pay heavy tribute money.

At the first skirmish of rebellion, which was normally provoked on purpose, the Assyrians intervened militarily. They installed a new king of their persuasion and further increased the tribute to create worse tension. This meant they had a reason to intervene again and annex the enemy's kingdom directly, taking away the ruling class and bringing in a new one, loyal to them. This happened even to the Northern Kingdom when, in 722 BCE, Samaria was destroyed and its ruling class deported. The Samaritan people came into being from this political event. The Assyrians were the first to carry out real imperialistic politics. They did not simply raid and subject nations. Their conquests were aimed at annexing people and territories in order to build a world empire.

Punished greed

The Assyrian ruling class, because of its greed, ended up by treating its own people badly. Their long and hard exploitation left them exhausted and so they were unable to resist the attacks of the enemies produced by their imperialistic politics. In 612 BCE Nineveh, the capital, fell into the hands of the combined armies of the Babylonians and the Medes. Its destruction was recounted by the prophet Nahum.

➡ Read *Nahum 2:12-14*.

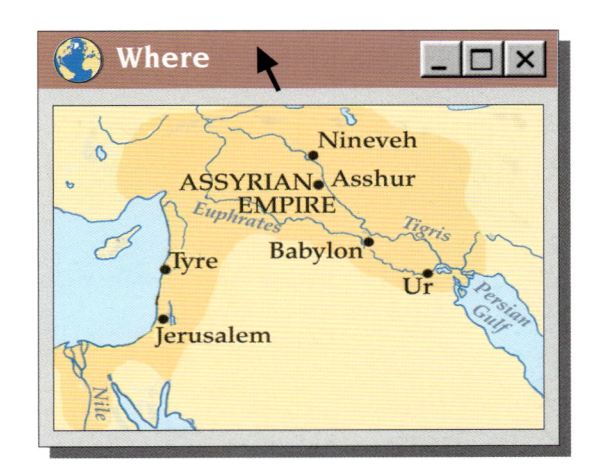

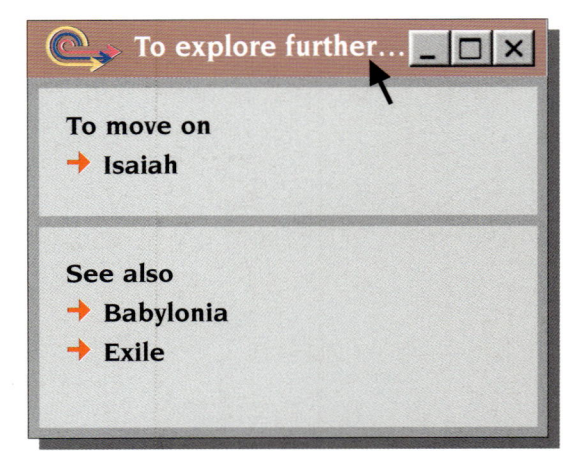

Where

To explore further…

To move on
➡ Isaiah

See also
➡ Babylonia
➡ Exile

BABEL
As high as the sky!

A controversial story

A huge tiered temple dominated the centre of Babylon. The sanctuaries of the gods were at the top of the temple tower. The tower represented the efforts of human beings to approach the divine. But the prophets and priests of Israel, exiled in Babylonia, did not agree with that: it was God who approached human beings and not the opposite way round. Never! They told a story to clarify their belief.

The tower

Once upon a time everyone spoke the same language. Then things changed. This is what happened. A nomadic people, always moving from one place to another, came to a vast plain and decided to settle there and build a city. The men were enthusiastic and wanted to become famous, so they also had the incredible idea of constructing a tower as high as the sky. Full of pride in their strength and skills, they quickly got organised and started the work.

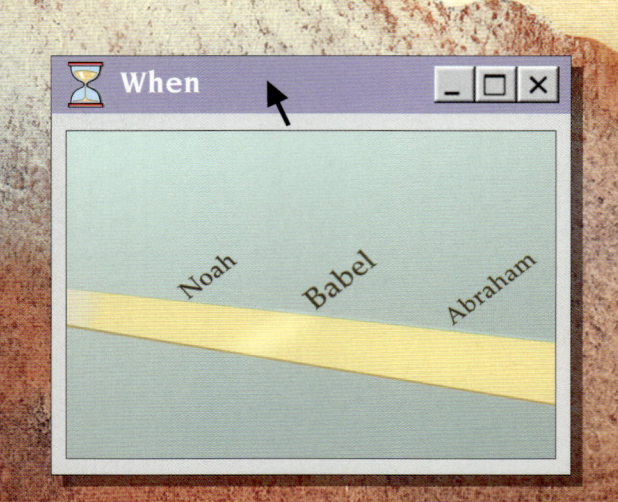

When

Noah — Babel — Abraham

Where

BABYLONIA

But wait and see!

One day God came down to take a look at the city and tower. Noticing the people's frenzied activity, God was worried and thought: 'With everyone united by the same language, they believe they are powerful enough to reach heaven. They have lost their heads! They have forgotten that they are merely human beings. And this is only the beginning! Encouraged by their success they will want to rule over other people and no one will be able to stop them any more. What should be done? I will confuse their speech so that they won't be able to understand each other any more, let alone organise themselves. And they will certainly not make the climb up to heaven!'

The end of a dream

And so it happened just like that! The people couldn't understand each other any more and took to the road in small groups heading in different directions. On the plain, the abandoned foundations of a city remained and in the middle, an unfinished tower: Babel.

Read *Genesis* 11:1-9.

To explore further…

To move on
➜ Abraham

See also
➜ Babylonia
➜ Religious life

BABYLONIA
Power and culture

Babylonia was the most splendid of kingdoms, the outstanding beauty of the Chaldees. The name 'Babylonia' referred to the region surrounding the city of Babylon. Historically it was associated with the name of Hammurabi. That great king had a code of laws inscribed on a stone column – the stele of Hammurabi. He is one of the first in the history of humankind to create an extensive, organised empire (nineteenth century BCE). Babylonia remained one of the major military powers in Mesopotamia throughout the centuries, even if after Hammurabi the Babylonians experienced good and bad fortune. It was certainly the chief promoter of culture in the region, partly because of its multi-ethnic character, created by the various peoples who, over the centuries, had been conquered and had been stationed there.

The tower of Babel and the exile

In the Bible, Babylonia was famous chiefly for two reasons. The first was the tower whose construction was described in *Genesis 11:9* as a symbol of human arrogance, which wanted to rise to the level of God. The tower was identified with the ziggurat, which was the huge construction at the centre of the temple of Marduk at Babylon.

The second reason was linked to its king Nebuchadnezzar II, who, in the very last period of the city's greatness, built an empire, which stretched from the Persian Gulf to the Mediterranean. During this expansion he conquered Jerusalem in 587 BCE and took the court and priests into exile in Babylonia. In 539 BCE the Persians conquered Babylonia. A slow decline led to the city being progressively abandoned and it soon became a desolate ruin.

Where

BABYLONIAN EMPIRE · Nineveh
Euphrates · Tigris
· Tyre · Babylon
· Samaria · Ur
· Jerusalem · Persian Gulf
Nile · Red Sea

A very ancient religion

The Babylonian pantheon was a mixture of the different gods belonging to the people who had been involved in the history of the city. The many gods of the Accadians, Assyrians and the Chaldeans were added to the original Sumerian gods. The religion was strongly linked to the cycle of nature, which the people tried to appease through rites and sacrifices, and to predicting the future through their highly developed astrology. Marduk was the chief god.

Babylonia – Rome

In Judaism, Babylonia symbolised the powerful enemy who had destroyed Jerusalem. As such, it was used to refer to absolute, oppressive power. In the book of Revelation and in *1 Peter 5:13* Babylonia became synonymous with Rome and its power.

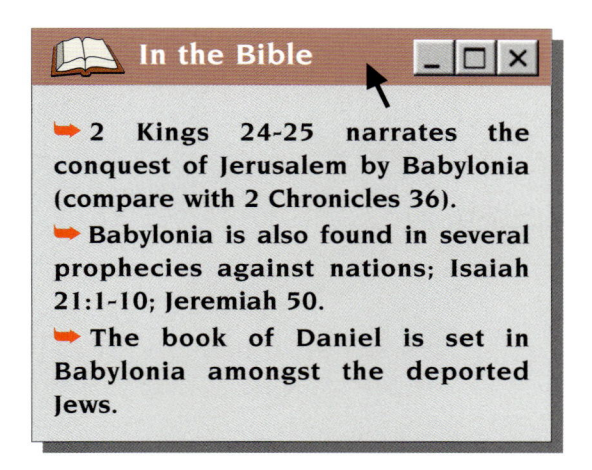

In the Bible

→ 2 Kings 24-25 narrates the conquest of Jerusalem by Babylonia (compare with 2 Chronicles 36).
→ Babylonia is also found in several prophecies against nations; Isaiah 21:1-10; Jeremiah 50.
→ The book of Daniel is set in Babylonia amongst the deported Jews.

To explore further...

To move on
→ Daniel

See also
→ Assyria
→ Exile; Judah
→ Return and rebuilding

BIBLE
The book of books

Removing a veil

The Bible is often defined as the revelation of God. It is like saying that the Bible removes a veil that hides something. God is hidden behind this veil and human beings cannot know him. But in the Bible, God reveals himself, by removing the veil and making himself known.

A word which is action

A better definition for the Bible is the revelation of the Word of God. But in the Bible God is not described as a professor who goes to the lecture platform, gives the lecture and then leaves. The Word of God in the Bible is at the same time, action. In *Genesis 1:1-2:2*, for example, in the creation narrative, 'God said' is repeated many times and with those words of God everything was made. Or in *Exodus 20:1-17*, the Ten Commandments are words of God. But they are words given by a God who had first of all acted by freeing Israel from slavery in Egypt.

The books

The word 'Bible' means 'books' in the plural. In fact, the Bible is made up of many different books bound together. The Bible should be thought of as a library in which many small volumes have been placed one beside the other.

Many authors, many styles

Each small volume is different from the others because each was written at a different time and by different authors. Each author has his own style. Each period has its own way of writing. Even today, a book written two centuries ago will be very different from one written only ten years ago.

The pleasure of story-telling

The books of the Bible have another characteristic, which distinguishes them from the books of today. Unlike a modern book, which the author would probably type on a computer, the volumes in the Bible were not written down directly. The Bible narratives were retold for a long time: by grandparents to parents, parents to children for many generations, before being written down. And often there was not a single author, but a group of people who collected all those stories together and put them down in writing.

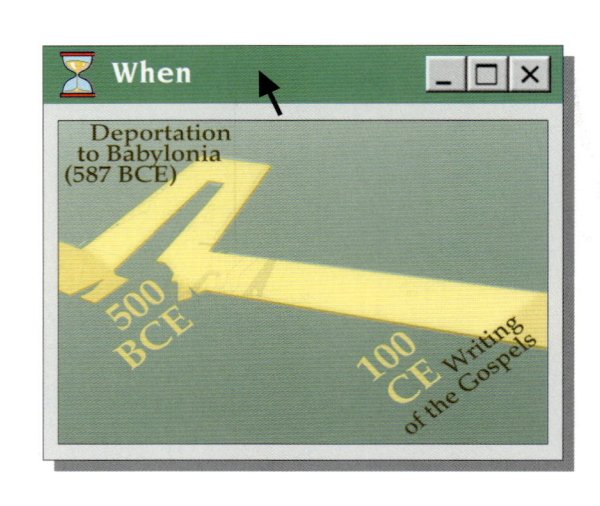

When

Deportation to Babylonia (587 BCE)

500 BCE

100 CE Writing of the Gospels

Manuscripts

When a modern author has finished writing a story, the disk is sent to the editor or it is forwarded directly by electronic mail.
Before the widespread use of computers, the author sent the manuscript to the editor by post. But the original manuscripts of the Bible no longer exist. So now there are only copies of the original manuscripts.
Fortunately, the scribes who copied these were very careful and meticulous. They knew they were copying very important texts and they took great trouble not to make too many mistakes.

Papyrus and parchment

The ancient scribes did not have pen and paper at their disposal. However, they had learned to use papyrus, a plant that grows in water with a stalk up to five metres high and a bunch of leaves around the stem top. They knew how to take out the white, spongy pith from those stalks. They cut the stalks into thin strips, then laid these out side by side to form a square shape. On top of this they placed a layer of strips horizontally. This square was then soaked with water and pressed well together. Finally, by gluing one square to another, a long strip was formed which could then be rolled up.
Later, people discovered a way of making a stronger material, parchment, from the skin of lambs, sheep or goats. The skins were soaked in lime, then dried and smoothed out. The oldest biblical manuscripts, kept in various museums, are on papyrus or parchment.

The caves of Qumran

Since 1947 a lot of parchment scrolls preserved in earthenware jars have been discovered in various caves close to the ruins of the 'monastery' of Qumran, near the Dead Sea in the Judaean desert. These texts, both complete and in fragments, are from books in the Bible as well as from various literatures and from the rule of conduct of that community. These date back (according to different scholars) to a period between the third century BCE and 66 CE, when the Roman troops of Titus devastated the 'monastery'. Perhaps it was an entire library, purposely hidden to save it from disaster during the war that disturbed Judaea from 66 to 73 CE. This was one of the most important and influential discoveries of the last century, because these parchments date back to about a thousand years before the oldest manuscripts of the Hebrew Bible recovered up to then, which are dated around 900 CE.

BIBLE

The Bible

For Christians, the Bible or Holy Scripture consists of two parts called the Old and New Testaments. The word 'testament' does not refer to the last will of a dead person. It would have been better to translate the original word as 'covenant', a word often used in the Bible: a pact that God made with human beings. But it would be even better to call these two parts: Jewish Scriptures and Christian Scriptures. The Jews, in fact, call only the first of the two parts the 'Bible'.

THE JEWISH SCRIPTURES

Old Testament

This is made up of thirty-nine books, written in Hebrew, which tell of God's intervention in the history of the people Israel. Another ten books can be added to these. They are often placed in the appendix. They are called the Apocrypha. The thirty-nine books are further divided up by subject matter into three main sections:

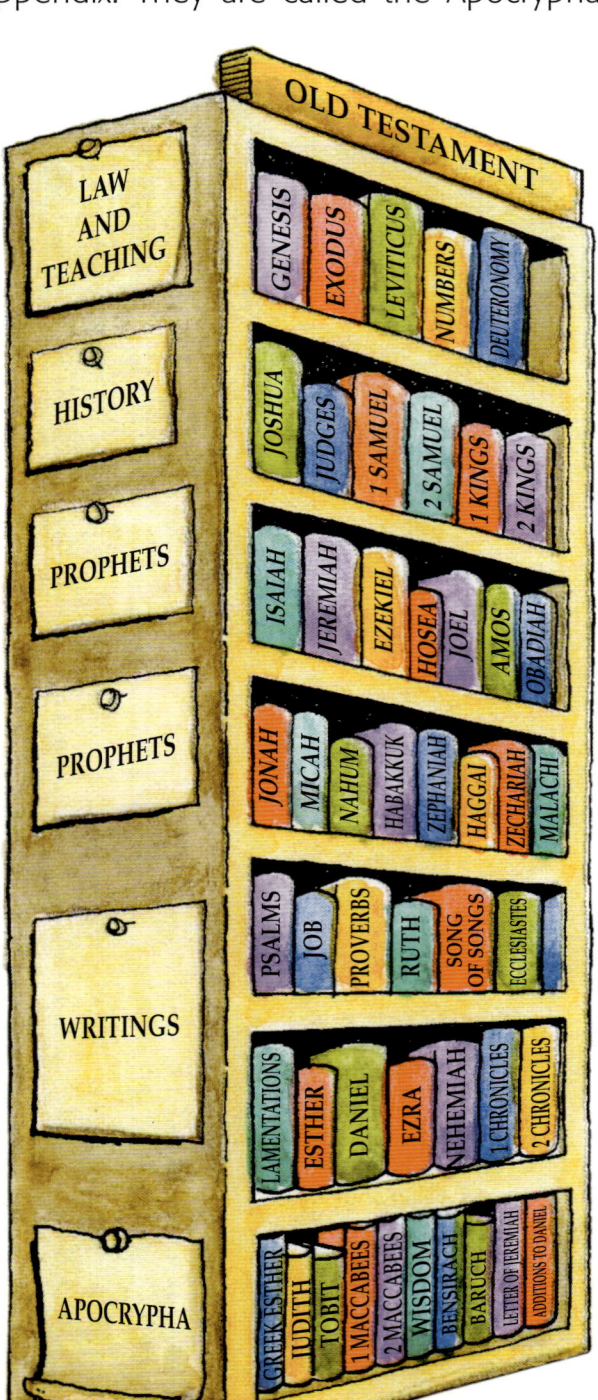

The Torah means law or teaching of God and includes the first five books. These are also called *the Pentateuch*, meaning five containers, that is, the five containers of the scrolls.

The Prophets are divided into two groups: the former prophets, also called *history books* and the latter prophets.

The Writings are various prayers, poetry, prophetic texts and stories.

The Apocrypha contains books found in the ancient Greek translation, (called the Septuagint) and in the Latin Vulgate, but not in the Jewish list of books. Some Bibles have these in an appendix.

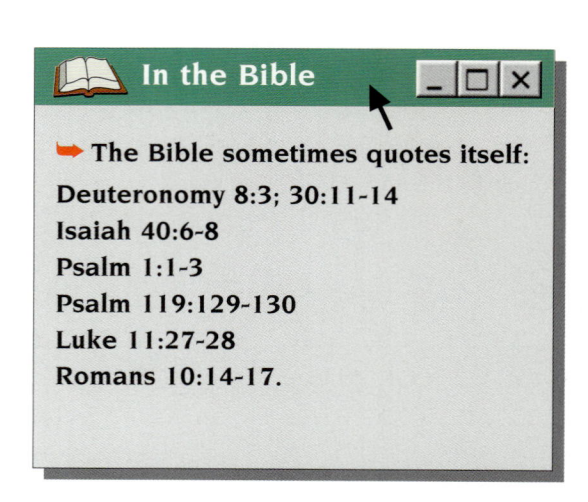

In the Bible

➡ **The Bible sometimes quotes itself:**
Deuteronomy 8:3; 30:11-14
Isaiah 40:6-8
Psalm 1:1-3
Psalm 119:129-130
Luke 11:27-28
Romans 10:14-17.

30

THE CHRISTIAN SCRIPTURES

New Testament

This is made up of twenty-seven books, written in Greek. It tells about the life of Jesus whose faith was based on the Jewish Scriptures, and about his first followers.

The twenty-seven books of the Christian Scriptures (or New Testament) can be subdivided into four main sections:

The Gospels contain the accounts of the life of Jesus, his actions, teaching and finally, the account of his trial, crucifixion and resurrection.

The Acts of the Apostles tells of the events in the early Church in which the two personalities of the apostles Peter and Paul stand out.

The Letters (or *Epistles*) are mostly written by the apostle Paul or his disciples. Other letters, called catholic ('general'), bear the names of Peter, John and Jude. *The Letter to the Hebrews*, whose author is unknown, quotes examples of the faith of important people from the Jewish Scriptures.

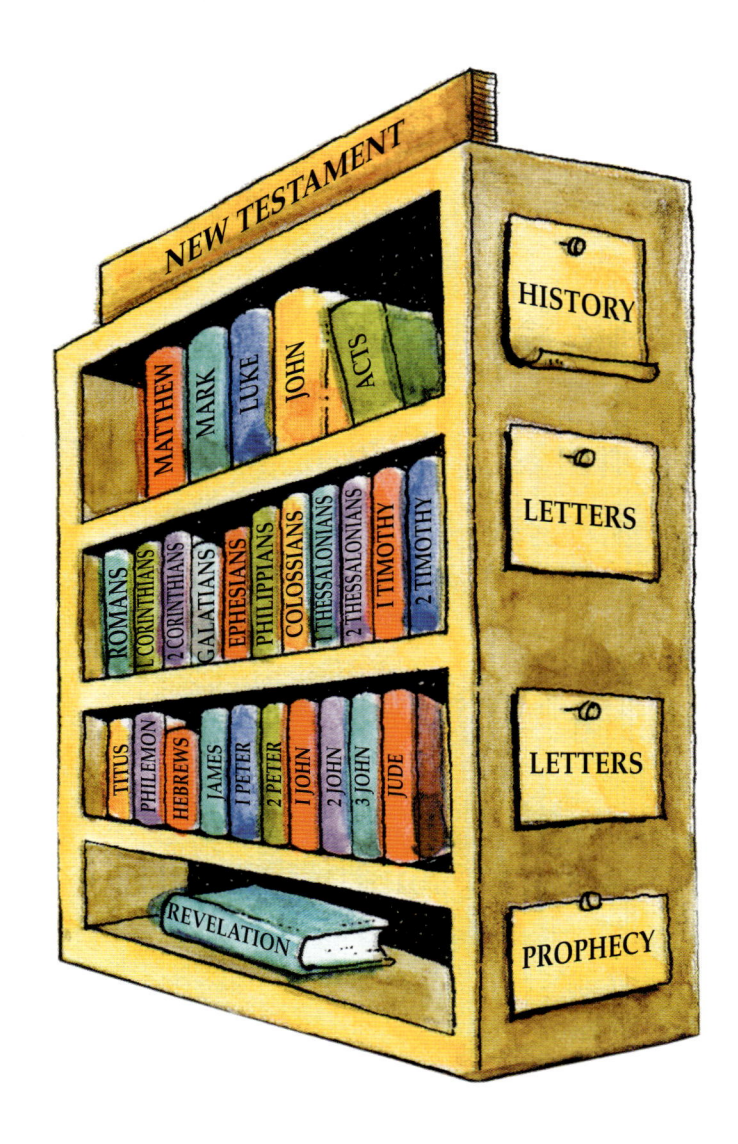

Revelation is the last book and has very particular characteristics.

Fixing the Canon

The list of books contained in the Bible is a closed list. No one can add or take away any writing. In ancient times it was not like that. Many other writings were in circulation and new ones were always being produced until both in Jewish and Christian circles, at different periods, the need to establish some rules was recognised.
The writings that were chosen were those which were considered more important for understanding how God had made himself known and how he had revealed himself. That was the measure applied. In those days a cane was used as a measure. From 'cane' the word 'canon' came. In fact today the terms 'Bible canon' and 'canonical books' are used.

Translations

The Bible is found all over the world. Nowadays, when a novel is translated into eight or nine languages it is reckoned to be a great success. The Bible has been translated into three hundred languages!
The first translation known about is that of the Old Testament in Greek, called the Septuagint. A very important Latin translation is the Vulgate, done by the great scholar Jerome.
After the invention of printing, Bible translations greatly increased and were more widespread. Translating the Bible into modern languages encouraged in many countries, the formation of a national language. The most famous example is Martin Luther's translation into German.

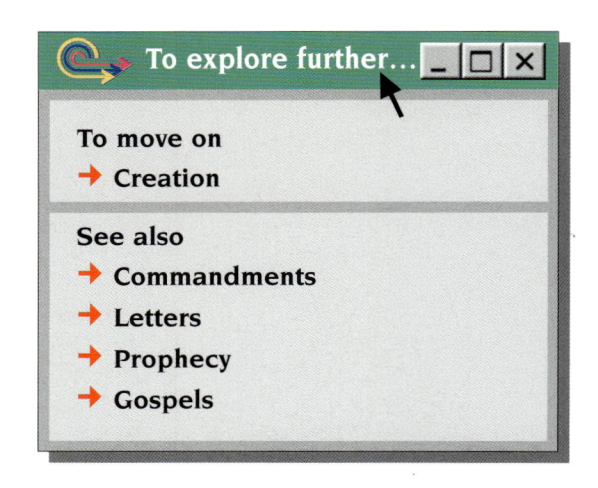

To explore further…

To move on
→ Creation

See also
→ Commandments
→ Letters
→ Prophecy
→ Gospels

BIBLE

A CLOSER LOOK AT THE JEWISH SCRIPTURES

Old Testament

The **Torah** is made up of:
– *Genesis* telling about the origins of the world, of humankind and the people of Israel. It can be divided into two parts: the prehistory (chapters 1-11), from creation to the tower of Babel, and the narratives of the patriarchs (chapters 12-50), Abraham, Isaac, Jacob, Joseph.
– *Exodus* narrating the exodus of the Israelites from slavery in Egypt. Their freedom was preceded by a period of oppression in Egypt and followed by a journey towards Sinai under the leadership of Moses. God gave them the Ten Commandments and other rules.
– *Leviticus* and *Numbers* containing both laws and rules as well as censuses and some episodes on the journey of the Israelites in the desert.
– *Deuteronomy* reporting Moses' discourses during the journey in the desert, new laws and ending with the death of Moses himself.

Prophets
– **Former Prophets** or historic books.
• *Joshua* and *Judges* narrate the history of the Israelites when they settled in Canaan, the land promised to Abraham. First, they were under Joshua's leadership and then under different leaders, called judges.
• *1* and *2 Samuel*, *1* and *2 Kings* carry on the story of Israel from Samuel, the last judge and prophet, to the kings, Saul, David and Solomon. Then they narrate the division of the kingdom between the North (kingdom of Israel) and the South (kingdom of Judah). In these the prophets Elijah and Elisha also appear. The account continues until the destruction of the two kingdoms. First the North was destroyed by the Assyrians and then the South, by the Babylonians.

– **Latter Prophets.**
These are made up of fifteen books reporting the words of prophets from various historic periods. The major prophets are:
Isaiah written by at least three authors who lived at different times: before, during and after the exile in Babylonia.
Jeremiah who lived through two important periods in the kingdom of Judah. The first was the reign of King Josiah following the discovery of Deuteronomy during the restoration of the Temple, which triggered an important religious reform. The second period was, in contrast, a difficult one with the arrival of the Babylonians, the fall of the kingdom and the deportation of the Jews to Babylonia.
Ezekiel was transferred to Babylonia in the first deportation. At first he took offence at his deported companions because they deceived themselves into believing that so long as the Temple was there, nothing very serious would happen to Jerusalem. But when news arrived that the Temple had been destroyed, Ezekiel called on the people to trust God's promises of freedom.

The Writings

- **Prayer and poetry:** *Psalms, Job, Proverbs.* The book of *Proverbs* belongs to the wisdom type of literature. It is a collection of proverbs or sayings, thought in part to come from Solomon.
- **Books of the great festivals:** *Ruth* is read at the Jewish Festival of Weeks (Shavuot in Hebrew), or harvest, or Pentecost; *The Song of Songs* is a collection of wedding hymns attributed to Solomon and read during the Festival of Passover; *Ecclesiastes* (or *Preacher*) is a book of wisdom which contains general reflections on life and is read at all the great solemn celebrations; *Lamentations* is a collection of laments, which are read in synagogue to remember the destruction of the Temple; *Esther* is a narrative set in the period of Persian domination and is read at the joyful and noisy Festival of Purim.
- **Books of prophecy and history:** *Daniel, Ezra* and *Nehemiah* tell of the return of the exiles from Babylonia and the rebuilding of Jerusalem, and *1 and 2 Chronicles* repeat, from their own particular viewpoint, the history of David, Solomon and the Kingdom of Judah.

The Apocrypha contains writings that are inspired partly by the message of the Old Testament and partly by later Jewish theology and Greek thought.

Not all Bibles follow the same order. Here the divisions correspond to those of the Hebrew Bible. The Christian Bible often follows the order of the Greek translation of the Old Testament called the Septuagint.

A CLOSER LOOK AT THE CHRISTIAN SCRIPTURES

New Testament

There are four **Gospels**. The first three, *Matthew, Mark* and *Luke* are called synoptic because they use a lot of common material. *Mark* is considered the oldest and is written in a simple and lively way; *Matthew* and *Luke*, in addition, narrate the birth and infancy of Jesus. The *Gospel of John* reports Jesus' life and discourses in a different way. All four Gospels give the majority of space to the passion and resurrection narratives.

The **Acts of the Apostles** is the sequel to the *Gospel of Luke* and the author is the same person. It narrates the spread of the gospel and, in particular, the activities of some of the apostles and the situation of different Christian communities.

The **Letters** give information about the life, organisation, problems and contrasting doctrines of the first Christian communities.

Revelation reflects an atmosphere of persecution and danger and encourages hope because at the end: 'God will make all things new.'

CANAAN
A contested land

A land promised to others

The region of Canaan positioned between Syria, Egypt and Arabia, was really rich and densely populated. That was the land promised by God to Abraham as the home of his descendants.

▸ Read *Genesis 12:7*.

According to the Bible, Canaan is spoken of as the land promised to the Israelites, sometimes forgetting that when the nomadic tribes, who were to become the people of Israel, arrived, that land had already been inhabited for centuries by various settled groups: the Canaanites, the inhabitants of Canaan meaning 'the country of the purple dye'. The Phoenicians were the most famous of those peoples. Grouped around their small, independent city-state and greatly influenced by Mesopotamia and Egypt, they built a rich civilisation, which would leave a lasting mark on the people of Israel.

▸ Read *Numbers 13:17-33*.

Conquest or assimilation?

From the book of Joshua, it seems that the taking over of Canaan by the Israelites was a ruthless conquest; in reality, the Canaanites, stronger politically and militarily, raised a serious obstacle to the invasion! Rather than an all-out conquest, it was largely a slow process of substitution and assimilation between the two peoples.

The Canaanites, as an independent people, disappeared for good during the reign of David, but their religion and their culture survived for many more centuries.

That religion was polytheism and the chief enemy of the prophets of Israel's one God. It was an enemy that had to be fiercely fought against before it was defeated once and for all.

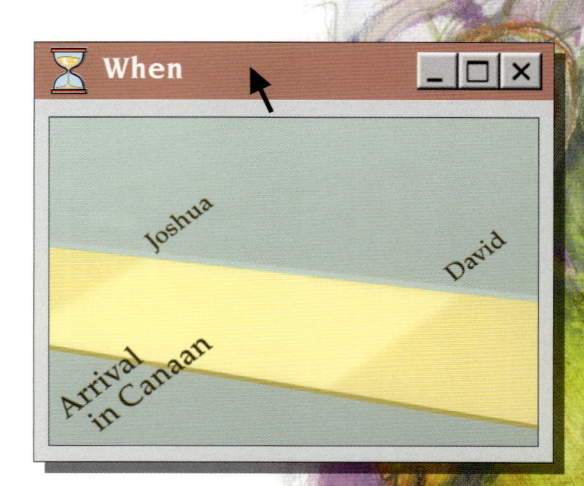

A cult of power and fertility

Canaan was a region that lived by agriculture. It depended totally on regular rainfall because of the lack of rivers. So, the religion that developed in Canaan was tied to seeking the favour of the gods who regulated the climate.

The pair of gods worshipped more than all the others was Asherah and Baal. They represented the earth's fertility and the fertilising power of the rain. Various demons were in the pantheon. Later on the pantheon was enriched by the deities linked to various localities.

It is very likely that the Canaanite cults influenced the way in which sacrifices were offered in the Temple at Jerusalem.

In the Bible

➡ The book of Joshua gives an account of the conquest of the country.
➡ The book of Judges speaks of the struggles between the Israelites and their Canaanite neighbours.

To explore further…

To move on
➡ Lot

See also
➡ Joshua; Judges; Idolatry; Religious life

CHURCH
Assembly of believers

After Jesus' resurrection, his disciples met together to pray. The Holy Spirit came down upon them in the place where they were gathered on the day of Pentecost.
While they maintained their links with the Temple for a certain period of time, they nevertheless kept up the practice of meeting and eating their main meal together, repeating Jesus' action of 'breaking the bread'. In those early days, the disciples shared their possessions and, in whatever way they could, they concerned themselves with those who were poorer or in worse conditions, like the widows. When new Christian centres sprang up in other places, they experienced that shared responsibility, in comparison with the Church in Jerusalem, which was in difficulty *(Romans 15:25-28)*.

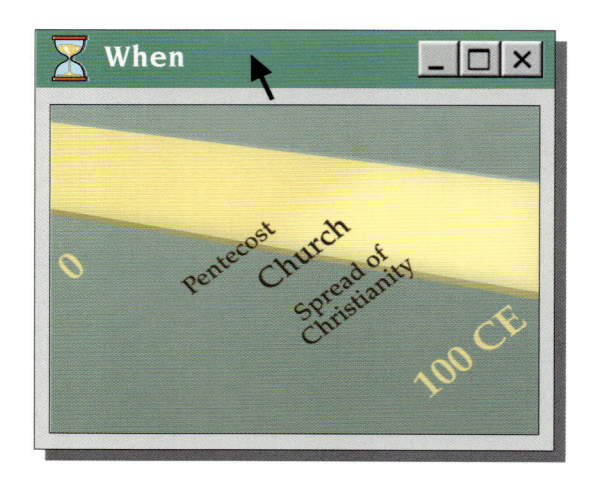

'Set apart'

The term 'Church' means an 'assembly' and is in fact a synonym for 'synagogue'. But Christians preferred the word 'Church' because it showed they were different. To begin with, 'Church' meant the religious gathering together of people, and later on it also referred to the place where this gathering was held. Those who believed in Christ were called 'saints' among themselves because they were conscious of participating in the holiness of God and being 'set apart' for their special task of proclaiming salvation.

Church worship

Worship was based on reading passages from the Jewish Scriptures, singing hymns and Psalms, remembering events in the life of Jesus and sharing news of other churches (the Gospels and Letters would be written down later). A special place was reserved for prayer and preaching, which involved explanation, encouragement and prophecy. Everyone was free to intervene and, in the wake of the enthusiasm that led some Christians to speak also in 'unknown tongues', the apostle Paul recommended the need for some order to be imposed. The Church recognised various gifts of the Spirit as genuine ways of serving God *(Romans 12:6-8)*. Whoever carried these out, whether a man or woman, was called a 'deacon' and only later did this term refer to a specific role.

Responsibilities

The most important decisions were taken in meetings of believers. Although the New Testament did not provide a unique model for the Church, the Church communities were the responsibility of the apostles, of the elders called 'presbyters' and then of the superintendents called 'overseers' and later 'bishops'. History was to confirm the role of the bishop. However, whoever wanted to become a bishop had to…

Read *1 Timothy 3:1-7.*

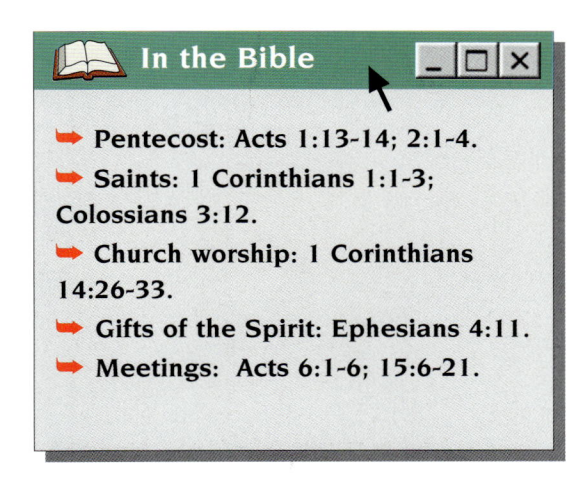

In the Bible

➡ Pentecost: Acts 1:13-14; 2:1-4.
➡ Saints: 1 Corinthians 1:1-3; Colossians 3:12.
➡ Church worship: 1 Corinthians 14:26-33.
➡ Gifts of the Spirit: Ephesians 4:11.
➡ Meetings: Acts 6:1-6; 15:6-21.

To explore further…

To move on
➡ Peter

See also
➡ Pentecost
➡ Synagogue
➡ Religious life

COMMANDMENTS
Laws for living in freedom

The Ten Commandments are also called the Decalogue, which means 'ten words.' According to the Bible these were written on tablets of stone given by God to Moses on Mount Sinai (*Exodus 19:16-19: 24:12-18*). The Ten Commandments are generally divided into two sections: the rules about relationships with God,

Read *Exodus 20:1-11*.

and those that regulate relationships between people,

Read *Exodus 20:12-17*.

Living in freedom

The Israelites had only just escaped from the terrible experience of slavery in Egypt. Now they had to learn how to live as a free people. It was similar to high-speed trains. The train travels fast and safely if the line is fitted with the latest technology and reliable tracks. The commandments are the sound rails and the latest technology, which God gave to his people so that they would not go off the tracks or have a serious accident, which would return them to slavery.

Before giving the Ten Commandments God reminded the people: 'I am the Lord your God, who rescued you from Egypt, where you were slaves.'

Read *Deuteronomy 5:6-22*.

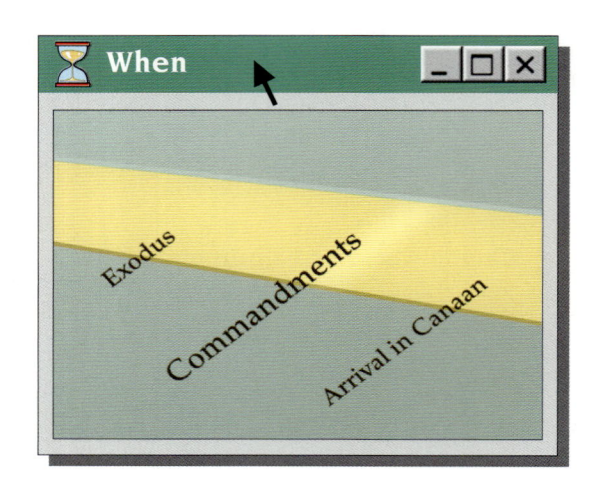

Where
Mediterranean Sea, CANAAN, Dead Sea, SINAI, EGYPT, Nile, Red Sea

When
Exodus — Commandments — Arrival in Canaan

38

Learning to live like free people

To learn to live as free people they had to do or not do certain things. But they should always remember that God, who had freed them, was the foundation of every command. For example: If God had freed them, they did not need to search out other gods.
God had freed them from forced labour in Egypt, so they should remember his day of rest.
They should not kill, because God had freed them from the constant threat of death in Egypt, so they should live in peaceful relations with others.
They should not steal, because God had given them many things and now God was teaching them not to take from others but to give to them.
They should not be false witnesses, because God had freed them from Egypt where they needed to be underhand and deceitful in order to defend themselves.

The Torah

The Ten Commandments are not the only laws to be found in the Bible. The first five books (the Pentateuch) were also called 'The books of the Law' – 'Torah' in Hebrew. It would be better to translate this word as 'teaching'. In fact it deals with God's teaching to his people not only concerning religion but also everything regarding human life and relationships.

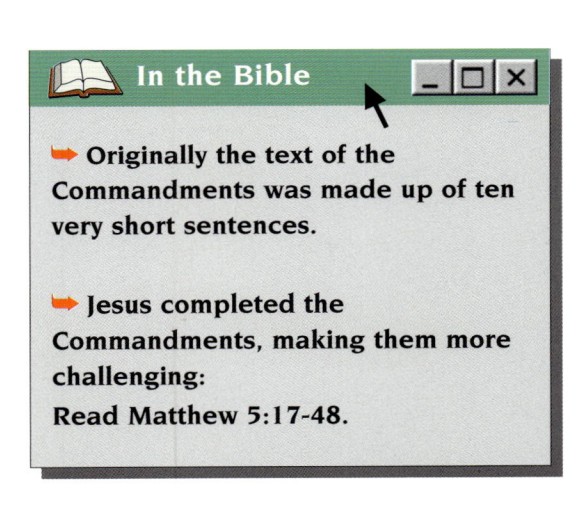

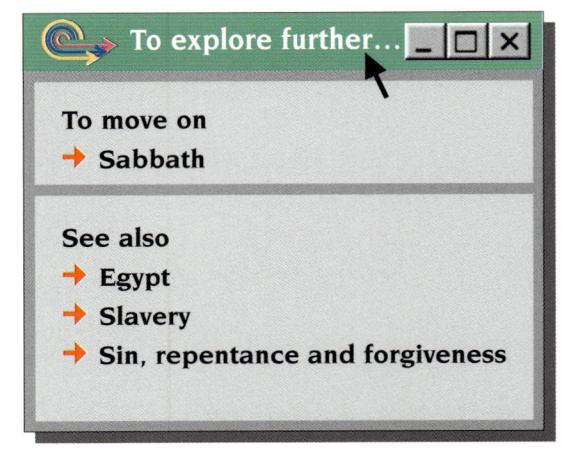

In the Bible

➡ Originally the text of the Commandments was made up of ten very short sentences.

➡ Jesus completed the Commandments, making them more challenging:
Read Matthew 5:17-48.

To explore further...

To move on
➜ Sabbath

See also
➜ Egypt
➜ Slavery
➜ Sin, repentance and forgiveness

COVENANT
Alliance with God

More than a contract – a relationship

In Israel a contract was first of all an alliance between people and was even more binding than family relationships: it was entered into by means of an oath sworn before God and sealed by a sacrifice; the partners committed themselves to mutual loyalty and responsibility *(1 Samuel 18:3-4)*. A contract could also be made between people of different classes, where the person who was wealthier or had a higher social status usually undertook to protect the other.

God and Israel: a covenant

The covenant became the chief image used to show the relationship between God and Israel. Obviously, it was not an agreement between equals but it came from God's initiative in choosing Israel and promising to walk beside her.

Read *Deuteronomy 7:7-11.*

Israel, for her part, agreed to the covenant, promising to acknowledge the Lord as God and to serve him; the covenant was solemnly sealed on Sinai. The tragedies of Israel's history, and especially the exile in Babylonia, came to be interpreted by her Scriptures as the consequences of Israel's breaking the covenant: nevertheless, even faced with Israel's betrayal, God declared his resolve to remain faithful, therefore keeping the covenant even on just one side *(Isaiah 54:1-10)*.

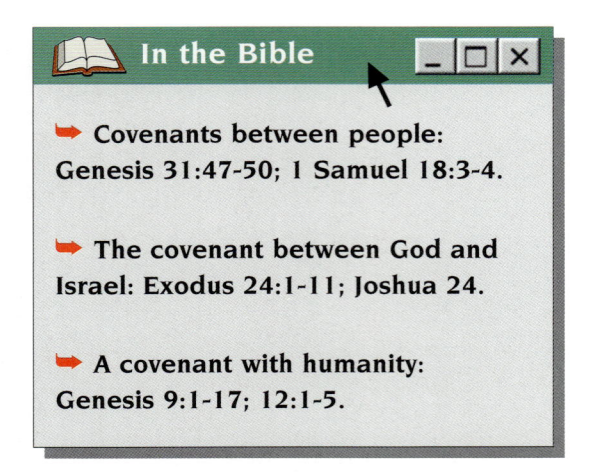

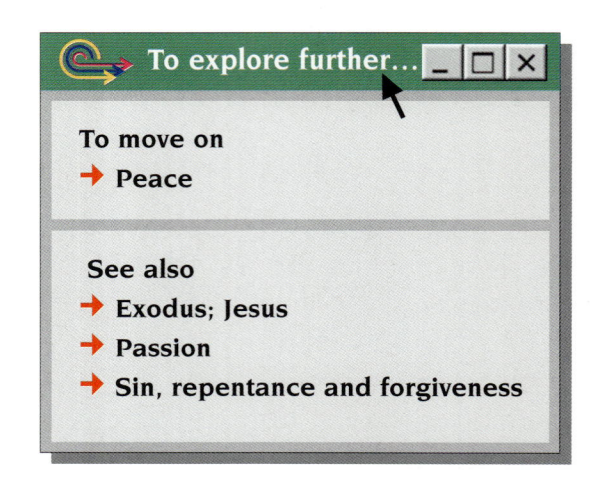

In the Bible

➡ **Covenants between people:** Genesis 31:47-50; 1 Samuel 18:3-4.

➡ **The covenant between God and Israel:** Exodus 24:1-11; Joshua 24.

➡ **A covenant with humanity:** Genesis 9:1-17; 12:1-5.

To explore further...

To move on
➡ Peace

See also
➡ Exodus; Jesus
➡ Passion
➡ Sin, repentance and forgiveness

The covenant with the whole of humanity

Reflecting on her own history with God, Israel understood that being the people God had chosen did not mean that God excluded the pagans from his love: in fact God had already drawn up a covenant with Noah, which embraced the whole of humankind and indeed the whole of creation, with the rainbow, which appeared at the end of the flood, as a sign; and Abraham was the partner of a covenant with God which was a blessing for all people of the earth.

The new covenant in Christ's blood

The life of Jesus embodied God's decision to be the faithful friend of Israel and humanity on the basis of one criterion alone, that of unconditional grace – his unconditional favour and mercy. The cross expressed a steadfast love, able to rescue life even from death, and the future from the oppressive actions of people. That was why, at the Last Supper, Jesus could say that the wine was: 'My blood which seals God's covenant.' It was the sign with which God expressed his special relationship with Jews and non-Jews who believe in Jesus.

Read *Mark 14:22-26*.

CREATION
God, the only Lord

The first account of creation

The first book of the Bible begins with a hymn of praise to God, Creator of heaven and earth. The work of creation was accomplished by God through his Word, in seven different moments of time, called days. The seventh day, the Sabbath, was God's day of rest. God subdivided creation to give order to it: at the centre of everything was humankind, man and woman, made in God's image. God blessed human beings and entrusted them with the responsibility of looking after the earth.

Read *Genesis 1:26-28*.

Of course, the account is based on the understanding of the cosmos in ancient times and does not aim to describe the origins of the world. Rather, it expresses faith in God, the one Creator and God of everything.

The second account of creation

There is a second account of creation in the Bible, which is an older narrative where the focus is not on the universe and the world but is placed on man, taken from the earth, moulded by the hands of God and brought to life by the divine breath. The narrative continues with the picture of God planting a garden for the man to live in with the task of cultivating the land and taking care of it. In the middle of the garden, amongst all the trees, God put two special trees, one giving life and the other knowledge. Man could eat the fruit from all the trees in the garden but not the fruit of the tree of knowledge.

'It is not good for the man to live alone,' observed God, and he moulded the various species of animal from the earth. But man still remained alone, for none of the animals was a helper equal to him. So God created woman.

Read *Genesis 2:21-25*.

CREATION

Disobedience

The tree of knowledge was the only thing out of bounds in the Garden of Eden because the knowledge of everything belonged to God, not to human beings. That was the reason for the prohibition and also the reason for the disobedience. The narrative is fiction and rich in unforgettable images, but the core of Adam and Eve's sin, the desire to be like God, was tragically inborn in human nature.

Read *Genesis 3:1-13*.

The harmonious situation that existed before their disobedience was shattered. The relationship between man and woman changed so that it was no longer one of equality. Even the harmony with nature was lost and human beings would be forced to work very hard in order to obtain food from the earth.

Read *Genesis 3:16-19*.

In the heart of the garden, near the tree of knowledge, was the tree of life. God was worried: 'What if man and woman were to decide to eat the fruit from this tree, too? It would be better to be cautious.' So Adam and Eve were driven out of the Garden of Eden. To the east of the garden, God placed guards with flaming and flashing swords.

In the Bible

➡ The Old Testament often mentions creation, for example: Psalms 8, 33, 89, 102, 104, 148: Isaiah 45:18; Job 9:5-9; 10:8-12.
➡ The New Testament: Mark 10:6; Romans 8:19-22.
➡ The new creation: 2 Corinthians 5:17; Galatians 6:15; Revelation 21-22.

Cain and Abel

Adam and Eve's firstborn son was Cain. Later Abel, their second son was born. Cain became a farmer, whereas Abel was a shepherd. As Cain was the firstborn his father's inheritance was due to him and his brother was expected to be subordinate to him. And yet Cain believed that God favoured his younger brother's offering and did not pay much attention to his. He was so angry and so jealous that he killed his brother. When God demanded an explanation from Cain about the murder, he denied any responsibility. God's punishment was very severe: Cain was placed under a curse. The earth that had been soaked in Abel's blood would not produce any more crops and he would be forced to flee far away. Cain cried out to God: 'My punishment is too much for me to bear! When I have run away to unfamiliar places, anyone finding me will kill me!' In order to protect Cain, God put a mark on him as a gesture of love towards a murderer. Abel's death must not lead to further deaths.

Read *Genesis 4:1-16.*

To explore further…

To move on
➡ Noah

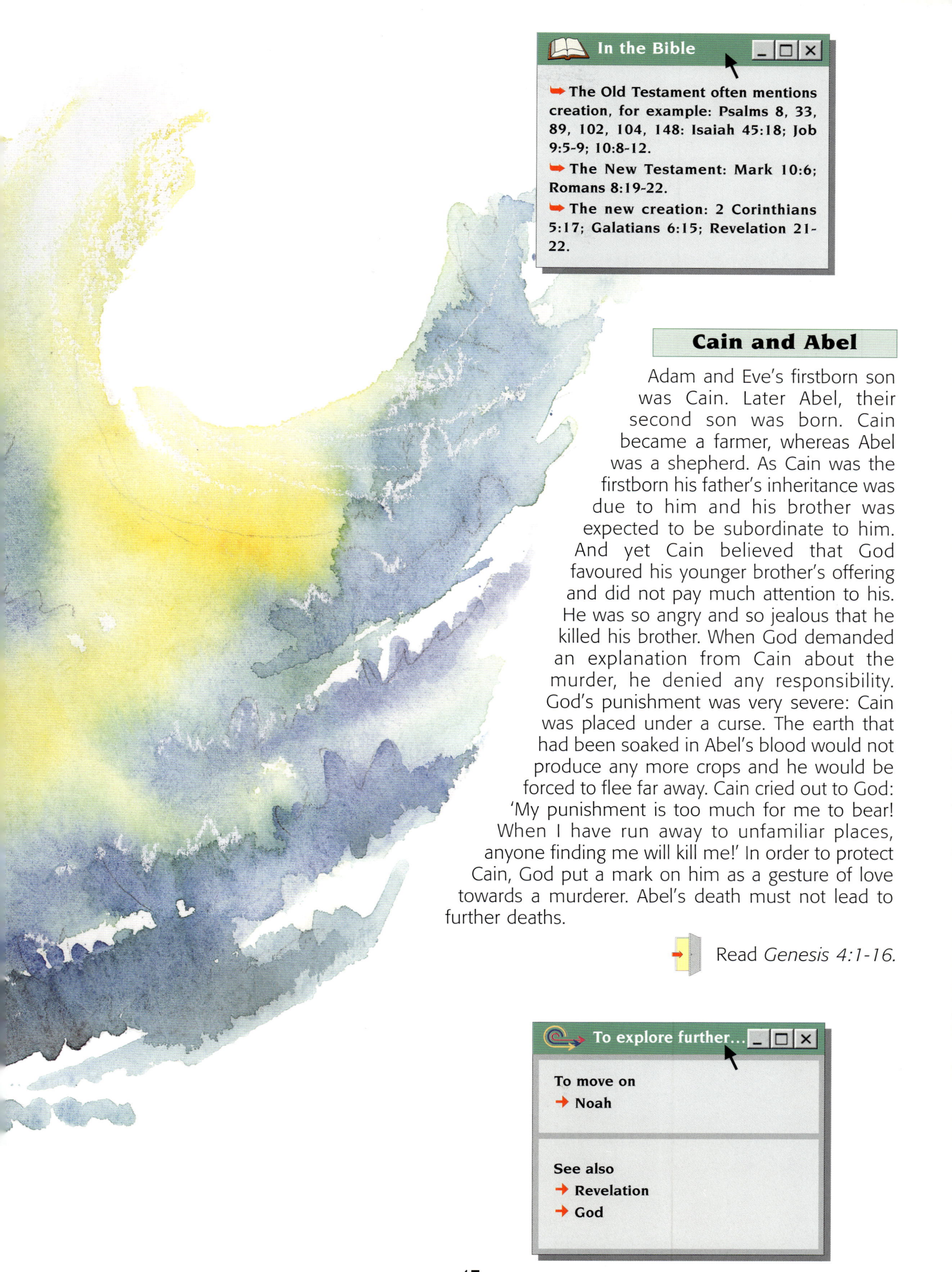

See also
➡ Revelation
➡ God

DANIEL
Stand your ground!

Daniel was a young Jew deported to Babylonia. He was chosen from among the noble Jewish families for service in the royal court, together with three friends, Hananiah, Mishael and Azariah. Those young men had to be free from physical defects, good-looking, strong, wise, intelligent and have common sense. They were to be taught to read and write the Babylonian language *(Daniel 1:3-4)*.

Their names were changed to emphasise their submission to the king.

The purpose of the book: to resist authority

The book of Daniel wants to encourage those faithful to God, to stand firm during a time of persecution.

In fact, the first six chapters tell about the faithfulness of these four young people in keeping God's Law, the Torah. With the vegetarian diet prescribed by their food laws, the four were healthier and stronger than the others.

Daniel interpreted the king's dreams three times, explaining that he did this only because God revealed their meaning to him.

The three friends refused to worship the statue of the king, honoured as a god. But they miraculously survived the flames of their punishment, thanks to the help of a fourth person who looked 'like an angel' *(Daniel 3:25)*.

Daniel prayed to God, in spite of the king forbidding it. Thrown into the lions' pit, he was miraculously saved, obtaining from the king….

Read *Daniel 6:1-26*.

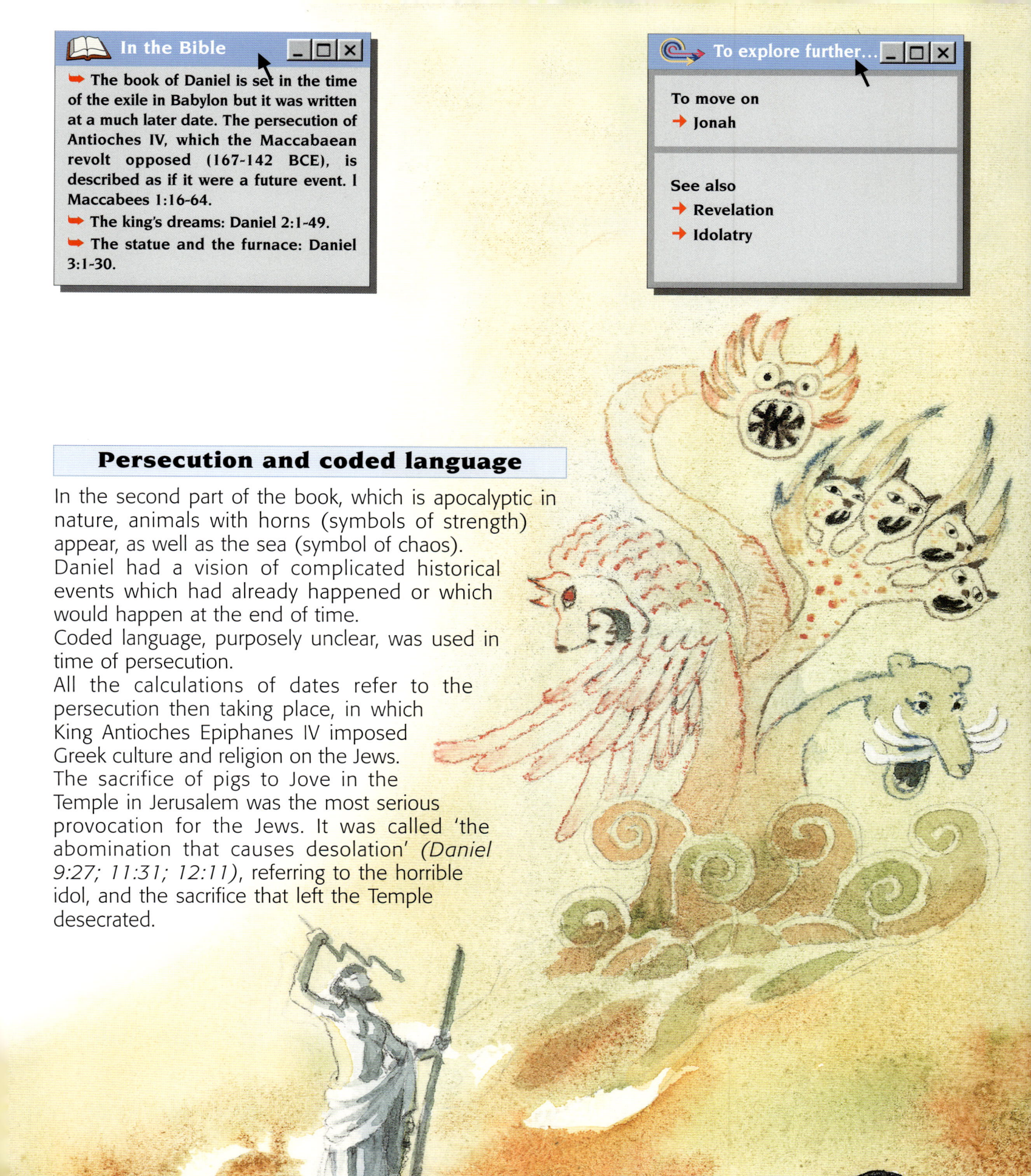

📖 **In the Bible**	↪ **To explore further...**
➡ The book of Daniel is set in the time of the exile in Babylon but it was written at a much later date. The persecution of Antioches IV, which the Maccabaean revolt opposed (167-142 BCE), is described as if it were a future event. I Maccabees 1:16-64. ➡ The king's dreams: Daniel 2:1-49. ➡ The statue and the furnace: Daniel 3:1-30.	To move on ➡ Jonah See also ➡ Revelation ➡ Idolatry

Persecution and coded language

In the second part of the book, which is apocalyptic in nature, animals with horns (symbols of strength) appear, as well as the sea (symbol of chaos). Daniel had a vision of complicated historical events which had already happened or which would happen at the end of time.

Coded language, purposely unclear, was used in time of persecution.

All the calculations of dates refer to the persecution then taking place, in which King Antioches Epiphanes IV imposed Greek culture and religion on the Jews. The sacrifice of pigs to Jove in the Temple in Jerusalem was the most serious provocation for the Jews. It was called 'the abomination that causes desolation' *(Daniel 9:27; 11:31; 12:11)*, referring to the horrible idol, and the sacrifice that left the Temple desecrated.

DAVID
The great king

David was considered the greatest king that Israel ever had. He began a family line that reigned for several centuries until Jerusalem fell to the Babylonians.
One of his descendants led the first phase of the return and rebuilding after the exile and, even in the time of the Romans, the whole nation expected that through a 'son of David' they would be freed from their oppressors. In fact, one of the characteristics of the Messiah was that he would be a descendant of David. Joseph, the husband of Mary, the mother of Jesus, originated from David's family as the genealogies in the gospels of Matthew *(1:1-17)* and Luke *(3:23-38)* point out.

The youngest

After a series of disobedient actions by Saul, God sent Samuel to Jesse's house at Bethlehem, to choose a new king. The choice fell on the last and youngest son of Jesse. God said to Samuel: 'Pay no attention to how tall and handsome he is … I do not judge as people judge. They look at the outward appearance, but I look at the heart.' *(1 Samuel 16:7)*. So David was anointed king while Saul was still reigning. Early on, the young boy was appreciated at court both for his skill in playing the harp and his poetry (very many of the hymns collected together in the book of Psalms were to be attributed to him) and because he killed a terrible enemy put forward against Israel by the Philistines – the giant Goliath. Armed only with a sling, David was successful in an impossible venture. With the help of God, he got the better of Goliath.

Read *1 Samuel 17:1-54.*

Abigail

King Saul wanted to kill his rival, so David had to flee into the territory of their enemies, the Philistines, where he pretended to be mad so that he would not be killed. Then he became the leader of a group of armed men, made up of people who were oppressed, in debt or dissatisfied with Saul.
At that time, David met Abigail, an intelligent woman. Going against her husband, Nabal's, decision, she helped David by giving him the rations his men needed and by preventing him from taking the law into his own hands. When Nabal died, David married Abigail.

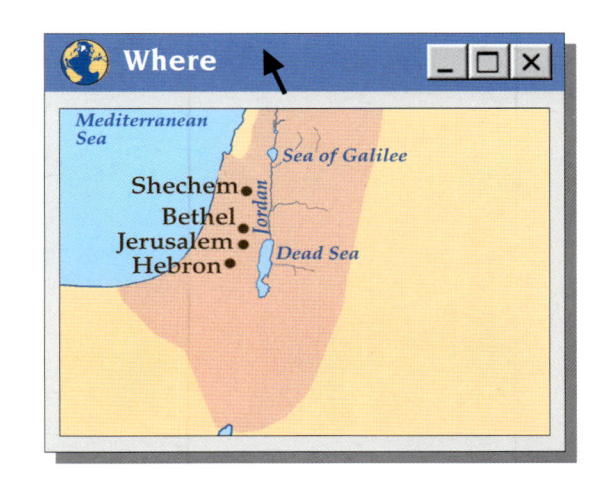

Read *1 Samuel 25*.

Where
Mediterranean Sea, Sea of Galilee, Shechem, Bethel, Jerusalem, Hebron, Jordan, Dead Sea

David reunites the tribes

David created a small autonomous state in the South of the kingdom, protected by the Philistines. But when the Philistines defeated and brought about the death of Saul, David, ordered by God, went to Hebron where the patriarchs were buried. There he was acknowledged as king by the tribe of Judah over whom he would reign for seven years and six months. After some years, David was recognised as king even by the tribes of the North (Israel) at Hebron and he would reign for more than thirty-three years over a reunited nation, which was internally at peace. Then David would die peacefully at an advanced age.
His descendants would reign for a long time over Judah, as God had promised *(2 Samuel 7:8-17)*.

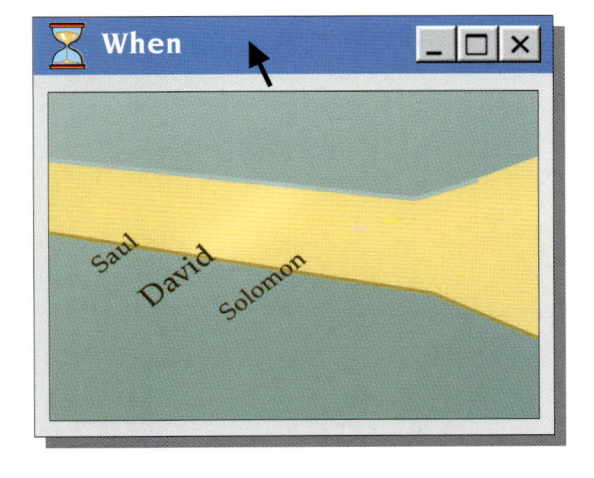

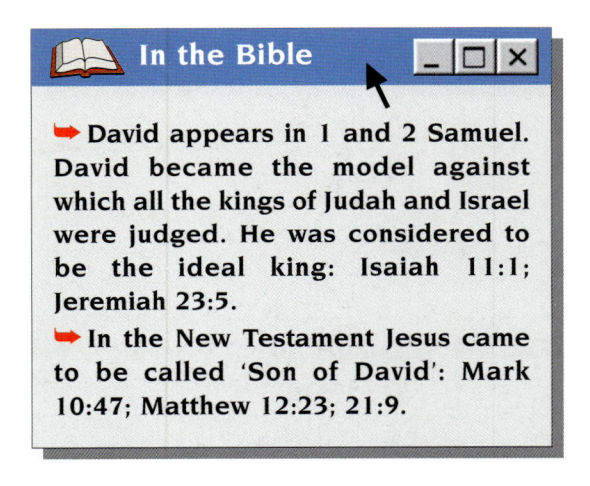

When
Saul, David, Solomon

In the Bible

➡ David appears in 1 and 2 Samuel. David became the model against which all the kings of Judah and Israel were judged. He was considered to be the ideal king: Isaiah 11:1; Jeremiah 23:5.

➡ In the New Testament Jesus came to be called 'Son of David': Mark 10:47; Matthew 12:23; 21:9.

DAVID

Jerusalem the capital city

King David's first task was to find a new capital city. He conquered Jerusalem and had the Ark of the Covenant taken there. It was a very joyful occasion: a festival for the whole population took place, with dancing and banqueting. Michal, one of David's wives and the daughter of Saul, did not approve of her husband's unkingly behaviour.

> Read *2 Samuel 6:12-23.*

But for David it was important to honour God and win the favour of his people who indeed, would always love him very much, unlike the more lordly but more distant and tormented Saul.
With the building of his palace at Jerusalem, the transfer of the ark, and the establishment of a new group of priests, David centralised political and religious power in one place and in this way maintained control.
The building of the Temple, planned by him was, however, to be accomplished only by his son and successor, Solomon.

The kingdom expanded

David's numerous victories led to his kingdom becoming very large and powerful. Only with Josiah, several centuries later and for a very brief period, would Israel be as vast as in the time of David and Solomon. Nevertheless, even David experienced difficult times, as when one of his sons, Absalom, rebelled against him and almost took his place. In addition, David was not perfect: no great figure in the Jewish Scriptures was immune from defects and blame.

To explore further…

To move on
→ Solomon
To learn more
→ Jerusalem

See also
→ Prophecy; Samuel

David and Bathsheba

One day, David took a fancy to Bathsheba, a very beautiful woman, who was the wife of Uriah, one of his generals. He had an affair with her. By deception, he arranged for Uriah to be killed in battle in order to be able to marry his widow and acknowledge his son who had been born in the meantime (2 Samuel 11). But that did not go unnoticed by God, who sent the prophet Nathan to David. Nathan told the king a story: 'A poor man had only one lamb…'

Read *2 Samuel 12:1-14*.

David repented of the wrong he had done and asked for God's forgiveness. The baby died, but God kept his promise concerning the king's descendants. David and Bathsheba would have another son to reign after him, Solomon.

DESERT
Desolation and hope

The deserted and stony land that is typical of vast areas of Palestine, especially in the south and east, is different from the sandy expanses of other deserts, like those in North Africa.
Even though water is very scarce, some plants and shrubs can grow, animals can find nourishment and human beings can survive, although with difficulty.

Fear and complaints

The desert was the place where the Israelites found refuge after their escape from Egypt and where they remained for a generation: forty years.
Those born and brought up in slavery were frightened of facing the risks of a free life and feared conquering a new land *(Numbers 13-14)*. Besides this, the ex-slaves, who were used to a hard but essentially protected life, were appalled by the hardship. So their complaints increased: 'We wish that the Lord had killed us in Egypt. There we could at least sit down and eat meat and as much other food as we wanted' *(Exodus 16:3)*.

Time of preparation

Only a new generation of people, born in freedom, hardened by the difficulties and used to trusting in God's help, could enter into the Promised Land. The desert, therefore, symbolised a time of preparation and, in general, a source of life for believers.

The protection of God

Right there in the desert Israel experienced the loving care of God. Amongst all God's gifts, the one of the manna particularly stood out. In the desert, God's invisible power and presence were confirmed by the fact that there God revealed himself and gave directions for living, in the Commandments.

Read *Exodus 16:13-36*.

Solitude and temptation

The desert was also the place of human solitude and the temptation to do without God. Already seen in Israel's Scriptures, it was also experienced by Jesus. Before Jesus began his ministry, he went into the desert to face a hard test. Should the Messiah make himself known through the schemes suggested by the tempter, or obey God totally?

Read *Matthew 4:1-11*.

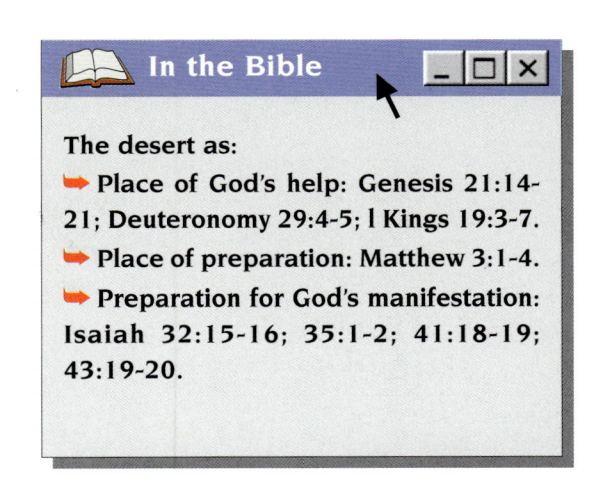

In the Bible

The desert as:
- Place of God's help: Genesis 21:14-21; Deuteronomy 29:4-5; I Kings 19:3-7.
- Place of preparation: Matthew 3:1-4.
- Preparation for God's manifestation: Isaiah 32:15-16; 35:1-2; 41:18-19; 43:19-20.

To explore further...

To move on
- Idolatry

See also
- Commandments
- Exodus

DIASPORA
Dispersion

A lost Diaspora

The word 'diaspora' which in Greek means 'dispersion' or 'scattering', still today refers to the Jewish communities outside the land of Israel.

Nothing is known of the destiny of the first Jewish Diaspora, made up of the tribes deported by the Assyrians when Samaria was destroyed in 722 BCE. However, the real Jewish Diaspora began with the Jewish exile in Babylonia where many remained even when, fifty years later, they were offered the possibility of returning home. They had in fact settled well in Babylonia and therefore they had no desire to face the risks of returning: what awaited them but the hostility of those who had remained and re-established themselves after the war? Thanks to their material and spiritual wealth, the Babylonian Diaspora had a strong influence on the whole of Judaism; take, for example, the Babylonian Talmud, the outstanding book of faith of Jews throughout the world.

In the Bible

➡ The book of Daniel tells of the problems for a practising Jew living among Gentiles.
➡ The prophet Jeremiah wrote to the Jews about their destiny in Babylonia. Read chapter 29.

From the Euphrates to the Tiber, via the Nile

In time Jewish communities formed throughout the whole of the ancient world. Round about the fifth century BCE, there was a colony of Jewish soldiers on the island of Elephantine, in the middle of the Nile. Very soon Jews were found in Alexandria in Egypt, where in the time of Jesus they made up the largest Jewish community outside Palestine (said to be tens of thousands of Jews).

In almost all the Mediterranean cities there were Jewish communities (like those at Tarsus, Ephesus, Thessalonica). Naturally there was an important Jewish group in Rome too.

To explore further...

To move on
➡ Ruth
To learn more
➡ Synagogue
See also
➡ Babylonia
➡ Exile
➡ Return and rebuilding

Remarkable citizens

The Jews always formed a lively element in cultural debates of their time; well-informed on the particulars of their monotheistic faith, they represented interesting debaters for the intellectuals of the time and their faith without doubt had a fascination for their contemporaries. Many converted from paganism and even more became God-fearers, that is, those who did not convert officially (perhaps for reasons of social convention) but lived according to the Law.
Unfortunately, even in the distant past, there were cases of fierce violence against the Jews.

● **Synagogues**

DISCIPLES
Following the Teacher

Discipleship

People who wanted to know about messages received from God gathered round the prophets. They in their turn told others about them *(Isaiah 8:16-18)*. So 'disciple' did not mean only 'pupil' but also 'follower' or 'successor'. John the Baptist had disciples and from this circle came those whom Jesus called to follow him.

▶ Read *Mark 1:16-20.*

Jesus' disciples continued to grow in number and included both men and women. That was new in a society which did not allow a woman to 'put herself at the feet' of a teacher, but forced her to occupy herself with family matters only. Jesus did not accept that sharp division of roles *(Luke 10:38-42)*.

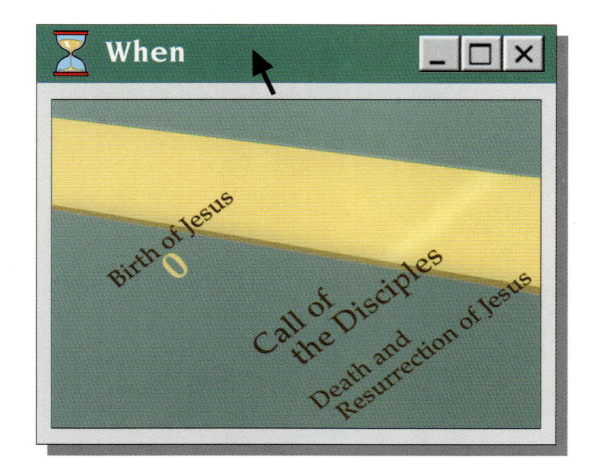

Where

Mediterranean Sea · Capernaum · Bethsaida · Sea of Galilee · Nazareth · Jordan · Jerusalem · Dead Sea

When

Birth of Jesus — 0 — Call of the Disciples — Death and Resurrection of Jesus

In the Bible

➡ Conditions for discipleship: Matthew 10:37; Mark 8:34-38; Mark 10:28-31; Mark 10:43-44; Luke 9:57-62; Luke 14:33; John 13:12-17; John 15:12-17.
➡ Women followers of Jesus: Matthew 28:1-10; Mark 14:3-9; Luke 8:1-3.
➡ Disciples called by Jesus: Mark 2:13-14; John 1:37.51.

To explore further...

To move on
➡ Parables

See also
➡ Church; Women in the Bible
➡ Jesus; John the Baptist

The consequences

With Jesus the disciples made their way on foot towards Jerusalem: they had left their homes, jobs and families. The recommendations Jesus gave to those who wanted to become his disciples were: do not be anxious about tomorrow; be available and ready for anything, even persecution and death; do not be held back by any special attachment to people or things; trust your own life to God, instead of seeking to save it with your own strength; be the servant of everyone. In the early Church there were still itinerant disciples, that is, without a steady job or a fixed home. But even those who did not make this radical choice were considered disciples all the same, in so far as they were followers of Jesus and would pass on his message.

The apostles

At a certain point in his ministry, Jesus chose twelve disciples, twelve like the tribes of Israel, for a particular task. This was to go in pairs and preach in the various towns round about and he gave them these instructions: 'When you set out....'

Read *Luke 9:3-5*.

These twelve were called apostles (from the Greek verb 'to send') – or those who were sent – and their names were: Simon nicknamed Peter, Andrew, James, John, Philip, Bartholomew, Matthew, Thomas, James the son of Alphaeus, Simon the Zealot, Judas the son of James (or Thaddaeus) and Judas Iscariot who would betray Jesus. After the resurrection, Matthias was chosen to replace the traitor and make up the group to twelve again. At the beginning, that group had an important role to play in Jerusalem: to bear witness to Jesus, from his baptism to his resurrection (*Acts 1:21-26*). The term apostle, however, was used also to refer to wandering preachers in general. Paul, for example, claimed that he himself was an apostle *(1 Corinthians 9:1-2)*.

EASTER
Freedom

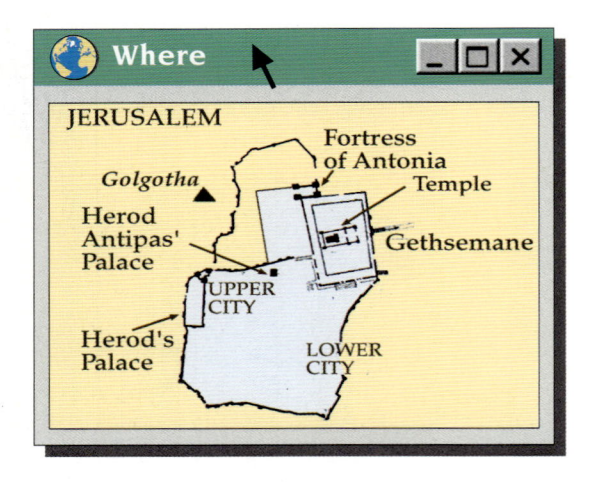

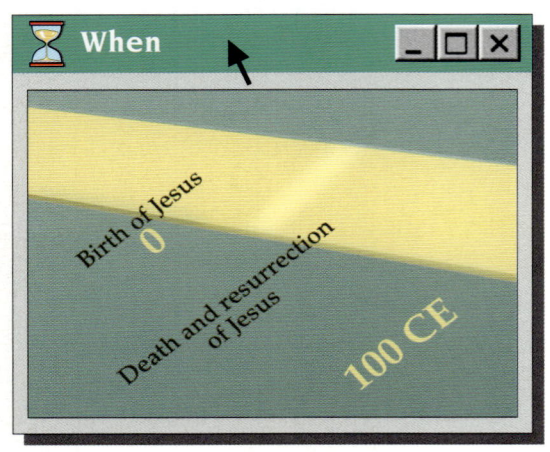

Where
JERUSALEM
- Golgotha
- Fortress of Antonia
- Temple
- Herod Antipas' Palace
- Gethsemane
- Herod's Palace
- UPPER CITY
- LOWER CITY

When
Birth of Jesus — 0
Death and resurrection of Jesus
100 CE

The Jewish Passover – freedom from slavery

The Hebrew word 'pesah' means 'passing over'. The Jewish Passover remembers the freeing of Israel from slavery in Egypt, guided by the hand of God *(Exodus 12; Deuteronomy 16:1-8)*. It is the great festival of freedom, when it was customary, in the time of Jesus, to go on pilgrimage to Jerusalem. It falls on the fourteenth of the month of *Nisan*, the first month in the Jewish religious calendar, which runs from the middle of March to the middle of April. Today at Passover, Jews still eat unleavened bread, that is, bread without yeast, to remember the departure of the Israelites from Egypt, which was so swift that there was no time to let dough rise *(Exodus 12:34)*. The annual Passover celebration reminds Jews that the freedom their ancestors enjoyed can be experienced today by following the path to freedom God has marked out for them, in other words, through obeying the Jewish Law.

Read *Exodus 12:1-14*.

To explore further…

To move on
→ Resurrection appearances

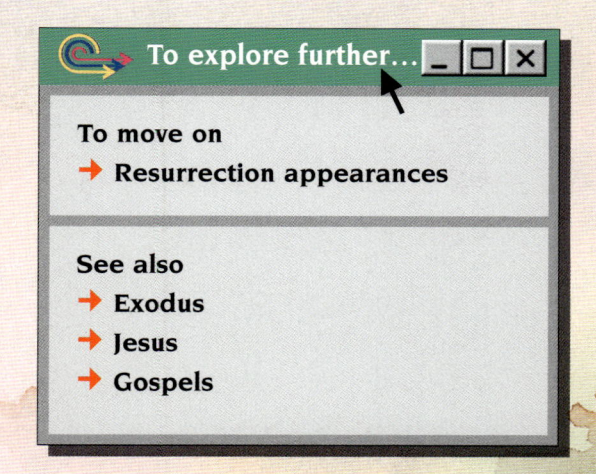

See also
→ Exodus
→ Jesus
→ Gospels

Jesus' resurrection – freedom from evil

On the first day after the Sabbath (Saturday) following Jesus' crucifixion, the tomb was discovered empty *(Mark 16:1-8)* and the crucified Christ appeared alive *(John 20:11-18)*. The resurrected Christ was not a ghost, nor even raised like Lazarus, who returned to life from the grave. Jesus was called by God to a new life, no longer threatened by death, to an eternal life. If Jesus was restored to life, it meant that God acknowledged that Jesus was right, it confirmed his message and personal identity: the God of Israel, the only God, was the God of the lowest of the low, the God of grace and mercy, like Jesus. Jesus' resurrection was God's triumph over the slavery of evil and brought freedom from death and sin.

→ Read *Matthew 28:1-10*.

A new creation – freedom for regeneration

Easter was the climax of Jesus' life on earth and it promised new life for the whole of creation. Jesus' resurrection, having conquered sin and death, signified the resurrection of every person and the recreation of the world. Everything that was alive, which reflected even a spark of God's life, (a small plant, an ant) would not be lost, but would be regenerated when God's kingdom would finally be established through God reigning truly in everything, at the last day. As God was at the beginning, so he would be at the end. God not death had the last word.

→ Read *1 Corinthians 15:1-28*.

EGYPT
A three thousand year old civilisation

E

Egypt was one of the cradles of human civilisation. It was there that one of the most evolved societies of ancient times was born and developed. Today it is famous for its pyramids and hieroglyphics. Egyptian civilisation experienced periods of splendour and decadence but, thanks to its fertile land irrigated by the Nile and protected by the deserts surrounding the country, it enjoyed a prolonged existence to which only the Romans were able to put an end, once and for all, after three thousand years of almost uninterrupted history.

Where

Mediterranean Sea
CANAAN
Nile Delta
Rameses
Pithom
GOSHEN
LOWER EGYPT
Memphis
SINAI
Nile
Red Sea
UPPER EGYPT

In the Bible

- **The arrival of the Israelites in Egypt: Genesis 37-50.**
- **The escape from slavery: Exodus 1-15.**

Egypt and Israel

Inevitably, such a culture and power as Egypt's influenced neighbouring Canaan. Famous murals show the kings of the Canaanite city-states submitting as vassals to the pharaoh. Only in a few periods of Egyptian weakness did Israel find space for herself: when the Israelites crossed the desert to escape from Egypt about 1300 BCE and especially when Israel established an independent kingdom under David.

An uncertain relationship

The Israelites always had an ambiguous relationship with Egypt because it was a land of refuge as well as that of a great enemy. On the one hand, Egypt was a place of refuge when the patriarchs Abraham and Jacob went there in times of famine to search for grain, or when some Israelites fled there from the court of Jerusalem to find asylum from the revenge of the Babylonians after one of many attempts at revolt.
On the other hand, Egypt was a great enemy when her army killed Josiah, King of Judah, and destroyed his army, and especially in the period of slavery when the Israelites, led by Moses, left Egypt.

Strange gods

Egyptian religion had two particular characteristics distinguishing it from the religions of Mesopotamia and Greece. First, there was the divine nature of the pharaoh, thought not so much to be a representative of the gods as a god himself, the god who gave reconciliation to the whole of Egypt. Second, there were the gods that were associated with animals. That very ancient tradition came from a time when the primitive tribes still depended on hunting for sustenance and so they had to gain the favour of the spirits of the animals in order to help the hunters capture them.

To explore further…

To move on
→ Moses

See also
→ Canaan
→ Exodus
→ Josiah

ELIJAH
A solitary prophet

Elijah lived about 860 BCE, and came from Tishbe, a village in the Northern Kingdom to the east of Jordan. He wore a skin cloak tied with a leather belt.
Elijah, a solitary prophet, appeared suddenly and announced to the king that there would be a terrible famine: 'In the name of the Lord, the living God of Israel, whom I serve, I tell you that there will be no dew or rain for the next two or three years until I say so' *(1 Kings 17:1)*.

The politics of King Ahab

Ahab was the king of Israel (about 869-850 BCE) whom Elijah challenged. He was an important character politically and militarily, but he had been disloyal to the faith of his ancestors. He had made an alliance with the Phoenicians and had married Jezebel, the daughter of the king of Tyre. That had officially brought the Phoenician religion into Israel, along with the triumphal entry of their local gods Baal and Asherah. That was not all: the queen and King Ahab had unleashed a fierce persecution against Israel's faith, killing the prophets of God. Besides that, influenced by the queen, Ahab thought that he should have absolute power and be above the law of Israel.

Read *1 Kings 21*.

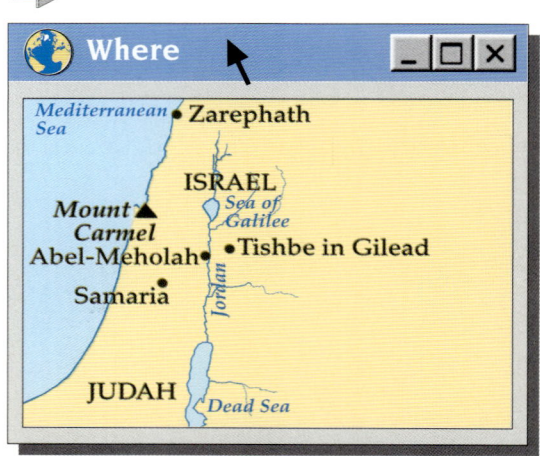

Where

Mediterranean Sea — Zarephath
ISRAEL
Sea of Galilee
Mount Carmel
Abel-Meholah
Tishbe in Gilead
Samaria
Jordan
JUDAH
Dead Sea

When

Northern Kingdom: Israel — Elijah, Elisha

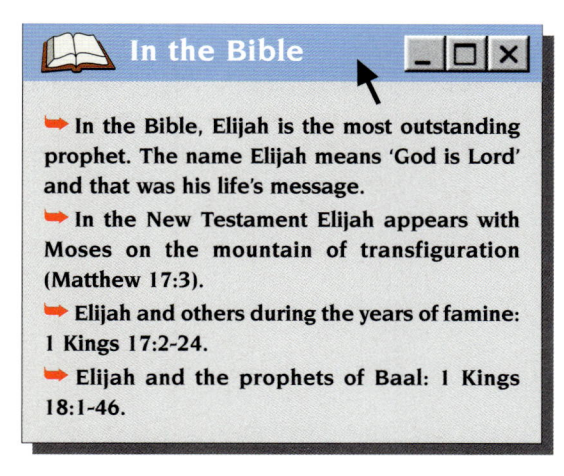

In the Bible

➡ In the Bible, Elijah is the most outstanding prophet. The name Elijah means 'God is Lord' and that was his life's message.
➡ In the New Testament Elijah appears with Moses on the mountain of transfiguration (Matthew 17:3).
➡ Elijah and others during the years of famine: 1 Kings 17:2-24.
➡ Elijah and the prophets of Baal: 1 Kings 18:1-46.

To explore further...

To move on
➡ Elisha

See also
➡ Idolatry
➡ Prophecy

God manifests himself

After three years of drought, Elijah confronted the king in a dramatic sequence of events. He proposed a test of fire with the prophets of Baal so that the people could see which was the true God. While the prophets of Baal failed, God responded to Elijah's prayers with fire. All the people shouted: 'The Lord is God! The Lord alone is God!' Now rain could return to the country. But Elijah took revenge and had all the prophets of Baal killed. However, he had to flee from the anger of the queen in order to save his life. Elijah ran away to Mount Horeb, the mountain of Moses. There, however, God manifested himself very differently from the way in which Elijah had imagined God. He was not in the violence of the flames, the earthquake or the whirlwind, but in the silence of intense listening.

➡ Read *1 Kings 19:1-18.*

Elijah had to name a prophet to take over from him. It would be Elisha. Elijah disappeared in a mysterious manner: 'A chariot of fire pulled by horses of fire came between them, and Elijah was taken up to heaven by a whirlwind' *(2 Kings 2:11).*

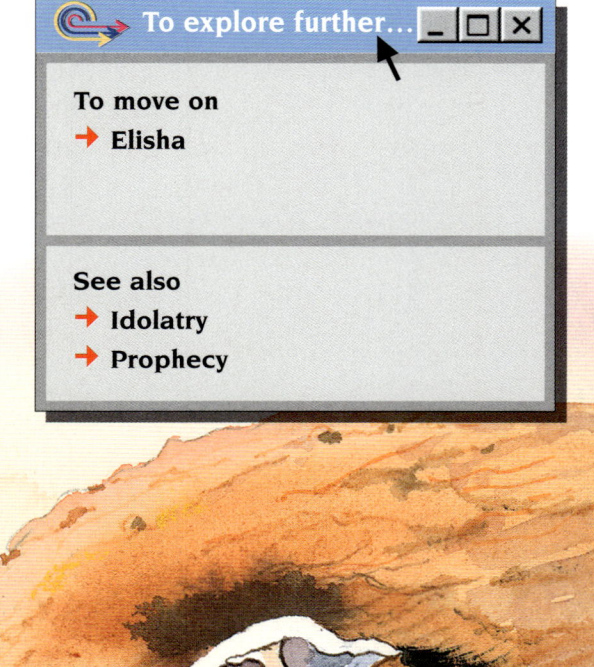

ELISHA
A *prophet of the people*

Elisha, in contrast to Elijah, was a prophet of the people. Throughout his life he would be always accompanied by a group of disciples. From the moment when Elijah chose him as his successor, Elisha showed his desire to be involved with those around him. So he prepared a great banquet with his workers and went to say farewell to his parents. But he also burnt the bridges behind him….

▶ Read *1 Kings 19:19-21*.

The real successor of Elijah

Elisha became Elijah's true successor. Not only did he witness the ascension of Elijah as an actual witness, but he also received Elijah's distinctive cloak. A group of prophets from Jericho recognised that 'the power of Elijah is on Elisha' *(2 Kings 2:15)*. Further, Elisha would rebuild faith and trust in the loving help of God, amongst the individual members of the people of Israel. To illustrate this, many events and miracles were narrated, regarding Israel and individual people, other nations and moments of war.

▶ Read *2 Kings 5:1-19*.

But Elisha would also become the agent of God's justice, which had been declared by Elijah against King Ahab, his family, and against other nations.

In the Bible
➡ Rebuilding the faith: 2 Kings 4-8.
➡ The slaughter of Jezreel: 1 Kings 21:17-21 and 2 Kings 9-10.

To explore further…
To move on
➡ Amos
See also
➡ Assyria
➡ Idolatry
➡ Prophecy

The slaughter of Jezreel

This final event involved Elisha in a real political revolt. The death of Ahab had happened earlier on….

Read *1 Kings 22:29-40*.

But the slaughter announced by the prophet Elisha against the family of Ahab would be terrible. Elisha had an officer called Jehu anointed king of Israel. Close to the city of Jezreel, Jehu would kill Jehoram, the king of Israel, and Ahaziah, the king of Judah, who had gone to visit him. Jehu would have Queen Jezebel thrown from a window and would have more than a hundred of Ahab's descendants cruelly killed.

The end of the Northern Kingdom

The cruel and revolting carnage, done in the name of God, would be interpreted a hundred years later as the cause of the end of the Northern Kingdom.
God would give the prophet Hosea a message in which he demanded an explanation from Jehu's descendants concerning the blood spilt by their grandfather on the plain of Jezreel. On that plain God would put an end to the Northern Kingdom and the dynasty of the kings of Israel, destroying its military power *(Hosea 1:4-5)*.

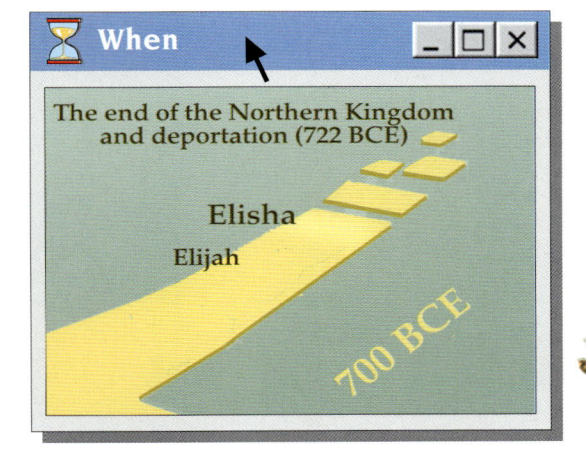

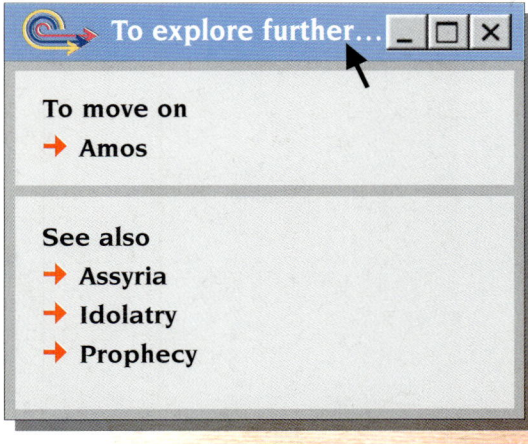

When
The end of the Northern Kingdom and deportation (722 BCE)
Elisha
Elijah
700 BCE

65

EXILE
The tragedy of a people

Where

In the early years of the sixth century BCE in the Near East, the power of the new Babylonian Empire led by Nebuchadnezzar II was growing, and Egypt tried to form a coalition of kings to stop its expansion.

The Kingdom of Judah also participated in the alliance, but the venture failed and Jerusalem was completely conquered in 587 BCE. The Babylonians destroyed the walls of the city and Temple, deporting a large part of the population – the king, courtiers, priests, and craftsmen. And so the exile began.

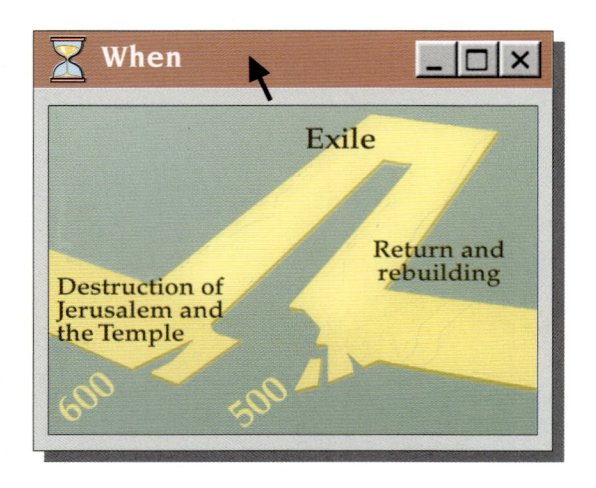

When

The exile was not bad at all!

Unlike the Assyrians, who scattered the defeated and deported people (as happened to the northern tribes of Israel, who were obliterated from history), the Babylonians arranged for the Jews to be placed in one region.

They had the opportunity to rebuild a normal life, keeping (more or less freely) their traditions and sometimes even to reach important positions in the Babylonian court. Certainly, there was a great deal of nostalgia, as reflected in Psalm 137, but the future was better than they had foreseen.

Saving their identity

However, the Jews chose not to forget who they were. Led by their priests, like the prophet Ezekiel, they gathered together the traditions of their faith and their history, emphasising those customs that distinguished them from other people, like the keeping of the Sabbath, circumcision and their food laws. They also wrote down the first draft of the Old Testament, in particular the Pentateuch (or *Torah*).

A decisive experience

The exile marked an unforgettable stage in the history of the Jews. Faced with the Babylonian culture and religion, the Jews sharpened up their own identity and their national consciousness. They defined precisely what the characteristics of the people of Israel and their faith were. They made up the first real Diaspora (scattering abroad) of the Jewish people. In the light of that dramatic experience, the people of Israel learned to reread all their history and remember who they were and what their mission in the world was.

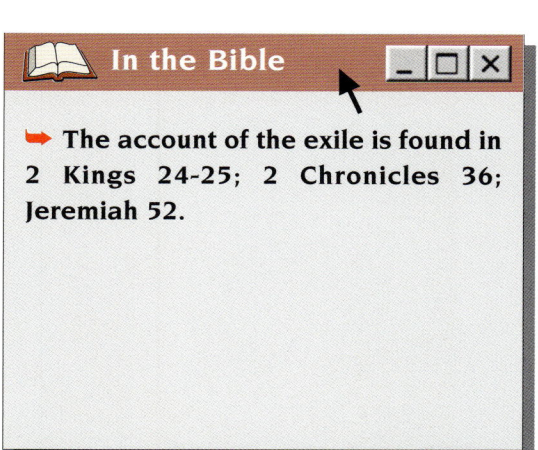

In the Bible

➡ The account of the exile is found in 2 Kings 24-25; 2 Chronicles 36; Jeremiah 52.

To explore further…

To move on
➡ Daniel

To learn more
➡ Babylonia

See also
➡ Diaspora
➡ Return and rebuilding

EXODUS
Towards freedom

A typical dictionary definition for the term 'exodus' might be: 'way out of; departure of a lot of people from the same place'. Then going further it might say: 'mass departure, for example, the May bank holiday exodus'. You can be sure that for the Israelite slaves in Egypt it was a departure but not an exodus for May bank holiday….

Crossing the Red Sea

The slavery of the Israelites had become more unbearable, but in Egypt awful events had occurred and the terrified pharaoh had ordered the Israelites to leave the country. The Israelites then began their exodus, their mass departure. But the pharaoh changed his mind about having let them go and ordered his army to follow them. The Israelites found themselves with the sea in front of them and the pharaoh's army behind them. What could they do?

Read *Exodus 14:1-31*.

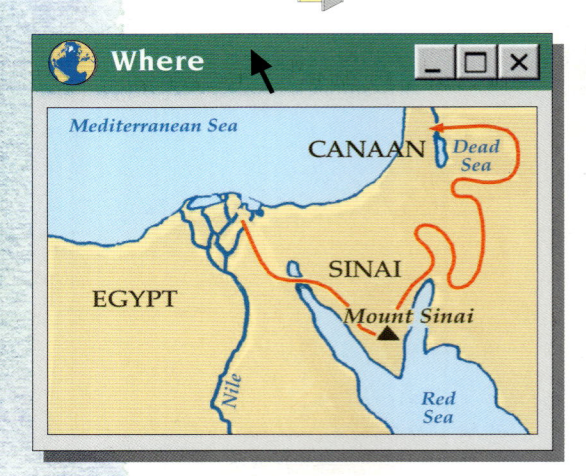

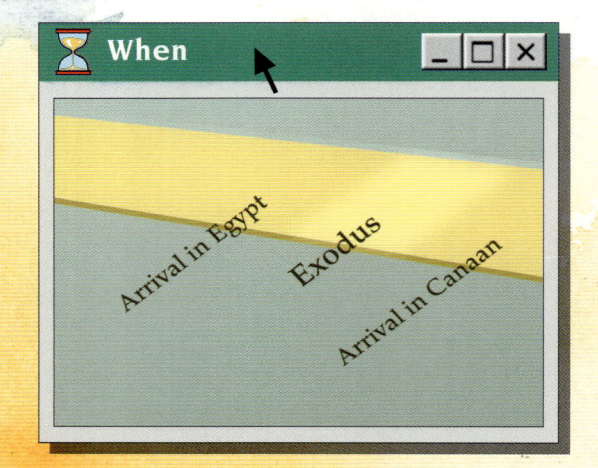

Where

When
Arrival in Egypt — Exodus — Arrival in Canaan

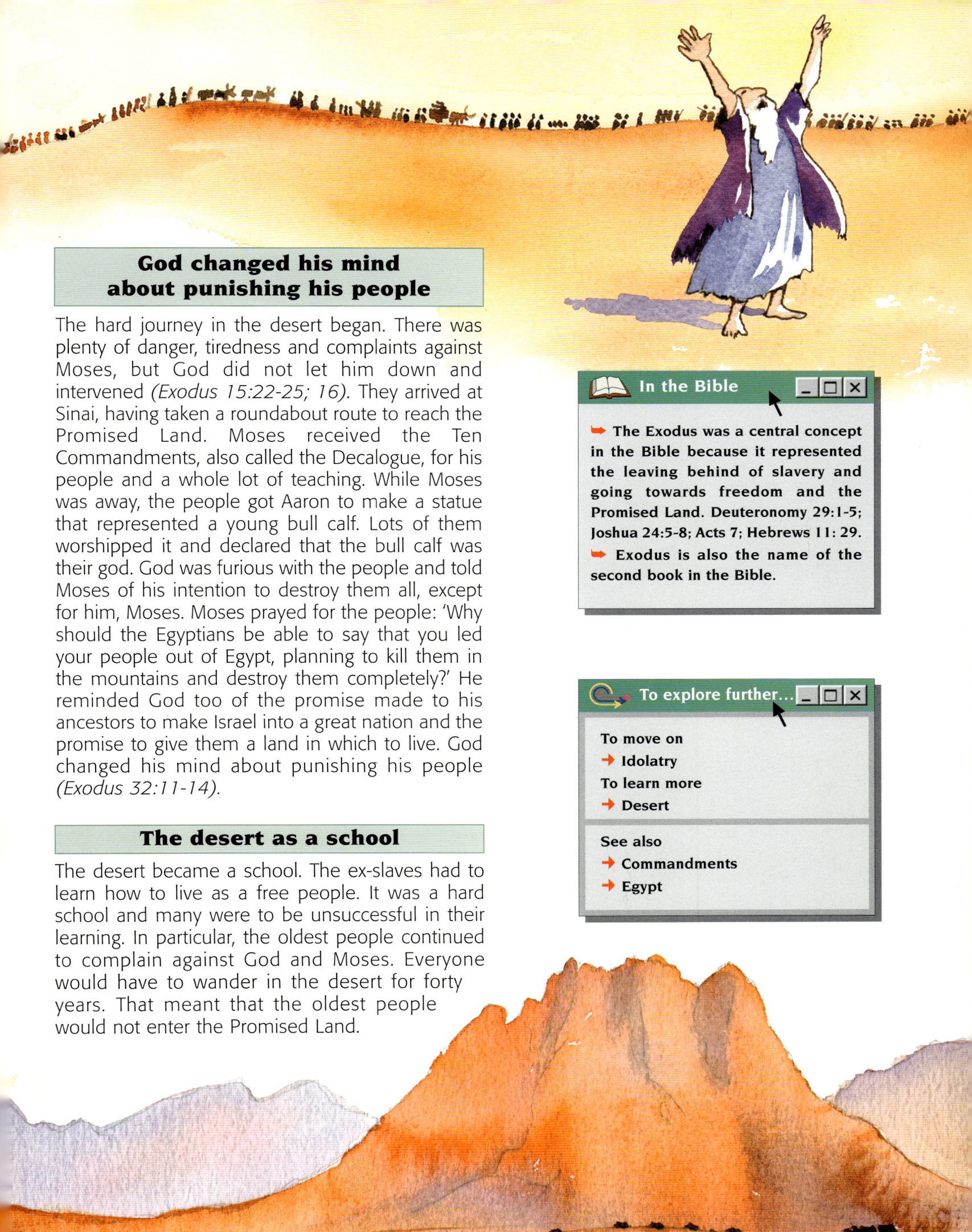

God changed his mind about punishing his people

The hard journey in the desert began. There was plenty of danger, tiredness and complaints against Moses, but God did not let him down and intervened *(Exodus 15:22-25; 16)*. They arrived at Sinai, having taken a roundabout route to reach the Promised Land. Moses received the Ten Commandments, also called the Decalogue, for his people and a whole lot of teaching. While Moses was away, the people got Aaron to make a statue that represented a young bull calf. Lots of them worshipped it and declared that the bull calf was their god. God was furious with the people and told Moses of his intention to destroy them all, except for him, Moses. Moses prayed for the people: 'Why should the Egyptians be able to say that you led your people out of Egypt, planning to kill them in the mountains and destroy them completely?' He reminded God too of the promise made to his ancestors to make Israel into a great nation and the promise to give them a land in which to live. God changed his mind about punishing his people *(Exodus 32:11-14)*.

The desert as a school

The desert became a school. The ex-slaves had to learn how to live as a free people. It was a hard school and many were to be unsuccessful in their learning. In particular, the oldest people continued to complain against God and Moses. Everyone would have to wander in the desert for forty years. That meant that the oldest people would not enter the Promised Land.

In the Bible

➡ The Exodus was a central concept in the Bible because it represented the leaving behind of slavery and going towards freedom and the Promised Land. Deuteronomy 29:1-5; Joshua 24:5-8; Acts 7; Hebrews 11: 29.
➡ Exodus is also the name of the second book in the Bible.

To explore further…

To move on
➡ Idolatry
To learn more
➡ Desert

See also
➡ Commandments
➡ Egypt

FAITH
Anchored to God

Israel's experience

In the Bible, the term faith points above all to the faith in God that allowed people to walk towards the light of his promise and was, therefore, a belief in a relationship with God. In the Old Testament, the model of faith is Abraham, who departed for the unknown relying only on the Word of God *(Genesis 12:1-5)*, obeying it even when it appeared cruel and absurd.

The opposite of faith is described in the narrative of the golden calf. Israel grew tired of waiting for God's Word, thinking God was absent, and they decided to put their faith somewhere else. The calf, which could be seen and touched, showed a solid reality which was actually present, whereas the God of Abraham, Isaac and Jacob – who knew where he was? But the statue was an idol that could not save. Faith went hand in hand with obedience. Faith was not to do with uttering religious words but with choosing which God to serve and behaving accordingly *(Joshua 24:14-15)*.

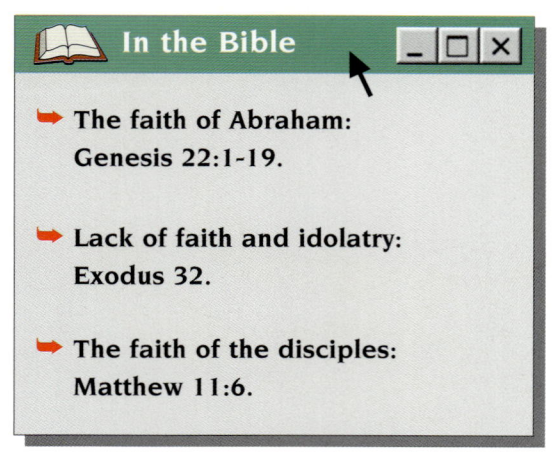

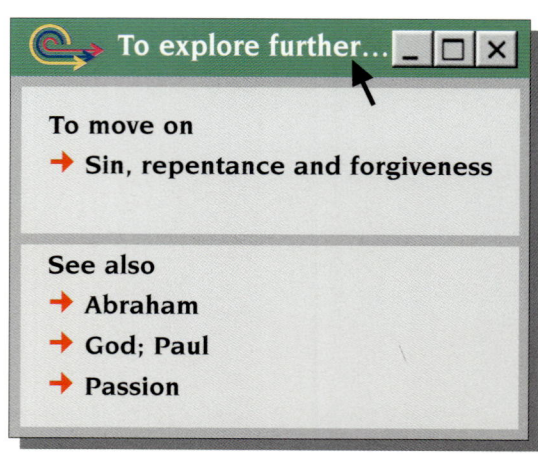

In the Bible

➔ The faith of Abraham:
Genesis 22:1-19.

➔ Lack of faith and idolatry:
Exodus 32.

➔ The faith of the disciples:
Matthew 11:6.

To explore further...

To move on
➔ Sin, repentance and forgiveness

See also
➔ Abraham
➔ God; Paul
➔ Passion

Belief in Jesus

The New Testament declares that God, as Jesus, was gracious to the poor and the outcasts of society and forgave the sinners. So faith in God meant finding in Jesus the source of a richer life of truth and fullness, in this world and the next.

The sick woman who was searching only for a cure for herself, but looked for it near to Jesus, had faith according to him *(Mark 5:34)*. Another woman had even more faith when she implored Jesus to save her daughter, overriding his unsympathetic reply and teaching him a lesson. That is the only gospel text in which Jesus is not portrayed in a good light.

Read *Matthew 15:21-28*.

But for the disciples, faith meant being available to follow Jesus, obeying his word without losing faith in him, even if his message and he himself were different from what they would have liked. *Mark 15:39* suggests that the centurion who recognised the crucified Jesus as the Son of God was an example of a person with faith. That was also central to Paul's message: faith recognises in the crucified Jesus the love of God which saves *(1 Corinthians 1:17-25)*, and Paul found such joy and strength from this good news that it became the centre of his whole life.

71

GOD
The Lord

The God of Freedom

God revealed himself to Israel as the one who 'brought you out of Egypt' *(Exodus 13:9)*. For the Israelites, he was above all the God of freedom, a powerful partner and a faithful friend.

However the freedom God gave was not gained once and for all, but had to be guarded. That was why God gave the commandments to his people – so that, freed from the pharaoh, the Israelites would not fall once more into the slavery of violence and selfishness.

God's name

According to *Exodus 3:1-14* God revealed his own name to Moses. It was a Hebrew word of four letters, YHWH, whose meaning is uncertain, even though most scholars translate it as 'Lord'. The Jews never pronounced God's name, out of respect, substituting other expressions, such as Adonai, which had the same meaning.

God had a name because he was not a concept or an idea, but a 'you' who spoke to his people and intervened in their history. When the Bible speaks of the name of God it is intended to refer not only to the word YHWH (the tetragram or word of four letters) but to God himself, in that he was present and acted in the events of Israel.

God and the people

In the ancient Near East, everyone, including Israel, was convinced that more than one god existed. Each nation believed it had a special relationship with its own gods and the Israelites considered YHWH to be their God and were convinced that he was 'a mighty king over all the gods' *(Psalm 95:3)*. According to Scripture, the God of Israel was not primarily interested in the fact that the people offered sacrifices or fasted. Above all, loyalty to God's Word meant they had to: 'break the chains of oppression and the yoke of injustice, and let the oppressed go free' *(Isaiah 58:6)*.

GOD

God is one

The biggest catastrophe in the history of Israel was the destruction of Jerusalem by the Babylonians and the deportation of a good part of the population in 587 BCE.

During the exile, Israel understood that their defeat did not depend on the fact that the God of Israel was weaker than the gods of the Babylonians. On the contrary, he was the only God, no other existed. YHWH, therefore, was also the God of the other nations, but those nations could understand that only through the witness of the nation God had chosen.

Many other names of God are found in the Bible: the Almighty God *(Genesis 17:1)*, the Most High God *(Genesis 14:18)*, the Everlasting God *(Genesis 21:33)* and others.

Those were only different ways of naming YHWH, the one true God. But if God who had brought Israel out of Egypt was in fact one, he was also the creator of the heavens and the earth: the whole world was his work. Throughout all the tormented events of its history, up to today, Israel has remained faithful to this profound belief and its faith can be reduced to the words of *Deuteronomy 6:4*: 'Israel, remember this! The Lord – and the Lord alone – is our God'.

The father of Jesus

The God of Israel was also the God of the Jew, Jesus of Nazareth and of the New Testament: there was no other God for Christians, too. Jesus presented God as his father ('*abba*', 'daddy') and everyone's father. He was affectionate, concerned about his sons and daughters and eager to gather them close to himself even and especially when they behaved badly towards him.

Read *Luke 15:11-32*.

For Jesus God was a 'good God' who, as in the Old Testament, did not want the cold observance of rules, but the health of the sick, the return to society of all those marginalised, like the lepers, or those who had betrayed their country like the tax-collectors who worked for the Romans; a God of Jews and non-Jews. The creator, nevertheless, did not leave the violence suffered by his creatures unpunished: Jesus stated that he himself and his father were present in the hungry, the thirsty, the stranger, those who were poor, sick and in prison: whatever was done to these people, was in fact done to God himself and the final judgement depended on that *(Matthew 25:31-46)*.

After the resurrection of Jesus, his disciples understood that God was exactly as Jesus had said, but above all, as Jesus was. No concept (not even the most lofty, such as grace, love, mercy) could describe God. Whoever wanted to know what the face of God was like must look at the life, death and resurrection of Jesus of Nazareth *(John 14:9)*.

To explore further...

To move on
→ Bible

See also
→ Commandments
→ Exodus; Jesus
→ Covenant; Holy Spirit

GOSPELS
Four witnesses

The word 'gospel'

The term 'gospel' comes from the Greek *'euangelion'*, which means 'good news'. The good news was that Jesus was the Christ, the Messiah, the hope of humanity. The Gospels were written in the commonly spoken Greek of the first century and report the different evidence that bore witness to Jesus of Nazareth's actions and words.

The Gospels were aimed at the Christian Churches and the far-reaching world surrounding them.

The names of the Gospels

There are four Gospels listed in the New Testament, under the names of Matthew, Mark, Luke and John, in that order. The names are found only in the titles and come from tradition. As the names of the authors are mentioned nowhere in the text of the Gospels, even scholars are not sure who the authors were.

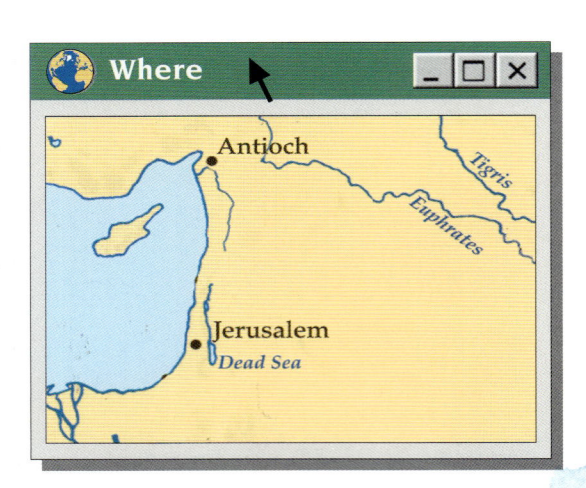

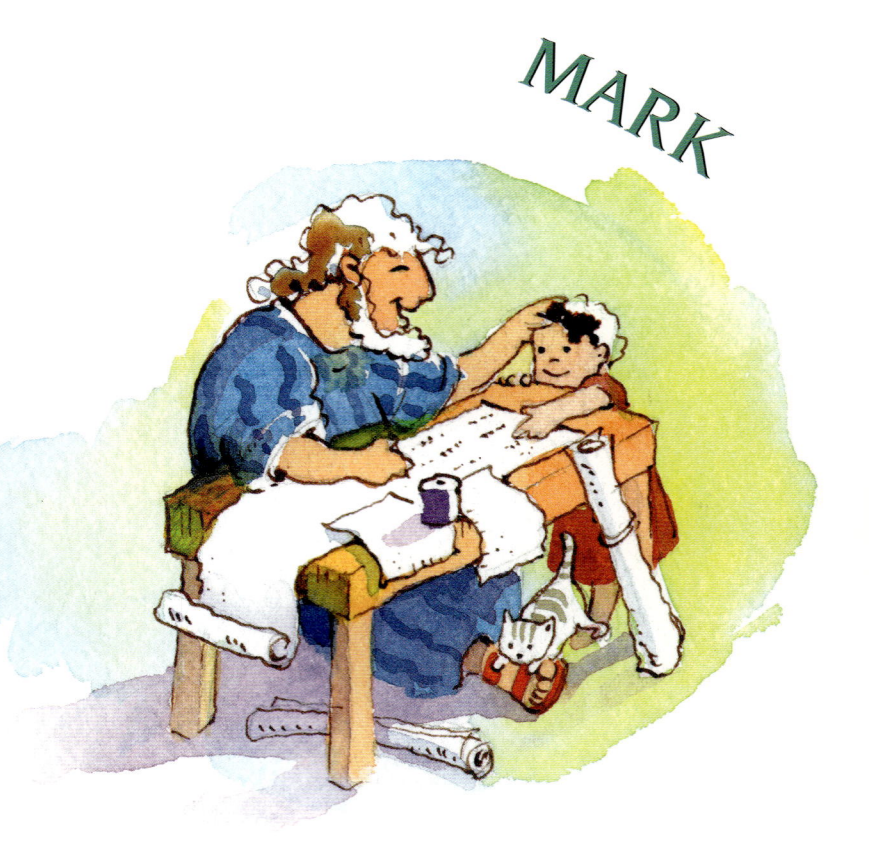

Where
- Antioch
- Tigris
- Euphrates
- Jerusalem
- Dead Sea

When
- 0
- Spread of Christianity
- Writing of the Gospels
- 100 CE

MATTHEW

MARK

The differences between the Gospels

All four Gospels were written after the tragic destruction of Jerusalem by the Romans, in 70 CE. Those of Matthew, Mark and Luke are called 'synoptic' because they used material from a common source, which resulted in some parts being very similar to each other.

Mark, the shortest Gospel, is more of a narrative and more straightforward. It concentrates above all on the facts of Jesus' life. It is recognised as the oldest Gospel (probably about 70 CE) and was perhaps translated from Aramaic, the language Jesus spoke.

Matthew made a lot of use of Mark for the facts of Jesus' life, adding to them five discourses of Jesus and many quotations from the Old Testament. He included a narrative about the birth of Jesus. This Gospel is addressed to a Christian Church not far from Palestine. As it is very critical of the Pharisees, it reflects the period of the break between the Christian Church and synagogue, probably between 80-90 CE.

Luke wrote his Gospel and the Acts of the Apostles in more correct Greek. He had a universal vision of the Christian mission. He outlined a story of salvation within the human story where Jesus Christ was Lord. He also used material from Mark and Matthew, as well as having his own particular source and his own narrative of Jesus' birth. He wrote after the Gospel of Matthew, probably about 90-95 CE.

John followed his own source, which was different from that of the synoptics in the timing of incidents in Jesus' life, in geographical information as well as in the language. It is thought to have been written towards the end of the 90s CE.

Only Luke, out of the four, explained how he came to write his Gospel….

Read *Luke 1:1-4*.

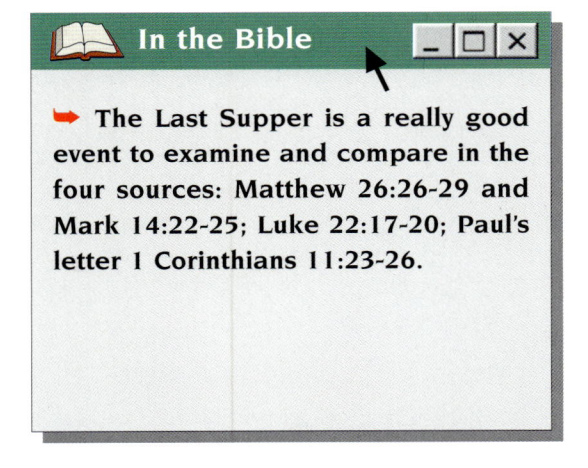

In the Bible

➡ The Last Supper is a really good event to examine and compare in the four sources: Matthew 26:26-29 and Mark 14:22-25; Luke 22:17-20; Paul's letter 1 Corinthians 11:23-26.

To explore further…

To move on
→ Jesus' Birth

To learn more
→ Rome

See also
→ Acts of Apostles
→ Disciples; Jesus

HOLY SPIRIT
The power of God

The wind of God

The Holy Spirit is the power of God in action. In Hebrew the same word was used for spirit, breath or wind, so the Spirit was described as the wind of God which ran through history, sometimes light and unobtrusive and at other times with a force that turned everything upside down. When Israel was oppressed by her enemies, the Spirit of God came down upon Samson, Gideon, Jephthah and the other judges and led their fight for freedom. It was the Spirit that placed the Word of God on the lips of the prophets. The Spirit was the source of knowledge and advised the leaders of the people when they wanted to listen to it. Above all, the Spirit would be the great strength of the Messiah, who would bring justice and peace to creation.

Read *Isaiah 11:1-9; 61:1-4.*

No one could take possession of the Spirit, which remained a gift from God. Israel waited however, for the great day when the Spirit would be given to the young and old, women and men, the free and slaves, all of whom would be prophets *(Joel 2:28-29).*

In the Bible

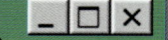

➡ The Spirit is the source of wisdom: Proverbs 1:23.
➡ The Spirit descends on Jesus: Mark 1:10.
➡ The Spirit is the power given to Jesus; Matthew 12:28.
➡ The Spirit is sent to the disciples: Acts 2:1-11.
➡ The Spirit is one: 1 Corinthians 12:4.

Jesus, the man of the Spirit

The Spirit descended on Jesus at the time of his baptism and directed his life, giving him the power to heal and save; it was the profound content of his words and the source of his prayer and his praise *(Matthew 11:25-27)*. Jesus' life was so deeply and wholly interwoven by the Spirit, that according to the Gospels of Matthew and Luke, it could be declared that he was conceived in Mary's womb by the action of the Holy Spirit *(Matthew 1:18; Luke 1:35)*.

To explore further...

To move on
→ Acts of the Apostles

See also
→ God; Jesus
→ Jesus' Birth
→ Pentecost; Gospels

The Spirit of Resurrection

After the crucifixion and Easter, the Spirit was sent to the disciples at Pentecost as a power to proclaim the gospel in words and deeds. The Holy Spirit explained, to the Church and the world, the meaning of Jesus' life and the story of the whole Bible in constantly new terms. It gave women and men the strength to live not against everyone else, but together with them and sometimes for them.

→ Read *John 16:5-15*.

In the Church the Spirit charged each and every one to put their own abilities to the service of others. The gifts were many, but the Spirit was one. The Spirit wanted everyone to find their happiness in doing what they were called to do because God's Spirit was the Spirit of joy.

IDOLATRY
Israel did not listen!

'Israel, listen to this! The Lord – and the Lord alone – is our God.' *(Deuteronomy 6:4)* This is the beginning of the 'Shema', the central Jewish prayer that is recited at home and synagogue. The Lord is one: no other God exists beside him. The commandment found in *Exodus 20:2-3* states this: 'I am the Lord your God who brought you out of Egypt, where you were slaves. Worship no god but me.' The God who liberates cannot have rivals.

The golden calf

God freed Israel from slavery in Egypt and gave them the Commandments to help in their new way of living as a free people. However, the people asked Moses' brother Aaron, the priest: 'Make us a god to lead us.' After having made the statue of a bull calf, Aaron said: 'This is your god who led us out of Egypt!' But that was impossible. God could not be imprisoned in any representation. Moses was furious: what would happen?

Read *Exodus 32:1-29.*

Baal and Asherah

The Commandments continued by saying: 'Do not make for yourselves images of anything in heaven or on earth or in the water under the earth.' It was not easy for the Israelites to live in Canaan, in the middle of a pagan people who worshipped other gods and who made lots of idols. The most popular gods were Baal, the god of the sky and Asherah, mother earth. The worship of the idols Baal and Asherah would ensure success in work in the fields. The Bible calls this idolatry.

The cause of trouble

The prophets of Israel often reminded the people that God, the Creator, was above all powers and all idols. They warned that idolatry was the cause of trouble: a violent king who sent people to their death; a hostile nation which invaded Israel; a deportation far from home, like the painful exile in Babylonia.

Jesus came to liberate

In the New Testament the theme is the same. Jesus had come also to give freedom from the need to make useless idols *(1 Corinthians 12:2)*. Even nowadays it is sometimes thought that inanimate objects have special powers: this is called superstition. Likewise, some people have an uncontrollable desire to possess things: '…greed (for greed is a form of idolatry)'. *(Colossians 3:5; Matthew 6:19-25)*

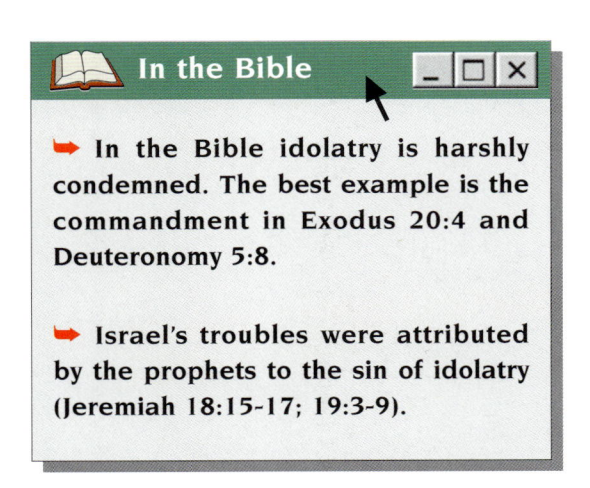

In the Bible

➡ In the Bible idolatry is harshly condemned. The best example is the commandment in Exodus 20:4 and Deuteronomy 5:8.

➡ Israel's troubles were attributed by the prophets to the sin of idolatry (Jeremiah 18:15-17; 19:3-9).

To explore further…

To move on
➡ Covenant

See also
➡ Elijah
➡ Moses
➡ Prophecy

ISAAC
The promised son

Isaac, the only son of Sarah and Abraham, was born when his parents were already old. Their joy was immense. Abraham, as God had promised, would have descendants. Sarah said: 'God has given me the joy of laughing.' Isaac grew up surrounded by his parents' affection.

Do not strike the boy!

Why did the angel of the Lord say that? What was Abraham doing with a large knife in his hand? And why was Isaac tied up on a stone, on top of a pile of wood?

▶ Read *Genesis 22:1-3*.

God tested Abraham. He had to sacrifice Isaac. But surely it was precisely Isaac his son, in whom God's promise would be fulfilled? And yet Abraham obeyed: he had absolute faith in God. When he left his camp with Isaac, he told the servants that they had to wait there: 'Then we shall come back to you.' To his son who asked him: 'Where is the lamb for the sacrifice?' he replied: 'God himself will provide one.' And the two of them walked on together. Abraham had faith in God, while Isaac had faith in his father. At the most dramatic moment the angel of the Lord intervened. Abraham threw away the knife. The mountain where Isaac was saved by God was named 'The Lord Provides'.

▶ Read *Genesis 22:9-14*.

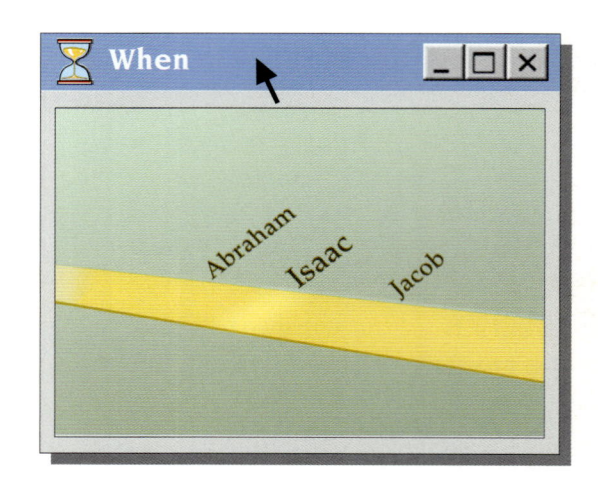

A wife for Isaac

Abraham was very old and had been on his own since Sarah died. It was time for Isaac to get married. But where would a wife be found for him? Among the Canaanite women? Never! No, there was another solution. Abraham called his most trusted servant: 'You must go to the land that I left so many years ago, to Haran, and choose a wife for Isaac from among my relatives there. God will guide you.' The servant took ten camels and as many of the best things as he could find, as gifts for those relatives in that distant place and he left.
Finally the small caravan reached its destination and stopped at the gate of the city near to the well where the old servant would meet the young Rebekah.

Read *Genesis 24:11-27.*

Abraham's family gave him a warm welcome. The servant told the story of his master and asked his hosts to give Rebekah in marriage to Isaac. The father and the brother of the young lady replied: 'Since this matter comes from the Lord, it is not for us to make a decision. Here is Rebekah; take her and go.' In the morning the caravan set out again with Rebekah and her servants.

The end of the journey

It was evening and Isaac was returning homewards. He had gone out at sunset to relax in the countryside. Lifting his eyes he saw camels approaching. Rebekah also looked up, saw Isaac and when she learned who he was, she covered her face and went to meet him. Isaac led Rebekah into his tent, married her and loved her.

To explore further…

To move on
→ Jacob

See also
→ Abraham

ISAIAH
Justice and hope

Prophet Isaiah

Isaiah was probably a young priest from Jerusalem in the Southern Kingdom. He was from a noble family and was used to going to the royal palace and the king's court. One day, in the year of the death of King Uzziah (about 740 BCE), something happened to Isaiah, which would change his life for ever. In the Temple he had a blazing vision of God, with angels singing 'Holy, holy, holy', in praise to God! It is not known what Isaiah saw. Only the consequences are known. In a flash his eyes were opened: he understood how truly real his own and his people's wretchedness, dishonesty and impurity were. He accepted God's forgiveness and the task of spreading God's message.

Isaiah's task

Isaiah would speak to the people as a prophet for about forty years. Everyone listened to what he had to say. Nevertheless, their eyes were incapable of seeing and their ears unable to hear. Only a small minority could understand the meaning of his prophecy. The sorrowful prophet asked: 'How long will it be like this, Lord?' And God replied that time was up for a people without ears to hear or eyes to see: a tree that did not produce fruit would be cut down!
The invasion of Assyrian troops in 722 BCE, and then the Babylonian army in 587 BCE, would be the instruments of that judgement! And yet, it would not be the end.
God declared….

Read *Isaiah 6:1-13*.

A terrible time

Isaiah's message was addressed to Israel and all the nations: it concerned a terrible period of time when there would be great disorder throughout the world. But, besides God's judgement, there was hope: God would save Jerusalem from the siege of the Assyrians and a new 'messianic age' was announced.

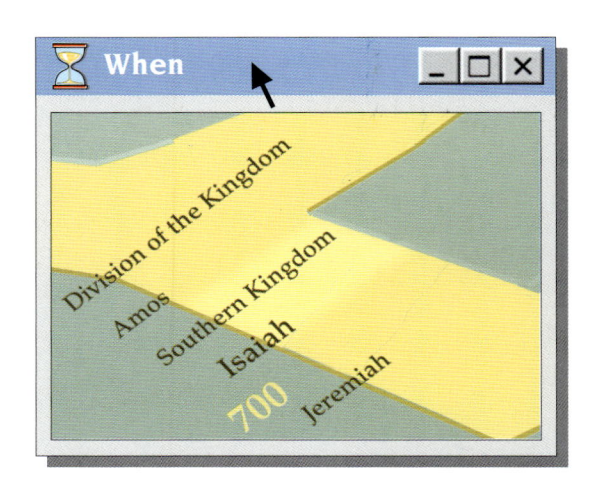

When

Division of the Kingdom · Amos · Southern Kingdom · Isaiah · 700 · Jeremiah

The book of Isaiah

The book of the prophet Isaiah, the longest of the prophetic books, was written by at least four authors at different times. 'First Isaiah' worked between about 750 and 700 BCE. Chapters 1-23 and 28-39 are attributed to him.
'Second Isaiah' worked towards the end of the Babylonian exile (about 540 BCE) and chapters 40-55 cover his writings. He announced poetically that Cyrus, king of Persia, was about to declare the release of the exiles.
'Third Isaiah' wrote chapters 56-66 when the exiles had returned to their homeland (about 500 BCE).
Finally, in chapters 24-27, there is an 'apocalyptic' passage, written in a later period.

In the Bible

➡ Isaiah's family: Isaiah 8:1-4.
➡ Isaiah speaks to his people: Isaiah 1:10-20.
➡ Jerusalem is liberated: Isaiah 36-38.
➡ The announcing of the 'messianic age': Isaiah 9:1-6; 11:1-9.
➡ Jesus quotes Isaiah: Luke 4:16-21.

Where

Mediterranean Sea · Sea of Galilee · Jordan · Jerusalem · Dead Sea · JUDAH

To explore further…

To move on
➡ Josiah

See also
➡ Assyria
➡ Babylonia

85

JACOB
Israel

Twins

Twins were born. Rebekah, their mother, and Isaac, their father, looked at them, puzzled, because they had never seen two newborn babies so different from each other. The babies grew up. Esau, the older one, became a hunter. Jacob, on the other hand, willingly stayed around their camp home. Isaac favoured Esau whereas Rebekah preferred Jacob.

One day, while Jacob was cooking some good soup, Esau returned from hunting worn out and hungry. 'I'm hungry, give me a bit of that stuff!' 'Yes, I'll give you some if you give me your rights as the firstborn, in exchange.' Esau raised his voice: 'I'm dying of hunger, what use is my birthright to me now!' 'Swear to it!' said Jacob. Esau swore away his birthright.

A blessing seized

Isaac had become old and was almost blind. It was time to speak to Esau: 'My son, I'm getting old and feel that I'll soon die. Go and hunt and prepare a nice tasty meal for me. I'll eat it and then I'll give you my blessing.' Rebekah had heard everything and she hurried to call Jacob….

Read *Genesis 27: 6-40*.

By trickery and cheating Jacob had got what he wanted, but his life was in danger: Esau wanted to take his revenge and decided to kill him. So Jacob had to run far away, alone.

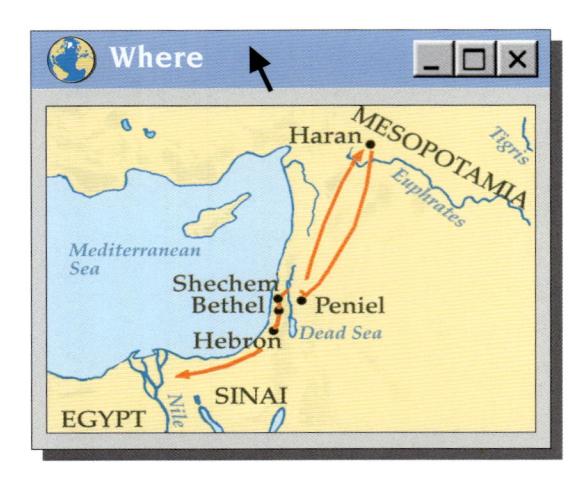

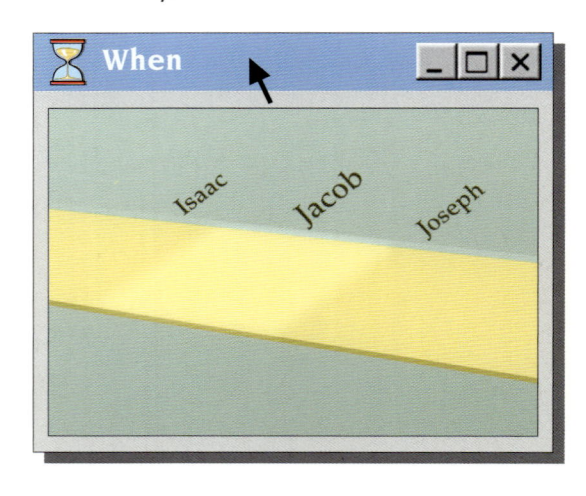

Where

When

86

To and from Haran

Jacob took refuge at his uncle Laban's home, at Haran. Laban had two daughters: Leah and Rachel. Jacob had fallen in love with Rachel and was prepared to work seven years for his uncle in order to marry her. At the end of seven years, Laban arranged the wedding feast, but….

Read *Genesis 29:23-30*.

The years passed and Jacob had become a wealthy man of property and had a large family: two wives, two slave-girls, eleven sons and a daughter. Rachel, his favourite wife had only given him one son, Joseph. One day God spoke to Jacob: 'Go back to your father's home and to your country and I will be with you.' It was time to leave.

Fear and making up

They were almost half way but the news was bad. Esau was coming to meet their caravan with four hundred men. Jacob was worried and afraid. He asked God for help. That evening his caravan stopped. Jacob sent gifts to Esau, then, in the middle of the night, he gathered together his wives, slave-girls and children and got them across the ford of the river, with all his possessions. Jacob was left alone. As the sun rose he was another man with a new name – Israel.

Read *Genesis 32:25-32*.

Jacob joined his family on the other side of the river and could make out Esau and his men on the horizon.
So Jacob went on ahead of everyone, bowing down seven times to the ground, as he approached his brother. But Esau went to meet him. He embraced him, threw his arms round him and kissed him. Both brothers wept.

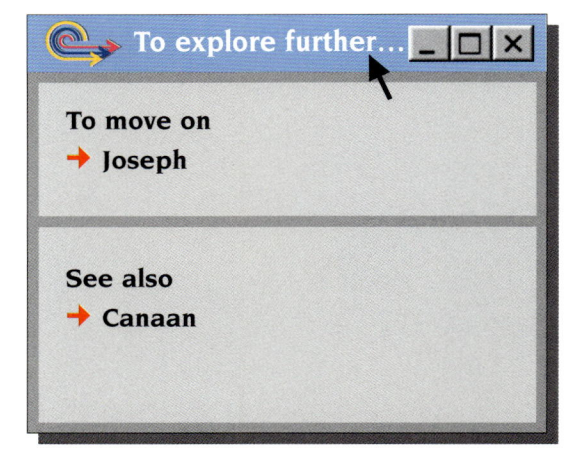

To explore further…

To move on
→ Joseph

See also
→ Canaan

JEREMIAH
A *prophet ignored*

Jeremiah and his time

Jeremiah was a priest in a town near Jerusalem. He lived in the most difficult and complicated time for the Southern Kingdom, positioned as it was between Egypt, Assyria and the rising empire of Babylonia. At Jerusalem opposing sides clashed. There were those who supported the older kingdoms of Assyria and Egypt while the others sided with the new empire of Babylonia.
Jeremiah was young when he was called to be a prophet. It was in the time of King Josiah, a little before his religious reforms (621 BCE). God said to him: 'Do not say that you are too young … Do not be afraid of them, for I will be with you to protect you … I am giving you the words you must speak. Today I give you authority over nations and kingdoms to uproot and to pull down, to destroy and to overthrow, to build and to plant.' *(Jeremiah 1:7-10)*

A dangerous speech

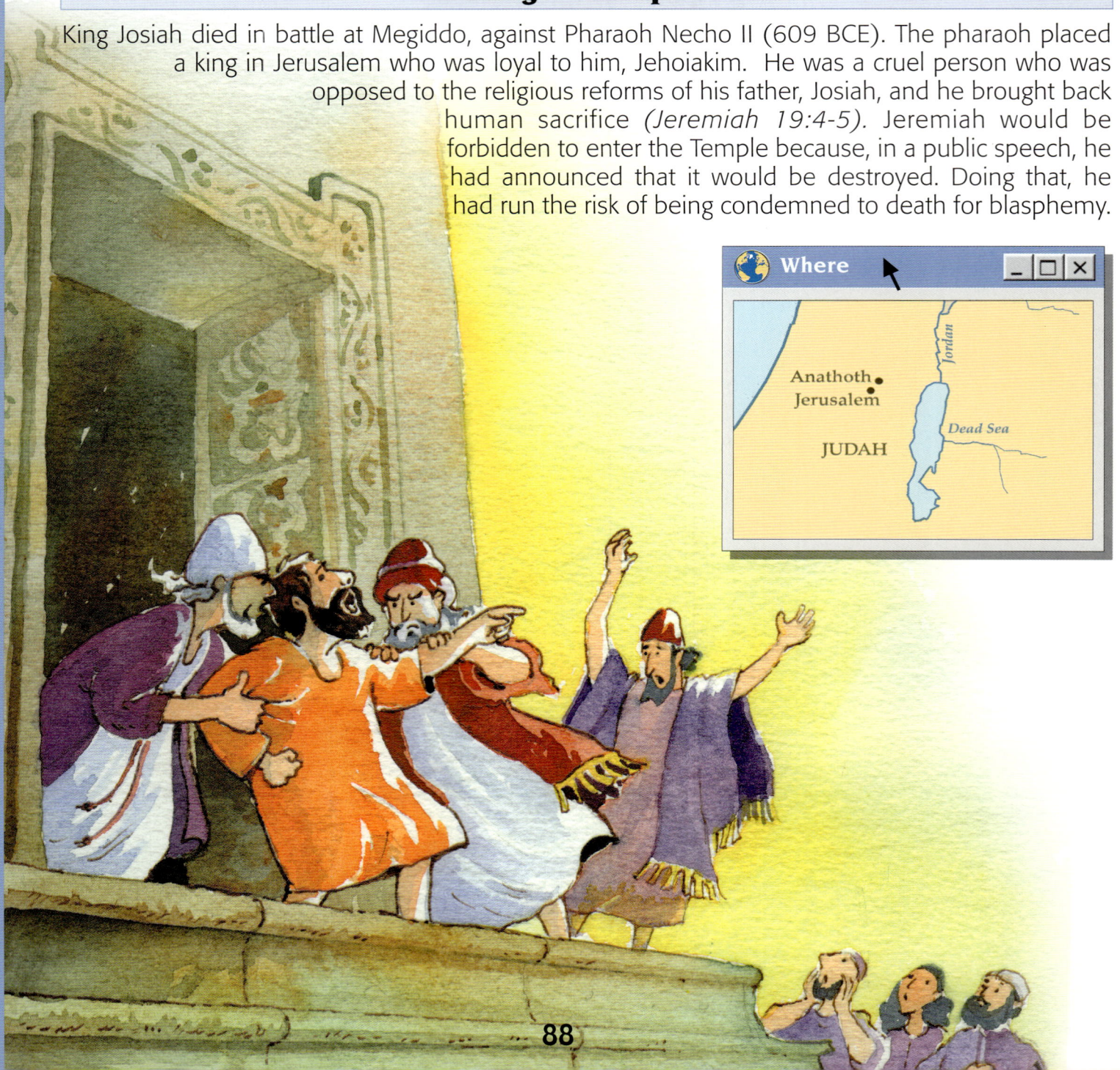

King Josiah died in battle at Megiddo, against Pharaoh Necho II (609 BCE). The pharaoh placed a king in Jerusalem who was loyal to him, Jehoiakim. He was a cruel person who was opposed to the religious reforms of his father, Josiah, and he brought back human sacrifice *(Jeremiah 19:4-5)*. Jeremiah would be forbidden to enter the Temple because, in a public speech, he had announced that it would be destroyed. Doing that, he had run the risk of being condemned to death for blasphemy.

Where

Anathoth • Jerusalem
Jordan
Dead Sea
JUDAH

The burnt scroll

At Carchemish, in 605 BCE, the Babylonians defeated Egypt who thus lost its three thousand year military dominance. Jeremiah, unable to enter the Temple any more, sent his secretary Baruch to whom he had dictated, on to a scroll, his speeches of the past twenty years. He had to take a message from God to King Jehoiakim: Jerusalem should surrender to Babylonia if it did not want to be destroyed. The king listened, tore the scroll into pieces and burnt them in a brazier. Eight years afterwards, Jerusalem would be conquered by Nebuchadnezzar II (598 BCE). In 587 BCE the city would be completely destroyed and a large part of the population deported to Babylonia. Jeremiah wrote an important letter to those people in exile from the first deportation….

Read *Jeremiah 29:4-14.*

Just suffering

Jeremiah would become the symbol for 'just suffering'. He was accused of blasphemy, defeatism and betrayal, thrown in a cistern and saved at the last minute, cut off like a false prophet. Jeremiah complained to God about all his suffering and pleaded for God's help. (*Jeremiah 20:7-18* illustrates this.)

Read *Jeremiah 38:11-13.*

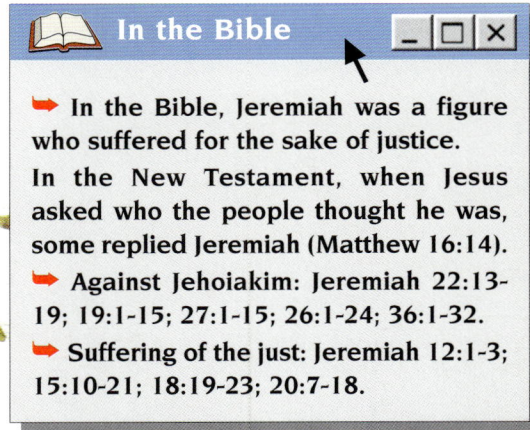

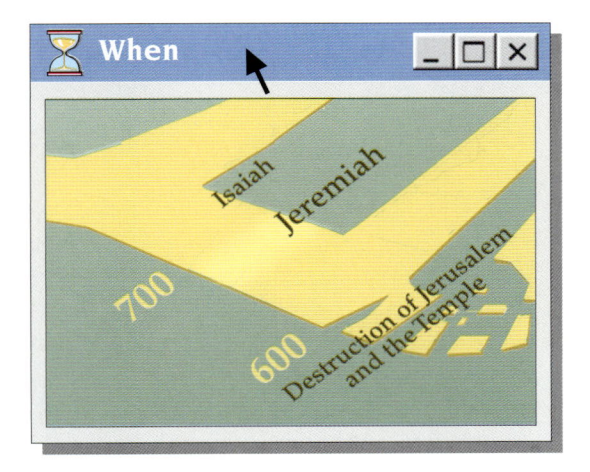

In the Bible

→ In the Bible, Jeremiah was a figure who suffered for the sake of justice.
In the New Testament, when Jesus asked who the people thought he was, some replied Jeremiah (Matthew 16:14).
→ Against Jehoiakim: Jeremiah 22:13-19; 19:1-15; 27:1-15; 26:1-24; 36:1-32.
→ Suffering of the just: Jeremiah 12:1-3; 15:10-21; 18:19-23; 20:7-18.

When

Isaiah
Jeremiah
700
600
Destruction of Jerusalem and the Temple

To explore further…

To move on
→ Exile

See also
→ Babylonia
→ Prophecy

JERUSALEM
The contested city

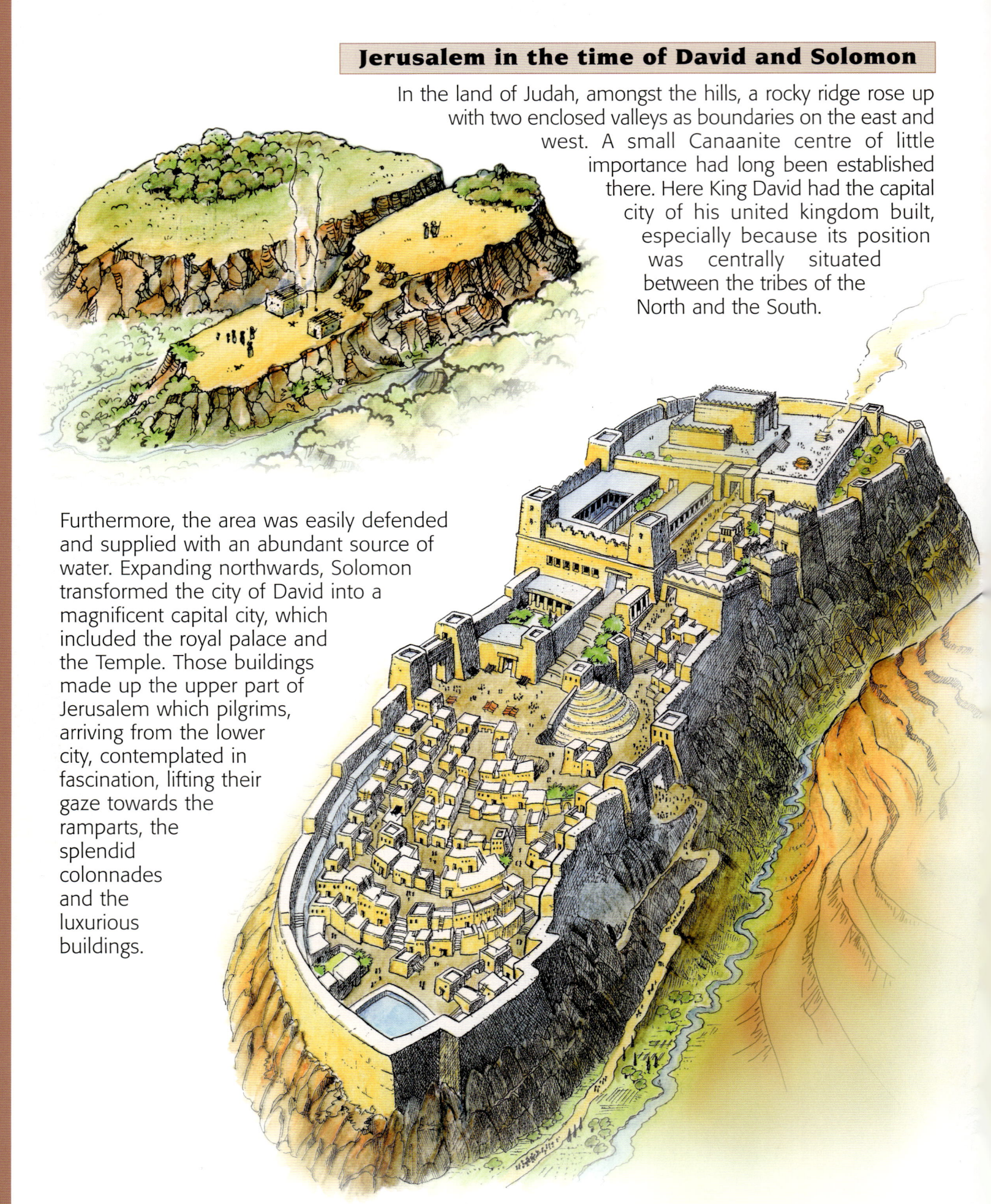

Jerusalem in the time of David and Solomon

In the land of Judah, amongst the hills, a rocky ridge rose up with two enclosed valleys as boundaries on the east and west. A small Canaanite centre of little importance had long been established there. Here King David had the capital city of his united kingdom built, especially because its position was centrally situated between the tribes of the North and the South.

Furthermore, the area was easily defended and supplied with an abundant source of water. Expanding northwards, Solomon transformed the city of David into a magnificent capital city, which included the royal palace and the Temple. Those buildings made up the upper part of Jerusalem which pilgrims, arriving from the lower city, contemplated in fascination, lifting their gaze towards the ramparts, the splendid colonnades and the luxurious buildings.

Jerusalem in the time of Herod

Jerusalem was destroyed by the Babylonian army in 586 BCE and rebuilt very slowly by the exiles who had returned home after Cyrus' decree in 539 BCE and by their descendants.

But the major reconstruction in the first century BCE was due to Herod the Great who had the royal palace, the Fortress of Antonia, the Temple and the formidable city walls built. The holy city regained its ancient splendour. The area of the monuments was spread out in the upper part, while the lower part was similar to any other town or village of the time with small houses, narrow and winding streets, labyrinths of steps, arches and courtyards, noisy crowds, confusion and filth.

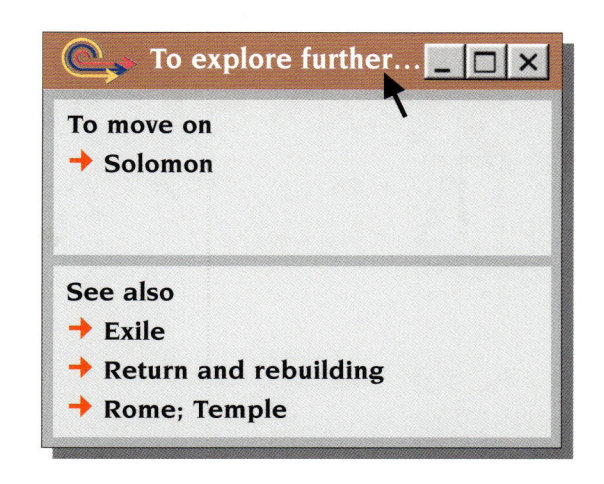

During the festivals, the population of about thirty thousand inhabitants was almost doubled and the area surrounding the city was transformed into a campsite where pilgrims crowded together, anxiously waiting to go up to the Temple.

The architectural restructuring begun by Herod the Great was still not completed when, because of the continuing rebellions, the Roman army invaded and destroyed Jerusalem with its Temple (70 CE). Later, after the second Jewish revolt (153 CE), the city was again destroyed and rebuilt as a pagan city from which the Jews were excluded.

To explore further…

To move on
➔ Solomon

See also
➔ Exile
➔ Return and rebuilding
➔ Rome; Temple

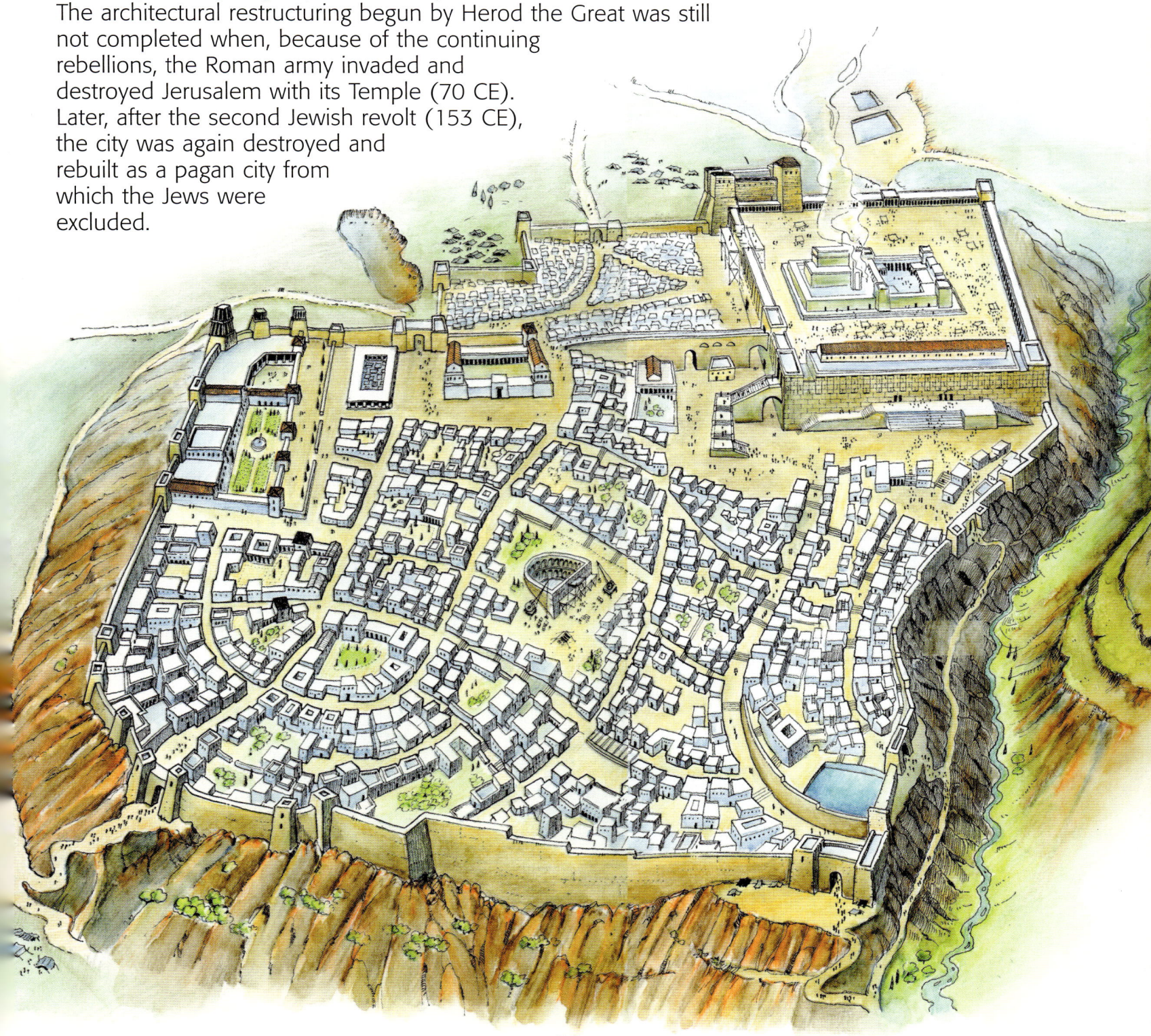

JESUS
A Jew

Jesus was a Jew who was born in Bethlehem, grew up in Nazareth and spent all his life in Palestine: his God was the Jewish God, his faith was Israel's, his Bible was the Old Testament, that is, the Jewish Scriptures, and his place of worship was the synagogue.

There are no portraits of Jesus, but he should not be pictured as blond with blue eyes, but rather dark-haired and dark-skinned, as an inhabitant of the Near East today. He was the son of a carpenter and as a young man he worked at that trade. He had brothers and sisters and was not married.

A wandering preacher

Jesus did not belong to the group of Pharisees, neither was he an official biblical scholar, nor a priestly Sadducee nor a Zealot. Jesus was a layman who did not belong to any of the main Jewish religious groups.

Before he began to preach he had been a disciple of John the Baptist who had baptised him in the river Jordan. Jesus was a wandering preacher and lived on what he and his disciples received from their supporters and from the people who lived in the places they visited.

An abandoned leader

Jesus called some men and women to live and to preach with him. That group followed him and were close to him for a long time, even though they did not always understand him. In particular, Jesus chose twelve men, like the twelve tribes of Israel, so that they could work more closely with him. They were not better than others: when Jesus was arrested, even they abandoned him and one of them, Judas, betrayed him. The twelve were, however, the people Jesus depended on to organise the life and activity of his followers.

A man who loved the freedom of others

Jesus deeply respected the Jewish Law, even though he held that the life and joy of men and women were more important than the Law; on account of that, Jesus did not hesitate to heal the sick on the Sabbath and always wanted to be near to all and everyone, but in particular to the people whom society and the well-off people rejected. He ate with tax collectors and other people of bad reputation, stirring up a lot of scandal.

Read *Matthew 9:10-13*.

Jesus saved a woman who had committed adultery, whom some wanted to stone to death, because that was what the Law demanded. He was not afraid to approach and heal lepers, who were regarded as unclean. For all those reasons, many people considered Jesus a rather strange and even dangerous character; but on the other hand, he was loved by the poor and by the outcasts of society *(John 8:1-11)*.

When

Birth of Jesus — 0
Death and resurrection of Jesus
100 CE

JESUS

A healer

Jesus was a great healer. His presence and his word were capable of healing the whole human person, body and spirit. He announced that God forgave sins, meaning that people's wrongdoing, no matter how serious, did not prevent God from being close to his sons and daughters and did not prevent them from beginning again, day by day, to love God and to be helpful to others.

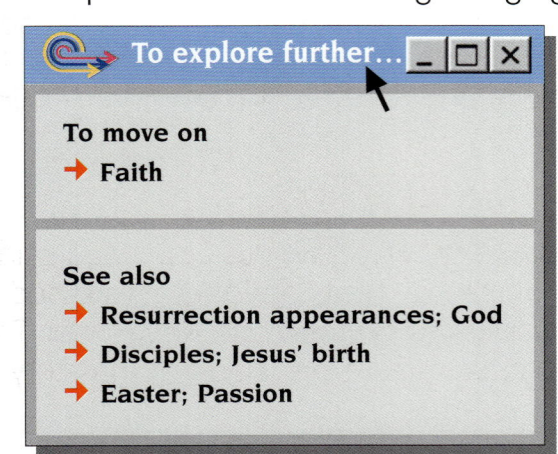

His miracles bore witness to the fact that the forgiveness of sins did not affect just the spirit but also helped the body to keep well by putting it at God's service. That is why Jesus said to a paralysed man: 'Your sins are forgiven' and at the same time, 'Get up, pick up your mat, and go home!' Jesus' miracles were not meant to be conjuring tricks to demonstrate his power, but signs of God's love and nearness.

Read *Mark 2:1-12*.

To explore further...

To move on
→ Faith

See also
→ Resurrection appearances; God
→ Disciples; Jesus' birth
→ Easter; Passion

The son of a good and loving God

Jesus lived in an intense and intimate relationship with God, so that he called him 'daddy', in Aramaic 'abba'. With his preaching and his deeds Jesus wanted to announce God's nearness, loving kindness and forgiveness for men and women, not only for those well-off but also, and more importantly, for the others. God was the 'daddy' of each and every one. According to Jesus, God was like the father of the prodigal son *(Luke 15:11-32)*, who waited full of fear and of hope for the return of his lost son. If the son returned only because 'my father's hired workers have more than they can eat, and here I am about to starve!', the father would receive him nevertheless, certain that his love could change him.

One Jesus, many ways of naming him

After the death and resurrection of Jesus, the disciples understood that God was as Jesus had said. So their faith in God remained closely tied to the message and person of Jesus and they expressed that by calling Jesus Messiah, Christ in Greek, Son of God, Son of David, Lord, Saviour, Redeemer. Those were all ways of saying that their faith in God would from then on always be linked to the story and person of Jesus.

JESUS' BIRTH
Through the will of God

Where
Mediterranean Sea, GALILEE, Sea of Galilee, Nazareth, DECAPOLIS, SAMARIA, Jordan, PERAEA, Jerusalem, Bethlehem, JUDAEA, Flight into Egypt, Dead Sea

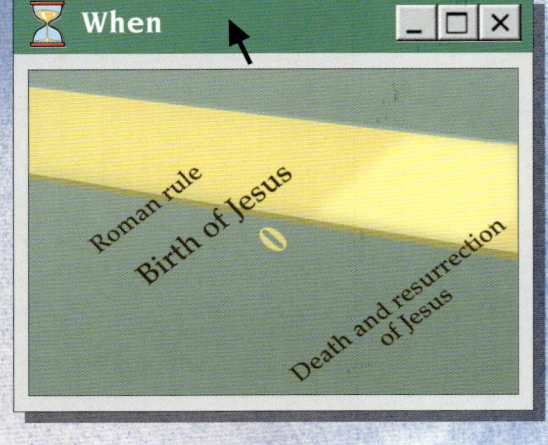

When
Roman rule, Birth of Jesus, Death and resurrection of Jesus

Whereas Mark and John began their Gospels with the preaching of John the Baptist and the baptism of Jesus, Matthew and Luke presented two full narratives, somewhat different from each other, relating to the birth of Jesus.

Jesus' parents were Joseph, a carpenter from Nazareth and Mary, who was very young. Her pregnancy was presented as the powerful work of God *(Matthew 1:20; Luke 1:26-38)*: Jesus' origin did not come from human desire but the divine will.

The long lists of ancestors found in Matthew and in Luke, were intended, in their different ways, to present Jesus as the climax of God's plan, which had run through the whole history of Israel. According to Luke, Jesus' life, right from its beginning in Mary's womb, paralleled that of John the Baptist. They were both God's messengers, rather different from each other, but united by a divine plan and both victims of the violence which sin produced.

Outsider and persecuted

Jesus was born in Bethlehem because, according to Luke, his parents, although living in Galilee, were originally from Judaea and they had returned there because of the census ordered by the Roman emperor. Jesus came into the world in a stable because his parents could not find lodgings in an inn. From the beginning he was an outsider. The news of his birth did not reach either Augustus or, at first, Herod, but shepherds: they were told that the baby of Bethlehem was the Saviour, the Lord and Christ, that is, the Messiah.

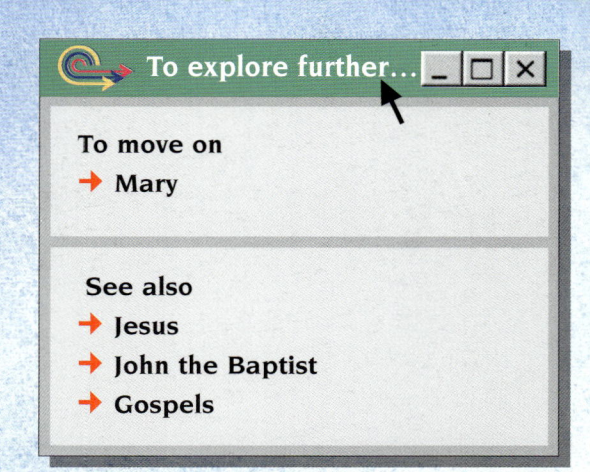

➡ Read *Luke 2:1-21*.

In Matthew, illustrious and mysterious people from the East reached Bethlehem to show their respects to the baby. These pagans found Jesus by following a star, while the theologians in Jerusalem searched for Jesus' whereabouts in their Scriptures, and in fact helped Herod to pursue the baby. The authorities feared that baby and started a violent murder campaign, but God saved Jesus, as he had done with Moses: Egypt was at first a place of safety, then the point of departure for a new 'exodus' towards the land of Israel.

➡ Read *Matthew 2:1-23*.

God's plans were accomplished in spite of human wickedness. The gospel accounts of Jesus' infancy, through means of narratives full of poetry but also drama, announce the good news of a mysterious God who was to reveal himself on the cross, that is, in a situation of great suffering and of unjust persecution.

To explore further...

To move on
➡ Mary

See also
➡ Jesus
➡ John the Baptist
➡ Gospels

JOB
A man cross-examines God

The patience of Job

'I need the patience of Job to deal with you.' Perhaps you have heard this phrase when someone's patience has been severely tried. But was Job, whose story appears in the Bible, really a patient man?

Job was a fair and honest man

Job was honest and fair and refused to do wrong. He was surrounded by a large family and was also very rich and happy.

But, all at once, he was hit by terrible troubles. The fierce plunderers of the desert robbed him of all his possessions: oxen, asses, camels. His sons, who were all together in the home of the eldest son, died when the house collapsed, caused by a very strong hurricane. Job himself was afflicted by a serious disease so his body was covered with irritating sores. Job had to scratch himself all day long.

> **In the Bible**
>
> ➡ The book of Job is found in the Jewish Bible amongst 'The Writings'. In several translations of the Old Testament into modern speech, Job is placed among the 'Poetry' or 'Wisdom Literature'. It is suggested that it was a play performed after the exile.

Friends arrived

Having heard about the terrible troubles that had come Job's way, three friends came to comfort him. They were wise and informed people and they were firmly convinced of one thing: suffering was a sign that the person had committed some bad act, and the person was punished because they were guilty. If the person admitted their guilt, God would cure them and would return them to health, happiness and wealth.

The three friends, joined by a fourth, tried their hardest to drive their belief into Job's head.

Job was not a patient man

Job rebelled. He could not understand for the life of him why so many afflictions had fallen upon him. But he was certain of one thing: his suffering was not a punishment. And he took it up with God. 'In anger God tears me limb from limb; he glares at me with hate.' *(Job 16:9)* Indeed, Job began to lose faith in God: 'Will no one listen to what I am saying? … Let Almighty God answer me. If the charges were written down so that I could see them….' *(Job 31:35)*

God did not answer – he asked questions

Job expected that, for once, God would explain everything to him. God, however, asked him a lot of questions like: 'Were you there when I made the world?' *(Job 38-39)* Job slowly began to understand. He had spoken against God only through ignorance. But God declared that Job had spoken the truth from his point of view, while the friends, with all their speeches, had not. Job had resisted the temptation to pay attention to the false statements of his friends.

Read *Job 42:7-8*.

To explore further…

To move on
→ **Return and rebuilding**

See also
→ **Creation**

JOHN THE BAPTIST
The last prophet

John the Baptist was a prophet. Jesus would say of him that he was more than a prophet, indeed that he was the greatest of them all, Elijah, who had returned to earth to bring about the beginning of the end times. *(Matthew 11:9,11,14).* Even John's clothes were like those of Elijah *(2 Kings 1:8; Mark 1:6).* According to some scholars, John would have experienced life in the 'monastery' of Qumran. That is quite possible since Luke records that John spent time in the desert on at least two occasions *(Luke 1:80; 3:1-2).* Following that, he would have left the 'monastery' in order to respond to his calling in a different way.

John the Baptist's message

John brought a new message. He said: 'Change your way of living because the Kingdom of God is on its way.' It was an announcement which made any false security crumble away, but which required at the same time a profound and daily renewal of a person's life, which their baptism in water emphasised. To be baptised meant to acknowledge oneself as a sinner in need of God's forgiveness. All Israel listened to the Baptist's preaching. Many people came to him to be baptised. Everyone considered him to be a prophet *(Matthew 21:26).* And yet he would have a horrible end….

Read *Mark 6:14-29.*

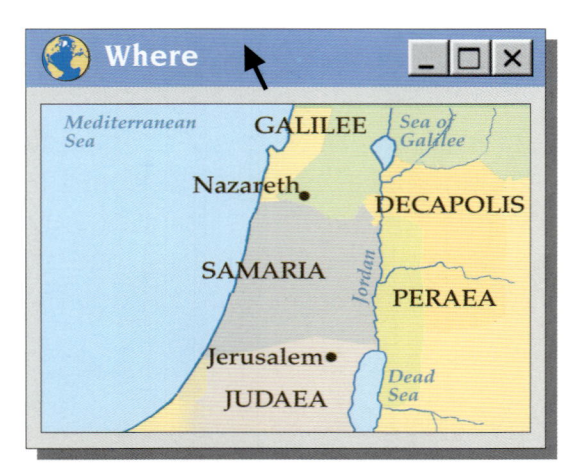

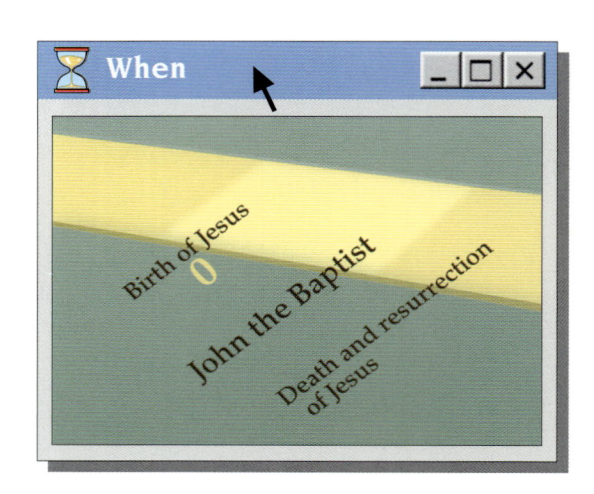

Where

When

John baptised Jesus

Even Jesus listened to John's preaching and he was baptised by him. In this way, he showed his sympathy with wrongdoers who needed God's forgiveness. But, the synoptic Gospels (see Gospels) also link Jesus' baptism to the announcement of a unique relationship between God and Jesus.

Read *Mark 1:10-11*.

John and Jesus

Jesus' public ministry began with his baptism. According to the fourth Gospel, Jesus spent a period of time with John the Baptist. It was John himself who persuaded two of his disciples, Andrew and one whose name is not given, to follow Jesus. Another three disciples, Peter, Philip and Nathanael, joined the first two. They also came from the area of John the Baptist's disciples *(John 1:29,35-49)*.
However, there was an important difference between John and Jesus. While the Baptist followed a strict way of life, of fasting and penance, Jesus, having seen the hard daily reality of the world, brought a joyful message and way of life.

Read *Luke 7:31-35*.

In the Bible

➡ John the Baptist is mentioned again in: Matthew 17:10-13; 21:23-27; Luke 7:18-30.

➡ John the Baptist's disciples: Mark 2:18; Luke 11:1; John 3:22-35; Acts 18:24-26; 19:1-7.

To explore further...

To move on
➡ Jesus

See also
➡ Desert
➡ Disciples

JONAH
A rebel

I'd rather run away

God ordered Jonah to go and preach at Nineveh, the capital city of the pagan and wicked Assyrian nation, but Jonah, not wishing in the least to do that, decided to run away. He went to Joppa and embarked on a ship that was going in the opposite direction.

Thrown overboard

When God wants to send one of his prophets to a particular place, it is difficult to escape from him. As Jonah embarked on the ship a terrible storm broke out. The sailors wondered who had done something bad against their God. In the end they found Jonah, who had gone away to sleep and they asked him who he was. Jonah told them everything and when the sailors knew that he was running away from an order given by God….

Read *Jonah 1:10-16*.

In the belly of a fish

A huge fish swallowed him. Inside there, in the darkness, Jonah reflected on his adventure: he had faced death in that stormy sea, with the water engulfing him and seaweed wrapping itself all around him. Jonah prayed to God. The fish vomited Jonah out on to the beach.

Where

Black Sea
Tarshish
Nineveh
Mediterranean Sea
Joppa
Red Sea

Better off dead

This time he obeyed God and he went to the vast city of Nineveh. Jonah crossed the city in all directions and continued to repeat the same thing. 'In forty days Nineveh will be destroyed.' *(Jonah 3:4)* The people of Nineveh listened to him and decided to change their way of life, so that God would not destroy the city. What a disappointment for Jonah! 'What!' he said to God, 'For day upon day I've announced destruction and now, are you going to forgive them? If that's how things are, I'm better off dead than alive!'

A plant isn't worth the life of so many people

Jonah was still furious with God. He threw himself on the ground. The shade of a castor oil plant protected him from the sun, but, the day after, it was already dead. Jonah was furious about the plant as well. God tried to calm Jonah down and make him understand the right way to act: 'If you are so angry over the plant, shouldn't I be worried about the fate of Nineveh, where amongst the population there are also one hundred and twenty thousand innocent children? Should I let them all die?' *(Jonah 4:9-11)*

In the Bible

➡ The purpose of the people of God in blessing other nations, was already found in the promise to Abraham: Genesis 12:2-3.

➡ The fish that saved Jonah is quoted also by Jesus as a sign of his death and resurrection: Matthew 12:38-41.

A parable

The book of Jonah is to be understood as a parable even if, in the Bible, it is included among the collection of the minor prophets. Its meaning is that the goodness of God is not limited to his people, but is also directed towards the other peoples on earth.

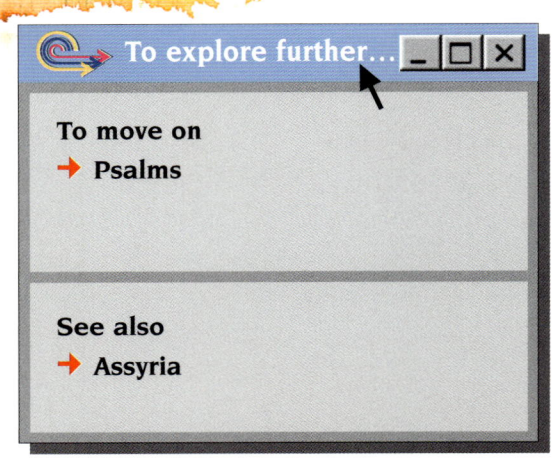

To explore further...

To move on
➡ Psalms

See also
➡ Assyria

JOSEPH
The Israelites in Egypt

The dreams

Joseph was the son of Jacob and Rachel, Jacob's favourite wife, who had died giving birth to Benjamin, the patriarch's last son. Joseph had a special place in the heart of his father, who spoilt him and had a very fine coat made for him. His older brothers hated him for that. Besides everything else, Joseph told them about a strange dream where it seemed that all his ten older brothers were bowing down before him. Immediately after, he told them about another, even worse, dream. But who did he think he was? Even Jacob told him off and was upset.

Revenge

One day his father sent Joseph to his brothers who were grazing their sheep far from home. Seeing him approaching, his brothers, mad with jealousy, decided to kill him, then changed their minds. They hit him, tore up his clothes and threw him in an empty cistern. Without taking any notice of Joseph's shouting and pleading, they calmly began to eat. A caravan of merchants, heading for Egypt, passed by. Why kill Joseph? It was better to sell him. He would disappear from their lives anyway.

In Egypt

Events in Joseph's life in Egypt alternated between successful and unsuccessful times, until he was made the administrator of the whole kingdom by the pharaoh himself. God had not abandoned him. The time of famine arrived and people, driven by hunger, went to Egypt to buy grain. Jacob also sent his sons, except for Benjamin. So Joseph, who, as the pharaoh's governor, was in charge of selling the grain, saw his persecutors arrive and recognised them. But he treated them as foreigners and spoke to them harshly.

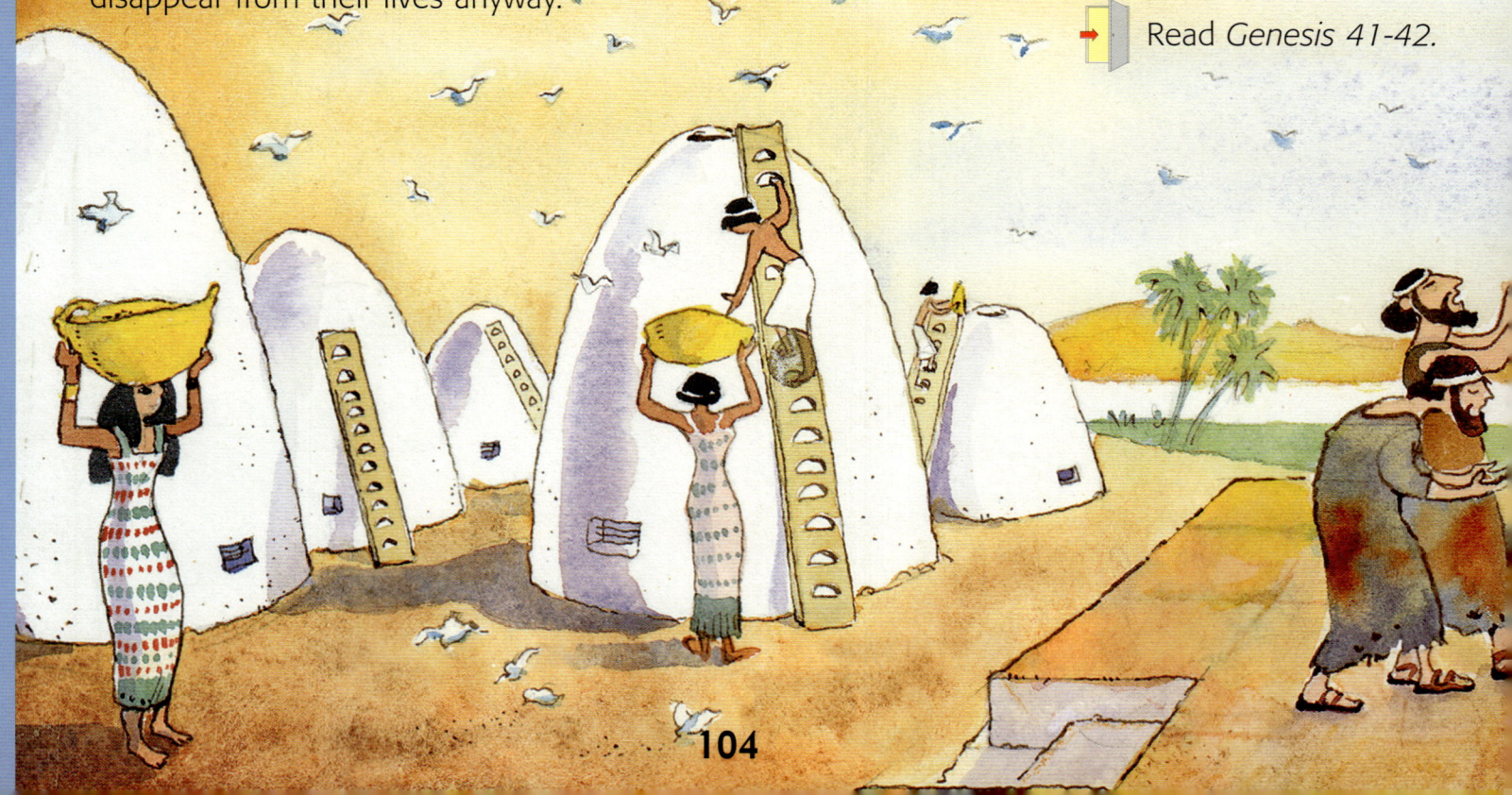

Read *Genesis 41-42*.

Where

When

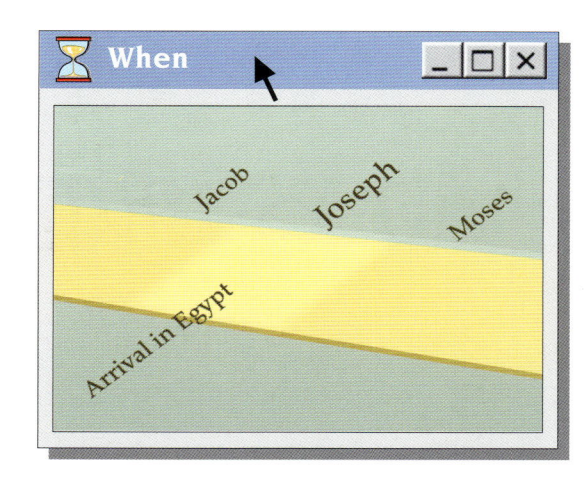

The old guilt

Joseph put his brothers into a very difficult position. Frightened and distressed, they remembered the fear of their young brother thrown into the cistern, his pleas for help and their silence. Their second visit to Egypt was vital because their stores of food had run out. But in order to have more corn, Benjamin had to accompany the brothers, as the governor required. When Joseph saw Benjamin, everything changed: they were all invited to dinner. It seemed as if the nightmare was over: they ate and drank merrily. But more trouble was looming on the horizon: Joseph wanted to test his brothers further to see if their hearts had changed.

➜ Read *Genesis 44-54.*

To explore further...

To move on
➜ Moses

To learn more
➜ Egypt

See also:
➜ Jacob

Jacob in Egypt

It was difficult for Jacob to believe that Joseph was alive. The pain of the loss of that son had become part of his life by then. But when he was convinced, he decided to move to Egypt with his sons, daughters-in-law, grandchildren, flocks, herds and everything he owned. After meeting Joseph, he settled in the land of Goshen where the grass grew high and the animals could graze.

JOSHUA
Moses' successor

Moses had died. Joshua, the son of Nun, became the new leader of the people, to guide them in the conquest of the Promised Land. 'Get some food ready, because in three days you are going to cross the River Jordan to occupy the land that the Lord your God is giving you.'

Two spies go to Jericho

Joshua needed information about the land and city of Jericho. Therefore, he sent two trustworthy men, who, when they had reached the city, went to lodge at the house of a woman called Rahab, a prostitute.

Read *Joshua 2:1-24.*

Crossing the river

It was harvest time. At that time the Jordan was in flood. The people took down their tents ready to cross the river. The priests set off in front of everyone, with the ark of the covenant. As soon as they put their feet in the Jordan the waters that came down from the north stopped and formed a wall. The priests stayed in the middle of the river until all the people had crossed the Jordan on dry ground.

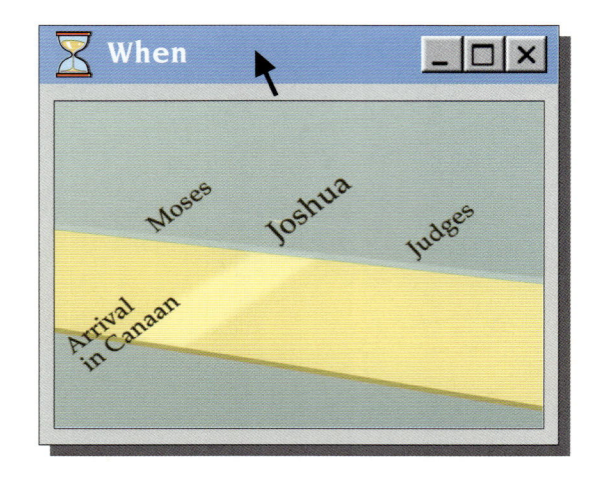

When

Arrival in Canaan — Moses — Joshua — Judges

To explore further...

To move on
→ Judges

See also
→ Canaan
→ Exodus
→ Moses

The conquest

The gates of Jericho were barred and barricaded for fear of the Israelites. No one left the city any more and it was impossible to enter it. Jericho was invincible but….

▶ Read *Joshua 6:2-21*.

With the help of God, cunning, weapons and by means of a treaty, a part of the Promised Land was in the hands of Joshua. The leader by then was old. God said to him: 'You are very old but there is still much land to be taken … You must divide the land among the Israelites, just as I have commanded you to do….'

A meeting at Shechem

Joshua assembled all the tribes of Israel at Shechem and reminded them that God's faithfulness to his promises required a commitment from the people in response. Living amongst a foreign population that did not know God, carried serious risks of unfaithfulness. Joshua, for this reason, asked for a solemn renewal of their covenant. The people were united in deciding to serve only God.

▶ Read *Joshua 24:1-28*.

The division of the land

JOSIAH
The reforming king

The Bible passes judgement on all the kings who succeeded to the thrones of Israel in the North and Judah in the South: 'He went (or did not go) against God's will.' Almost none of the kings of the Northern Kingdom, upset by numerous government coups, is judged positively. Some of those of the Southern Kingdom, on the other hand, all descendants of David, are judged better. One of those was Josiah, who would be one of the last kings of Judah.

His achievements

Josiah has gone down in history as a reforming king. He tried hard to rid his country of idolatry, as his great-grandfather Hezekiah had tried to do in the time of the prophet Isaiah and of the fall of the Northern Kingdom through the action of the Assyrians in 720 BCE. After Hezekiah, Manasseh had reintroduced a large number of pagan cults modelled on neighbouring peoples. Having ascended the throne, Josiah took advantage of the weakness of the Assyrians whose empire was about to fall on account of the attacks of the Babylonians, and he was able to restore the boundaries of the kingdom almost to where they were in the time of David. In addition, like his ancestor, he tried to centralise political as well as religious power, giving new splendour to Jerusalem and the Temple.

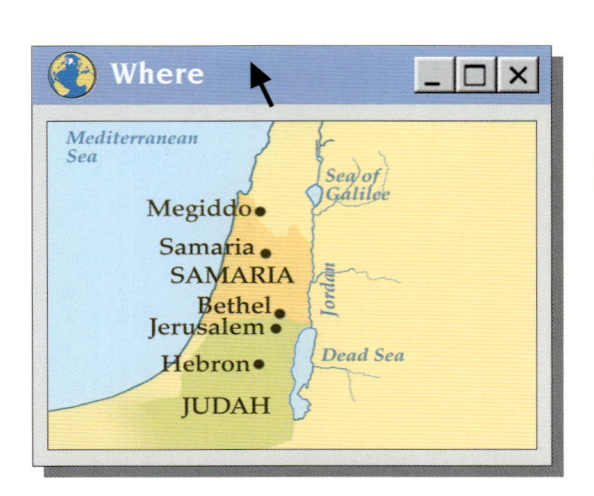

Where

Mediterranean Sea
Megiddo
Samaria
SAMARIA
Bethel
Jerusalem
Hebron
JUDAH
Sea of Galilee
Jordan
Dead Sea

The book is discovered

During the restoration work, 'the book of the Law', which had been forgotten for a very long time, was discovered. After Josiah had read it and consulted the prophetess Hulda, he promised to observe what was written in it.

Read *2 Kings 23:1-3*.

So, Josiah began to sweep away all the idols and the objects dedicated to other gods: Baal, Asherah, the Moon and the Sun, first in Jerusalem, then in the territory of Judah and lastly also in the North of the country. He hunted out the unfaithful priests and killed those of other cults. He desecrated and eliminated various altars, including the furnace where babies were burnt as sacrifices to the god Marduk. Finally, he ordered the people to keep the feast of Passover again, in remembrance of their freedom from slavery in Egypt: a festival that had not been celebrated since the time of the judges.

Read *2 Kings 23:21-23*.

Towards the end

In 609 BCE Josiah died in battle against the Egyptians and the country fell under their power. So the new king, Jehoiakim, forced by his rulers, reintroduced idolatry.

In vain the prophet Jeremiah, who had already been close to Josiah, tried to oppose that: from the political standpoint, he invited the government of Judah to place their trust in the Babylonians and from the religious one, to return to God. The government did neither and the consequence would be the fall of Jerusalem, the destruction of the Temple and exile for the people.

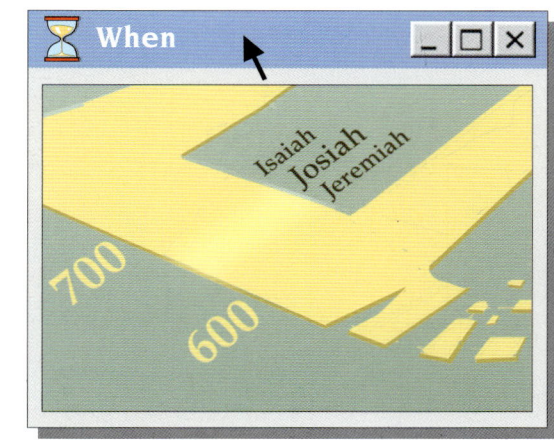

When
Isaiah
Josiah
Jeremiah
700
600

In the Bible
- Hezekiah: 2 Kings 18-20.
- Josiah: 2 Kings 22:1-20; 2 Kings 23:4-14, 28-30.

To explore further...
To move on
- Jeremiah

See also
- Women in the Bible
- Idolatry

JUDAH
A land, a tribe, a kingdom

J

A glorious and mysterious promise

'Judah is like a lion … Judah will hold the royal sceptre and his descendants will always rule. Nations will bring him tribute and bow in obedience before him.' *(Genesis 49:9-10)*

That was Jacob's prophecy to his son when he blessed him from his deathbed. As long as his descendants remained faithful to God, that prophecy was fulfilled. They were aggressive warriors, occupying the large area to the south of Jerusalem. David the famous king who united the twelve tribes of Israel in one kingdom, was from that tribe. According to the Scriptures, the Messiah would be a descendant of David.

A poor but important kingdom

After the death of Solomon, the kingdom divided into two parts: to the North, Israel with its capital Samaria, and to the South, Judah with Jerusalem as its capital, where God's Temple was situated. Even if poor – the region was almost completely desert and sparsely populated – the kingdom of Judah was very important for the faith of Israel because there, especially after 722 BCE, when the kingdom of Israel was destroyed by the Assyrians, the fundamental beliefs of its faith in only one God were worked out.

Where
Mediterranean Sea
ISRAEL
Sea of Galilee
Jordan
Shechem
Jerusalem
JUDAH
Dead Sea

In the Bible

- **Some narratives about Judah, son of Jacob, are told in Genesis 37-38.**
- **The history of the kingdom is in 1 Kings 12-2 Kings; and also in 2 Chronicles 10f.**

Two exceptional kings

Two kings of Judah distinguished themselves through their faith in God: Hezekiah and Josiah. Both were famous for their religious reforms, which opposed the widespread polytheism in their kingdom by applying the principles of the preaching of monotheism by prophets like Isaiah and Hosea.

A long-lasting kingdom

Precisely because Judah was poor and politically unimportant, the kingdom remained independent for longer: from 922 BCE to 587 BCE when the Babylonians destroyed Jerusalem and carried the population away into exile. While the Northern tribes were scattered by the Assyrians and disappeared from history, the tribe of Judah, together with part of the tribes of Benjamin and Levi, survived both in the Diaspora (Jews living outside Israel) and in the land of Israel, after the return from exile in Babylonia (539 BCE).

To explore further...

To move on
➜ Elijah

See also
➜ David; Exile; Josiah
➜ Return and rebuilding
➜ Solomon

JUDGES
O God, help!

The entire book of Judges is a reflection on history. After the conquest of the Promised Land, Israel's history depended on the relationship between the people and God. When Israel was unfaithful to God, she was oppressed by neighbouring peoples. When she repented and called for God's help, God listened and raised up courageous commanders from within Israel, the Judges, who freed her.

Deborah

The Canaanite king, Jabin, had been harshly oppressing the people of Israel for twenty years. From the depths of their torment the Israelites asked God for help. At that time the prophetess Deborah was Judge and head of Israel. She met the people who asked for justice and advice, under a palm tree.

➡ Read *Judges 4:6-10,12-16*.

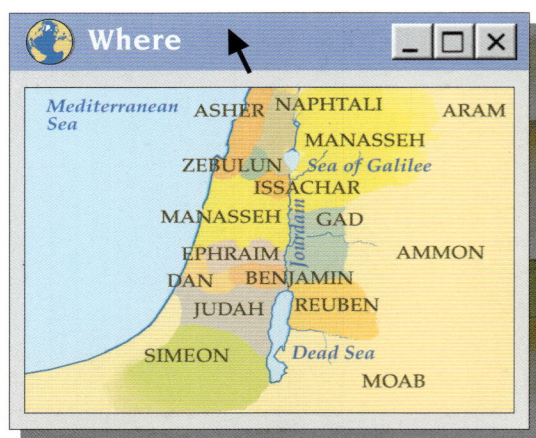

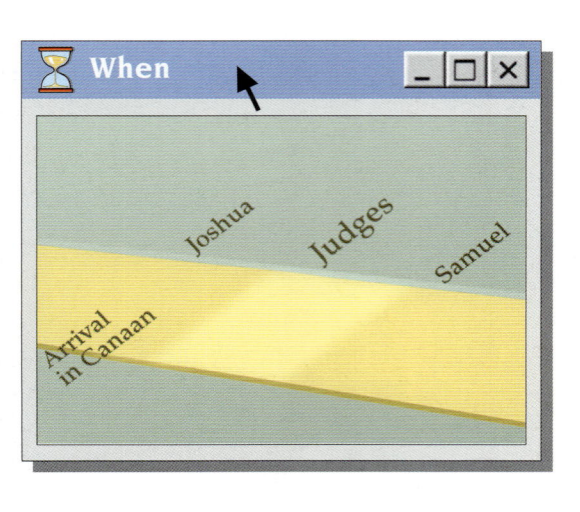

Where

Mediterranean Sea, ASHER, NAPHTALI, ARAM, MANASSEH, ZEBULUN, Sea of Galilee, ISSACHAR, MANASSEH, GAD, Jordan, EPHRAIM, AMMON, DAN, BENJAMIN, JUDAH, REUBEN, SIMEON, Dead Sea, MOAB

When

Arrival in Canaan — Joshua — Judges — Samuel

In the Bible

➡ The book of Judges presents the situation of the tribes of Israel after the death of Joshua. It recounts, sometimes briefly and sometimes in detail, the undertakings of the judge-commanders and ends with some episodes that describe the disorder and confusion which reigned before the establishment of the monarchy.

Gideon

Again Israel went against God's wishes and fell under the power of the people of Midian. The Midianites were like swarms of locusts; wherever they passed by, they devastated, plundered and destroyed.

The desperate Israelites sought help from God. The angel of the Lord went to Gideon who was threshing the wheat, hidden inside a winepress so that the Midianites would not find him. The visitor politely said: 'The Lord is with you!' but Gideon was downhearted….

→ Read *Judges 6:13-16*.

A trumpet, a jar and a torch

The Midianites and the other desert tribes joined forces. Gideon, guided by the Spirit of God, had the trumpet sound the signal for war and sent messages to the tribes. Lots of men assembled.

→ Read *Judges 7:16-22*.

Samson

Again Israel was disloyal, so for forty years God let the Israelites fall under the control of the Philistines. A baby boy was born in the tribe of Dan, Samson. The baby grew up blessed by God, developing exceptional strength so that he became a terrible enemy of the Philistines.

But the day arrived when they could get their own back: the Philistines managed to capture him. They gouged out his eyes, tied him up with a double chain of bronze and forced him to turn the millstone.

One day, the Philistine chiefs came together to offer a great sacrifice to their god. Caught up in the celebrations, they sent for Samson to be brought…

→ Read *Judges 16:26-30*.

To explore further…

To move on
→ Prophecy

See also
→ Joshua
→ Ruth
→ Samuel

LAW and JUSTICE
God's gift

The people of the Law

The Jews are known as the people of the Law. Christianity, on the other hand, is often called a religion of love. These descriptions are misleading since, for Jews, the Law is never opposed to love. The God of the Bible loves and judges the world at the same time.
In Jewish tradition it is said that God sits on two thrones, one of justice and the other of mercy. He cannot sit on one or the other for long because if he sits only on the one of justice, the whole world will be condemned, but if he stays too long on the mercy throne, the crafty people will take advantage. Jesus, too, who was merciful to wrongdoers, said he had not come to do away with the Law.

Do this and you will live

The Hebrew word that is translated 'Law', means also 'teaching' or 'revelation'. The Law was considered to be a precious gift from God to teach his people to live freely after their slavery and exodus from Egypt. Their Law was seen by Israel not as a burden placed on them, but represented a practical way in which they could respond to God's love.
Faith for the Israelites was to be experienced through actions, a way of life. Real knowledge of God came more from actually doing something rather than from abstract reflection on the Scriptures. That is why after Moses handed over the tablets of the Law, the people replied: 'We will obey the Lord and do everything that he has commanded.' *(Exodus 24:7)*

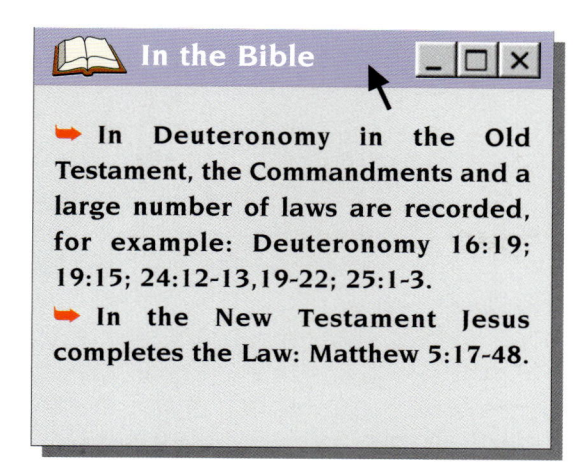

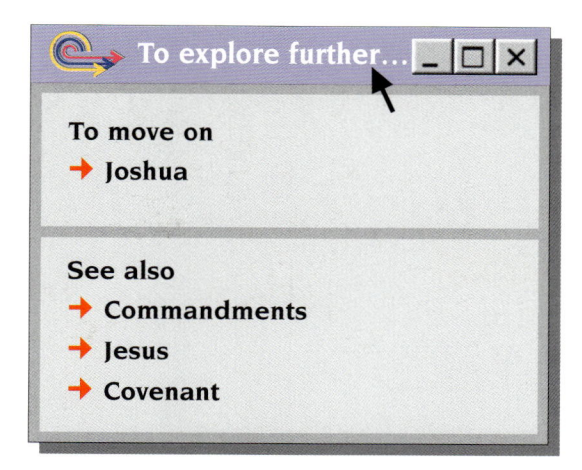

> **In the Bible**
>
> ➡ In Deuteronomy in the Old Testament, the Commandments and a large number of laws are recorded, for example: Deuteronomy 16:19; 19:15; 24:12-13,19-22; 25:1-3.
> ➡ In the New Testament Jesus completes the Law: Matthew 5:17-48.

> **To explore further...**
>
> To move on
> ➡ Joshua
>
> See also
> ➡ Commandments
> ➡ Jesus
> ➡ Covenant

Officials of justice

In the Bible there were different officials who guaranteed justice for people.
At the city gates there were the elders who were consulted to resolve disagreements among the citizens. In the time before the monarchy, the judges, who were really rulers, appeared and after those it was the responsibility of the king to administer the law. The law protected the poor, the widows, the orphans and foreigners, but human shortcomings in guaranteeing full and lasting justice brought about an expectation amongst the people of the 'just judge', who would finally bring justice: the Messiah.

➡ Read *Psalm 72*.

Jesus and the Law

Jesus summed up the entire Law of God in two rules: love the Lord your God and love your neighbour as yourself. He had criticised all those who felt right before God and in their relationships with other people because they kept the Law. He also condemned the ease with which some people distorted the meaning of God's rules and hid behind those distortions in order to avoid helping neighbours or to seek approval from others rather than God.
That was the nature of much of Jesus' criticism of the religious people of his time.

➡ Read *Mark 3:1-6*.

Here Jesus replies to critics who accuse him of breaking their ancient traditions.

LETTERS
To keep in contact

The twenty-one letters of the New Testament make reference to five different authors: Paul, James, John, Jude and Peter. There is no reference to the author of the letter to the Hebrews.

Why write letters?

It was necessary to keep in contact with the Christian Churches that sprang up in the Jewish Diaspora (Jews scattered outside Palestine) and in the various cities of the Roman Empire. The Churches told the apostle Paul about difficult problems they had concerning faith and community life and asked for his advice on how to resolve them.

Paul definitely wrote seven letters to identifiable Churches.

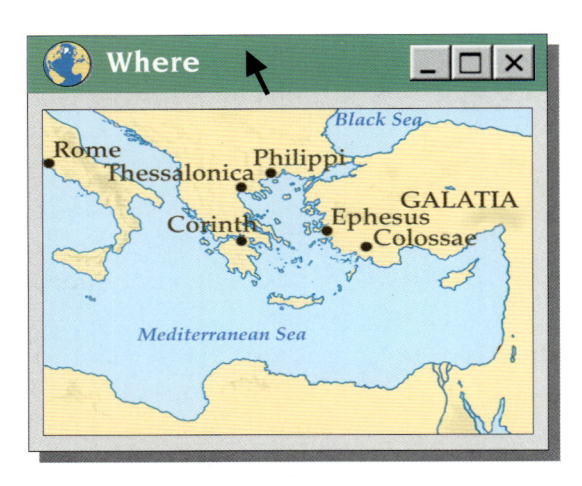

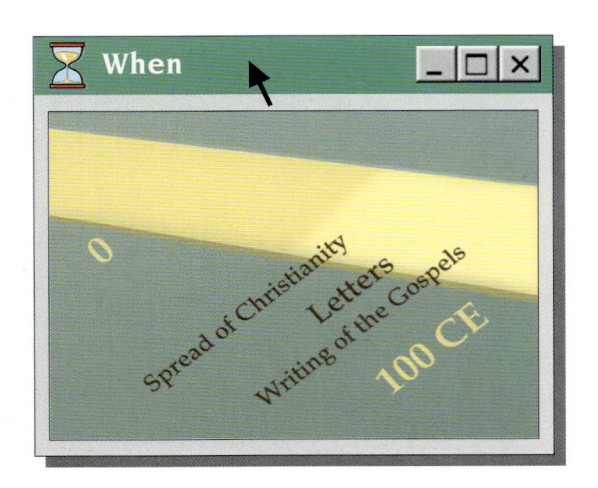

Where

Rome, Thessalonica, Philippi, Corinth, Ephesus, Colossae, GALATIA, Black Sea, Mediterranean Sea

When

0 — Spread of Christianity — Letters — Writing of the Gospels — 100 CE

How to date Paul's letters

The Bible lists Paul's letters beginning with the longest and ending with the shortest. *Acts 18:1-2,12-13* helps to establish dates for the seven letters that are definitely Paul's. There it is stated that Aquila and Priscilla, Paul's companions at Corinth, were part of a group of Jews expelled from Rome by the Emperor Claudius between 49 and 50 CE. In addition, at Corinth, as in the whole of Greece, L. Junius Gallio was the Roman proconsul. An inscription found at Delphi shows that Gallio was proconsul of Greece between 50 and 52 CE. Starting from Paul's visit to Corinth around the year 50, the book of Acts allows the following reconstruction of the dates:

1 Thessalonians, during Paul's second journey about 50 CE; *1 and 2 Corinthians, Philemon, Philippians, Galatians* and *Romans*, during the third journey, between about 53 and 57 CE.

➡ Read *1 Thessalonians*.

Circular letters

The letters to the Ephesians and the Colossians were circular ones to be read by all the Churches in a wide area.
The three pastoral letters were addressed to the person responsible for the community (Timothy or Titus) in view of the task that he had to carry out.

➡ Read *2 Timothy*.

Other letters passed on valuable messages without specifying to whom they were sent. These are called the catholic letters because of the universal nature of their message. Among these was material for catechumens (those taking instruction before baptism into Christianity), like *1 Peter*, or the preaching of encouragement and teaching to a Church in crisis *(Letter to the Hebrews)*.
Finally, others, like *1 John*, warned against incorrect interpretations of doctrine about Jesus Christ.

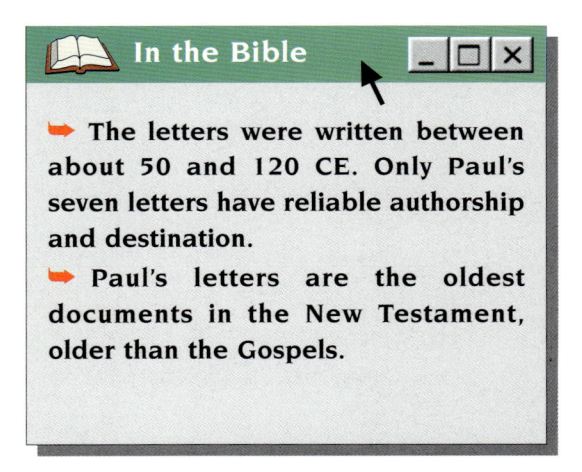

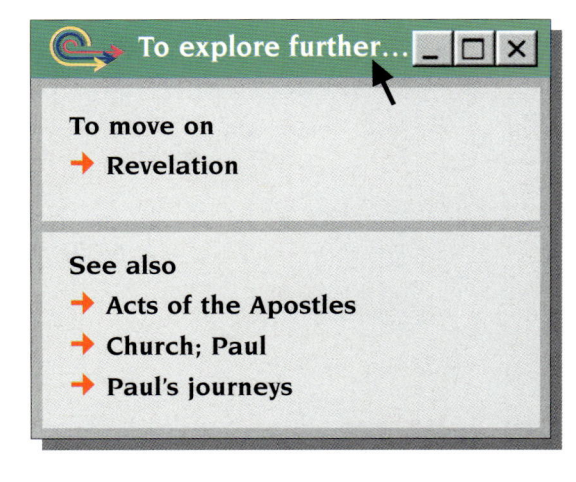

In the Bible

➡ The letters were written between about 50 and 120 CE. Only Paul's seven letters have reliable authorship and destination.

➡ Paul's letters are the oldest documents in the New Testament, older than the Gospels.

To explore further...

To move on
➡ Revelation

See also
➡ Acts of the Apostles
➡ Church; Paul
➡ Paul's journeys

LOT
An ordinary man

Lot, Abraham's nephew, followed his uncle on his wanderings. His father had died. They journeyed together but they were different in character: Abraham had a vision, which made him look to the future. Lot thought only of the present.

With the passing of time the flocks of uncle and nephew steadily increased. The pastureland was no longer adequate for all of their animals. The shepherds from the two camps quarrelled. They could no longer go ahead like that. Abraham discussed it with Lot and the two went their separate ways.

God announces the destruction of Sodom

After the visit of the messengers who announced the birth of Isaac, Abraham accompanied his guests along a stretch of the road, almost as far as Sodom.

Meanwhile, God wondered: 'Should I perhaps keep hidden from Abraham what I intend to do? I have chosen him so that he may teach his sons to follow my way, doing what is good and just.'

So God spoke to Abraham: 'There are terrible accusations against Sodom and Gomorrah, and their sin is very great. I must go down to find out whether or not the accusations which I have heard are true.' Two angels of God set out towards Sodom, where Lot then lived.

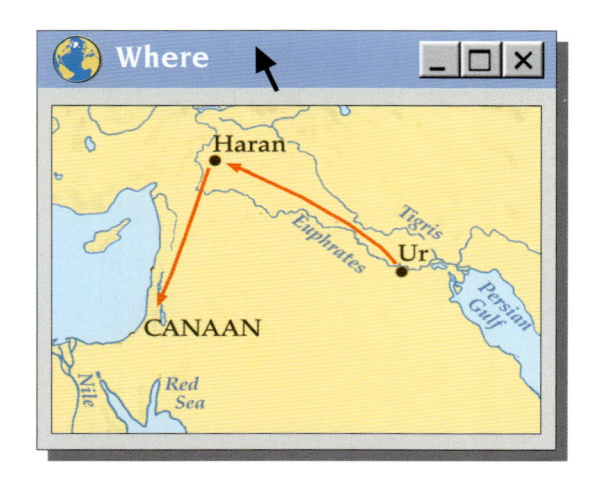

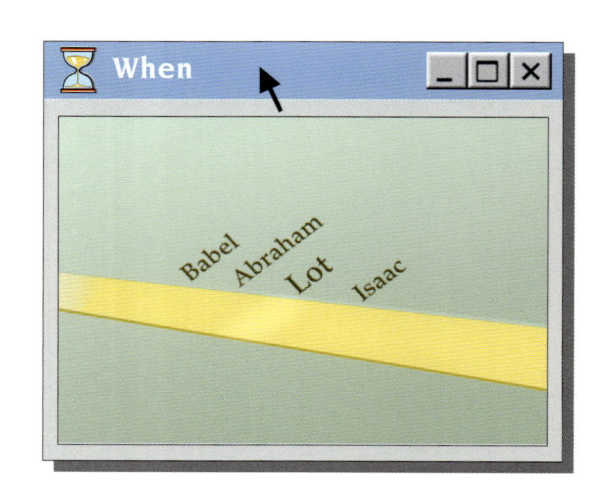

118

To explore further…

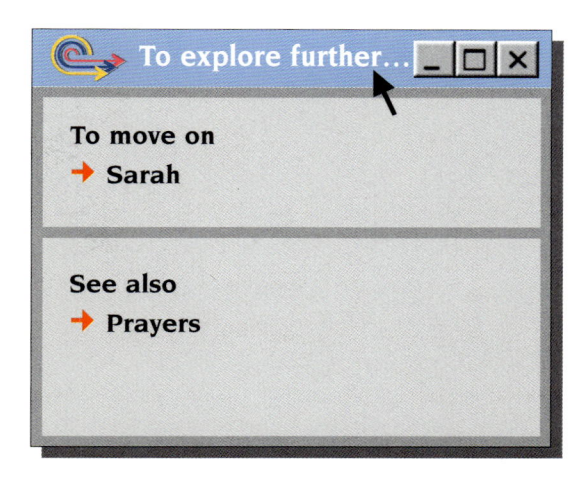

To move on
→ Sarah

See also
→ Prayers

Abraham argues with God

Abraham remained standing in front of God. He then approached him and said: 'Will you really destroy the guilty and the innocent together? Perhaps there are fifty innocent people in that city, do you really want them to be killed? Why don't you rather forgive that city for love of those fifty people?' 'If I find fifty innocent people in the city of Sodom', replied God, 'I will pardon the whole city because of my love for them.'
Abraham continued to say: 'It could be that instead of fifty innocent people there are five fewer! Would you destroy the city if there were five fewer?' 'No!' replied God, 'I would not destroy it if there were forty-five innocent people there!' Abraham continued….

Read *Genesis 18:29-33*.

The destruction of Sodom

The inhabitants of Sodom were unbelievably violent and no one tried to stop them. Where were the good people? The two angels of God said to Lot: 'God has sent us here to destroy this place, because the outrage against its inhabitants has been so great that it has reached him. Therefore, make all of your family who live in the city, leave'. Lot, the man whose life revolved around the present, did not understand and he hesitated. So the angels of God took him by the hand, with his wife and two daughters and made them leave the city. 'Run for your lives! Don't look back. Don't stop in the plain! Run to the hills so you will not be overtaken by disaster.' But Lot's wife looked back and became a statue of salt.

MARY Chosen by God

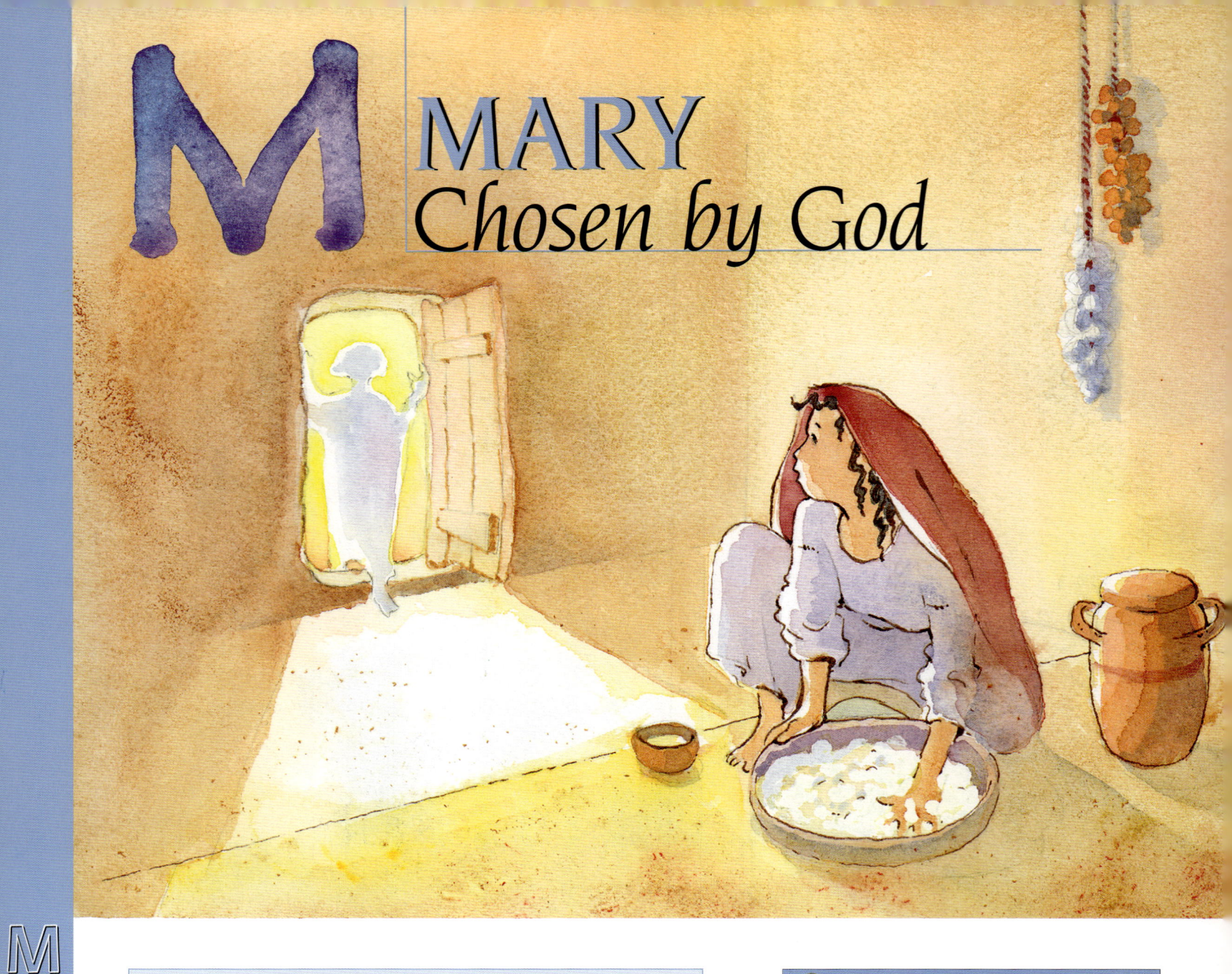

Mary in the Gospels

The evangelist Luke presents Mary as a key figure in the events of Jesus' infancy narrated in the first two chapters of his Gospel. God burst into Mary's life, and so, from being a simple girl on the sidelines, not yet officially engaged to a man, she found herself taking on the role of the mother of Jesus, the Son of God. Nevertheless, even though God entered overpoweringly into her life and filled her with grace, she did not remain passive. Before everything else she asked: 'How is that possible?' Only after she had understood the meaning of that divine intervention did she decide to believe God's words – words which did not go to her head, leaving her stunned, but got her moving: in fact she went to help her relative, Elizabeth, who was shortly to give birth to her baby.
It was in just those circumstances that Mary, using words from the Jewish Scriptures, uttered a hymn of thanks and praise for the great things that Almighty God had done for her.

Read *Luke 1:46-55*.

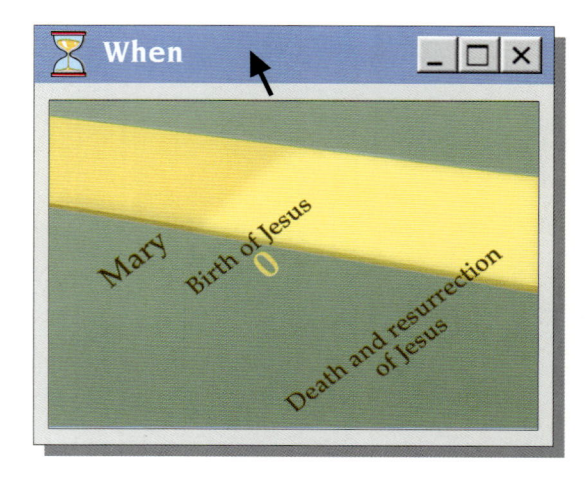

Mary, a disciple

Mary gave birth to Jesus, who had been conceived by the Holy Spirit. That comment about the virgin birth, reported by Luke and Matthew, was meant to point out that the Messiah was not of human origin: God alone could bring full salvation to humanity. But humanity had been invited to take an active part in God's plan, like Mary, who followed Jesus as a disciple even when she did not understand him, as in the Temple incident, where the twelve-year-old Jesus abandoned his parents to devote himself to matters of his Father, God. Or later on, when she felt rejected by her adult son who was a wandering preacher. Her greatness did not lie so much in her having given birth to Jesus but rather in having listened to him and lived out his teaching: *Luke 8* says that that was the only way to become a member of Jesus' family. Mary was a disciple of her son, a persevering disciple, capable even of getting the times of divine intervention in history brought forward, as in the episode of the wedding at Cana in *John 2*, where, just because of his mother's insistence, Jesus decided to perform the first sign in public that announced God's Kingdom. Mary followed Jesus right to the foot of the cross and, after the announcement of the resurrection, continued to live in faith, constant and united in prayer together with the other believers.

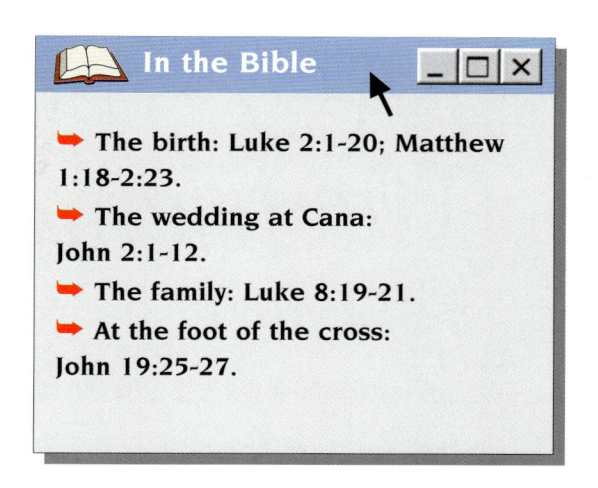

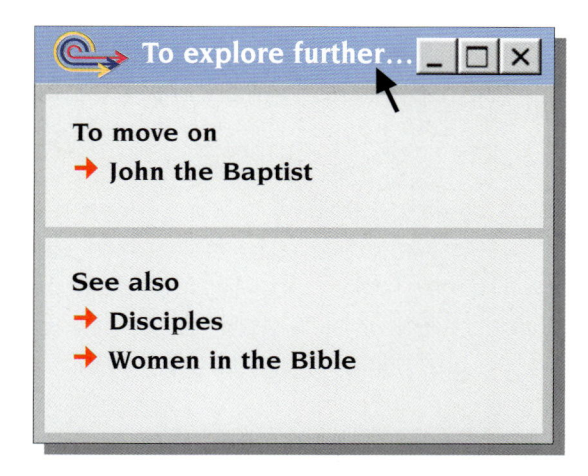

Read *Acts 1:12-14*.

In the Bible

➡ The birth: Luke 2:1-20; Matthew 1:18-2:23.
➡ The wedding at Cana: John 2:1-12.
➡ The family: Luke 8:19-21.
➡ At the foot of the cross: John 19:25-27.

To explore further...

To move on
➡ John the Baptist

See also
➡ Disciples
➡ Women in the Bible

MOSES
The friend of God

Moses, saved from the water

According to the biblical narrative 'Moses' means 'drawn out of the water.' In Egypt, the descendants of Joseph had become a large people. A new ruling dynasty, which was hostile to foreigners, had come to power. At that time, the pharaoh considered the Israelites a danger for Egypt and decided to reduce their numbers. Among the other anti-foreigner measures, it was decreed that all the newborn male babies of the Israelites were to be put to death. But one of these little baby boys was put in a waterproof basket, which floated on the water of the river Nile. It was Moses: saved from the water.

Moses, son of the princess

But according to an ancient Egyptian word, the name 'Moses' means 'son'. The basket floated on the water of the Nile. The princess, daughter of the pharaoh, saw it.
She had it brought to the bank. She realised that the baby was an Israelite and decided to bring him up as her son. Moses became the son of the Egyptian princess. How would the princess have managed to feed a newborn baby?

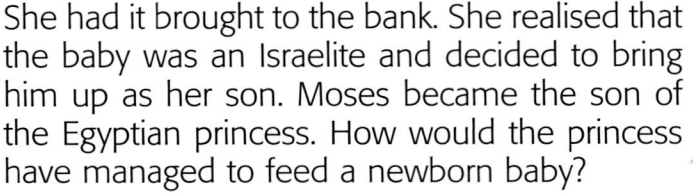

Read *Exodus 2:1-10*.

Moses, an Egyptian or an Israelite?

Moses grew up in the court of pharaoh and he became an adult. He knew he had Israelite parents, but he was an Egyptian prince. One day, he went to visit the places where the Israelites worked and he happened to see the ill-treatment of an Israelite by an Egyptian overseer. Moses killed the overseer and hid him under the sand. But people got to know about his deed and Moses was forced to escape far away from Egypt.

A peaceful life in Midian. And in Egypt?

Moses fled to a nomadic tribe of the country of Midian, on the east coast of the Gulf of Aqaba. He was welcomed by the local priest, whose daughter, Zipporah, he married. He also became a shepherd and lived a peaceful life.

But in the meantime, in Egypt, the oppression of the Israelite slaves had increased. An enslaved people could not rebel by themselves. But then something new happened. God listened to the moaning of the slaves and, remembering his covenant with the patriarchs, *(Exodus 2:23-25)* he decided to free his people. Who would help him to free them?

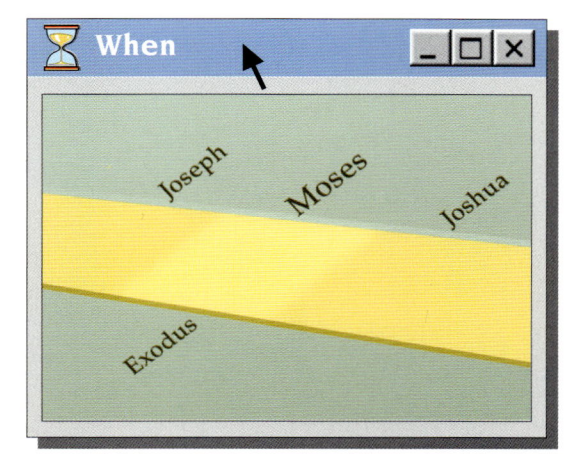

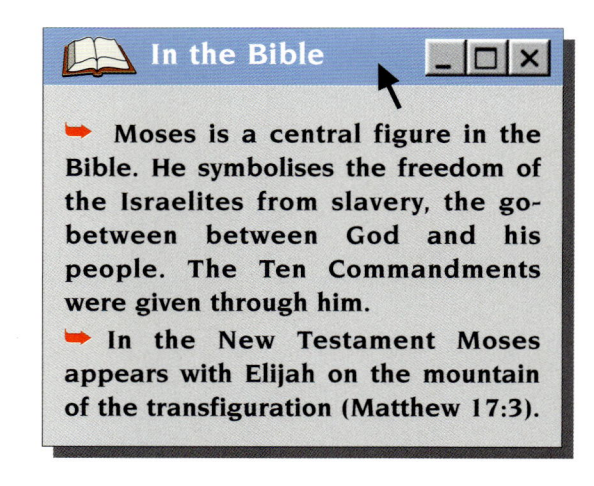

When

Joseph — Moses — Joshua
Exodus

In the Bible

➡ Moses is a central figure in the Bible. He symbolises the freedom of the Israelites from slavery, the go-between between God and his people. The Ten Commandments were given through him.

➡ In the New Testament Moses appears with Elijah on the mountain of the transfiguration (Matthew 17:3).

123

MOSES

Get my people out of Egypt

The burning bush was a mysterious event. It kept on burning and yet did not turn into ashes! Moses had ventured on a great distance, as far as Horeb, known as the mountain of God. He saw that bush which was not being burnt up, and he could not explain the phenomenon. God called him by name and Moses responded. It was the same God of Abraham, Isaac and Jacob. He said to Moses: 'Now I am sending you to the king of Egypt so that you can lead my people out of his country.' *(Exodus 3:10)*

After several excuses to get out of the assignment, Moses asked God: 'But if the people ask me what you are called, what shall I tell them?' 'I am who I am. The one who is called **I AM** has sent me to you.' *(Exodus 3:13-14)* God did not say his name: the name of God could not be uttered.

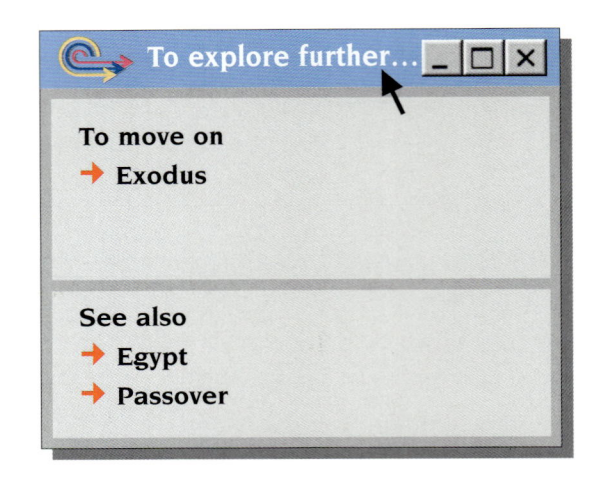

To explore further...

To move on
➡ Exodus

See also
➡ Egypt
➡ Passover

Let my people go

Moses returned to Egypt and with his brother Aaron at his side, he went to the pharaoh. He said: 'The Lord, the God of Israel, says, "Let my people go, so that they can hold a festival in the desert to honour me."' *(Exodus 5:1)* Why should the pharaoh give up his large and cheap workforce? Indeed, to show who really had power, the pharaoh made the slaves' work conditions worse: he gave orders to their slave-masters to demand the same production of bricks, without supplying any more of the straw needed to make them. Moses was desperate and said to God: 'Lord, why do you ill-treat your people? Why did you send me here? Ever since I went to the pharaoh to speak for you, he has treated them cruelly. And you have done nothing to help them!' *(Exodus 5:22-23)*

The ten plagues

What could be done to sway the tyranny? Well, God sent ten punishments, which would strike the Egyptians and the pharaoh. Those became known as the plagues of Egypt. Calamities of various types came one after the other: an invasion of harmful and annoying insects, illnesses, the deaths of animals and terrible weather conditions.

The Passover

'Every family is to get a lamb or goat. Before cooking them, take some of their blood and with that paint the outside part of the door of the house.' Moses gave that and other instructions to the people of Israel. The blood of the lambs, brushed on the door of every Israelite family, would be the sign that would save them. When the final punishment from God arrived, the death of all the firstborn children in the country, the Israelite homes would be saved from this calamity. It would be the signal for their freedom. The Israelites were to leave Egypt, carrying with them bread that had not had time to rise: unleavened bread.

NOAH
God's project

This is an account of the judgement of guilty and wicked humankind and of a new creation: the story of an ending and a new beginning. Ten generations had followed on after the unsuccessful experiment of the creation of Adam and Eve. Evil increased and multiplied on earth. God was sorry he had created human beings: 'It's necessary to destroy everything and begin again. Shall I return everything to the state of chaos? Supposing I were to do that, but with a plan in mind?' There was a man, Noah, with whom God was pleased: he would be the new project, he and his family. 'And what about the animals? Must I really remake everything? Perhaps it is better to save the models – a couple for every species. Yes! That's the best thing to do!' God called Noah: 'Build….'

Read *Genesis 6:14-22*.

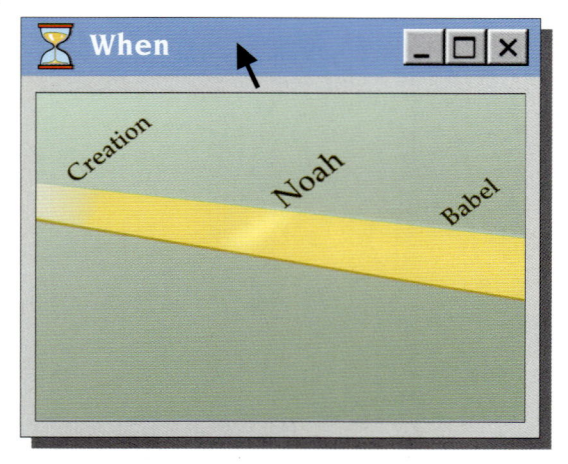

The Flood

Exactly on Noah's birthday the underground waters, as if mad, surged up in torrents and with an unheard-of violence, from the springs; the large vault of heaven, which held the waters of heaven, was flung open, releasing torrents of water from above as well. Now was the time to enter the ark. Noah was in control of the embarkation: sons, wives, daughters-in-law and all the animals in pairs and in an orderly way. God himself shut the door of the ark, the guarantee of his life-saving project. The flood raged on for forty days: all living beings were swept away and died. Only Noah was saved along with those in the ark with him. They were in God's hands.

When
Creation — Noah — Babel

To explore further…

To move on
→ Babel

See also
→ Creation
→ Covenant

A wind blows on the earth

The ark drifted for one hundred and fifty days. But God did not forget his friend Noah, the man whom he had chosen to make a new start. Wind was made to blow on the flooded land, the springs stopped, the vault of heaven closed. Slowly the waters began to subside.

➡ Read *Genesis 8:8-12*.

Thank you, God!

A year had passed since the flood began. Noah took off the roof of the ark. The land was dry. God himself let everything disembark from their large shelter: 'Go slowly, in an orderly way, without pushing!' Noah, full of emotion and gratitude, built an altar and offered a sacrifice. God accepted the offering and reflected on human wickedness.

➡ Read *Genesis 8:21-22*.

The Rainbow

God blessed Noah and his sons and made a covenant with his new humanity. There were some rules to protect life and a generous commitment: the flood would never be repeated. 'I have placed my rainbow among the clouds. It will be the sign of my promise to the world.'

PARABLES
Speaking in riddles

What is a parable?

The word parable means comparison. It can be a brief illustration or a complete story, full of detail. However, every parable in the Bible always has one point, or rather its own unique key point, which is a secret to be discovered. The attempt to explain every detail of the parable, therefore, would create only confusion.

The aim of parables

The aim of the parables was to attract the attention of those addressed and to make them reflect on the actions, words and life of Jesus. The parable was, in fact, like a riddle or an enigma, which demanded attention and reflection, because it not only illustrated but also, at the same time, hid the message of the gospel. Jesus often spoke in parables about the Kingdom of God.

The Kingdom of God, present and hidden

The Kingdom of God was the proclamation in words and actions, in cures and miracles, that God was the God of this world and wanted to save it. But this Lordship of God was often hidden and contradictory, even if it was already in operation on this earth. It was because of this that Jesus often said at the end of his parables: 'Who has ears to hear, let him hear!'

What gave rise to each parable?

Every parable had its own background, that is, a specific reason or actual incident that led Jesus to tell it. We have to look first for the situation that prompted Jesus to tell each parable.

Three parables

Read *Mark 4:1-9*.

Mark 3:6 and *3:21,31* give the setting. It was after the first death threat against Jesus by the religious people (Pharisees) and people friendly with the governor Herod Antipas (friend of the Romans). Then there was the worry of members of Jesus' family and the accusations of his enemies. From then on Jesus changed his style and spoke in parables. What riddle and what secret did Jesus hide in that strange story, which could be called the parable of the mad sower?

Read *Luke 10:30-37*.
Setting: vv.25-29.

Read *Luke 15:11-32*.
Setting: vv.1-2.

To explore further…

To move on
→ Prayer

See also
→ Jesus

129

PASSION
The heart of the gospel message

The word 'passion', originating from 'to suffer', refers to the final stage of Jesus' earthly life, from the entry into Jerusalem to the crucifixion. Mark's Gospel has been described as the passion narrative with a long introduction and the same could be said of the other Gospels: the events of that last week make up the heart of the New Testament's message. The resurrection allowed the Christian community to understand those events in a new light.

At Jerusalem

Jesus went to Jerusalem for Passover with the group who had followed him along the roads of Palestine. His fame must have gone ahead of him among friends and enemies: in any case his entry into the city is described as a triumphal march. Jesus, who rode a donkey like the meek king proclaimed by the prophet Zechariah, was acclaimed by the crowd as 'the one who comes in the name of the Lord.' *(Psalm 118:25-26)* The crowd who applauded him then would shout a few days later to demand his death.

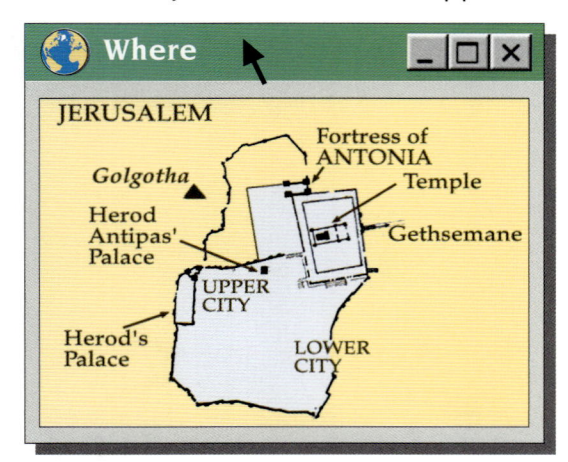

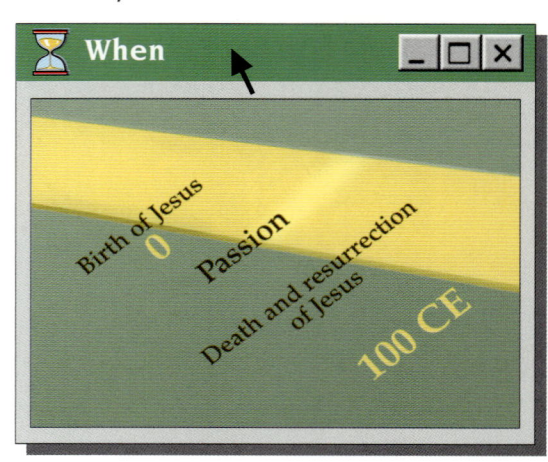

Where

JERUSALEM
- Golgotha
- Fortress of ANTONIA
- Temple
- Herod Antipas' Palace
- Gethsemane
- UPPER CITY
- Herod's Palace
- LOWER CITY

When

- Birth of Jesus — 0
- Passion
- Death and resurrection of Jesus
- 100 CE

In the Temple

The day after, according to the first three evangelists (John placed the incident at the beginning of Jesus' ministry), Jesus went to the Temple in Jerusalem. There he turned the stalls of the traders upside down and threw into the air the tables of those who exchanged money and the stools of the dealers in pigeons. The money-exchangers collected ordinary coins with the emperor's image on them, which could not be used in the sacred space of the Temple, and gave in exchange, special Temple money, which could be offered. The pigeon-sellers supplied the animals for the sacrifices: they were therefore providing a useful service for religious ceremonies, not a tourist market of sacred items. Jesus explained his action by quoting *Jeremiah 7:8-11*, where the prophet says that as pirates completed their raids then took refuge in caves along the coast, so religious people shamelessly sinned then went to the Temple to perform their rituals, as if God's house was in fact a den of thieves in which to find refuge. Religion without the practice of justice was blasphemous, disrespectful to God. Jesus' action upset the Jews and worried the Romans, who wondered whether he was actually the dangerous rebel that some people said he was.

PASSION

The Last Supper and the betrayal

Jesus was conscious that his enemies were closing in on him. Before the end he wanted to share a meal once more, with his friends. According to Mark, Matthew and Luke it was the Passover meal and during that meal Jesus broke the bread and distributed it together with the wine. Jesus urged his disciples to continue this practice in memory of him. So, accepting Jesus' invitation, the Christians celebrate the Lord's Supper, also called the Eucharist or Mass, in remembrance of his death *(1 Corinthians 11:23-26)*.

Even Judas participated in the meal. He had already decided to hand over Jesus to his enemies. Why did he betray him? The Bible does not say.

In Gethsemane

After the meal, Jesus withdrew to pray in the garden called Gethsemane, asking his disciples to stay awake with him. He turned to his Father: 'Abba, my Father, you can do everything. Take this cup of suffering away from me! But if it has to be like this, let your will be done, not mine'. The disciples could not keep awake so Jesus was alone. The guards arrived, led by Judas, and they arrested him.

The execution

Jesus was condemned to death by the Romans because the chief Sadducees made him out to be subversive. According to the gospel narrative, even the ferocious crowd wanted his death and preferred to ask for mercy for a certain Barabbas who probably was indeed a political rebel. As was the custom in these cases, before being crucified, Jesus was whipped and bullied, then forced to carry the cross beam of the cross on which he would be nailed, until his fainting prevented him from continuing. The evangelists record some differences in the details of the final scene: Mark presents Jesus alone, without friends or family, only a few women watched from a distance and even the two wretches who were crucified with him insulted him. Jesus died with a loud cry. Still in Mark, a Roman centurion, who was probably the chief of the execution squad, seeing the dying man defeated, tortured and alone, recognised in him the revelation of a different kind of God, whose strength was revealed in weakness and he claimed: 'This man was truly the Son of God'.

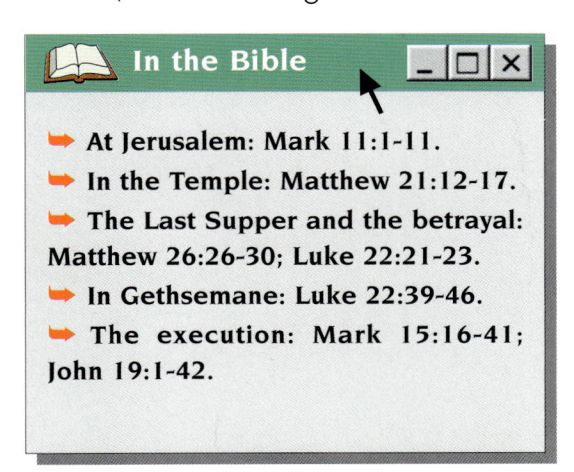

In the Bible
- At Jerusalem: Mark 11:1-11.
- In the Temple: Matthew 21:12-17.
- The Last Supper and the betrayal: Matthew 26:26-30; Luke 22:21-23.
- In Gethsemane: Luke 22:39-46.
- The execution: Mark 15:16-41; John 19:1-42.

To explore further...

To move on
- Easter

See also
- Resurrection appearances
- Jesus
- Gospels

PAUL
A *worldwide mission*

In his letters Paul talks about himself on several occasions. The Acts of the Apostles supplies us with a lot more information about him.

Who was Paul?

Paul was a Jew of the Diaspora, meaning he lived outside Palestine, originating from Tarsus in Cilicia. He was the son of a practising Jew and he himself, belonging to the group of the Pharisees, was a strict observer of the Law of Moses. Paul had had a good Greek education and studied at Jerusalem under the famous teacher Gamaliel. His Jewish name was Saul, his Latin one, Paul. He enjoyed Roman citizenship, like his father. His father, as a conscientious Jew, had also made sure that his son had learnt a trade and so Paul was a tent-maker.

More than once Paul reported that he had been an active persecutor of the Christian Church. But one day, when he was travelling on the road towards Damascus in Syria, with the task of getting the Christians of that city arrested, something extraordinary happened to him.

Read *Acts 9:1-19*.

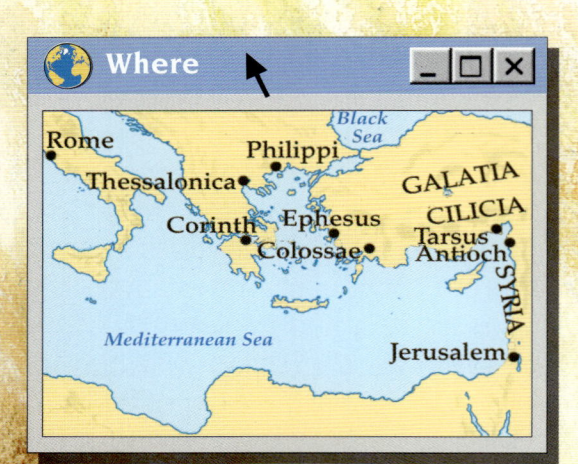

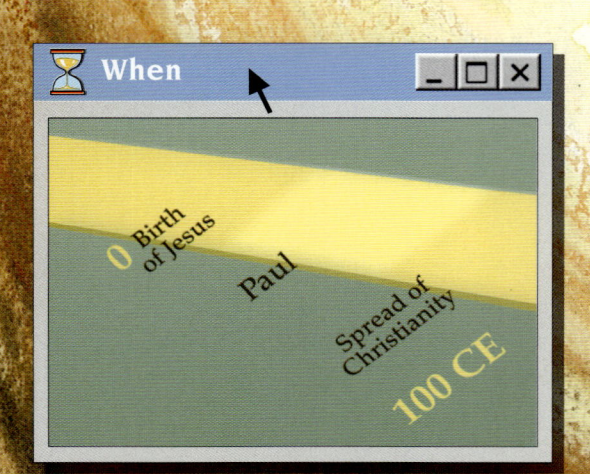

Where

Rome • Philippi • Black Sea • Thessalonica • GALATIA • Corinth • Ephesus • CILICIA • Colossae • Tarsus • Antioch • SYRIA • Mediterranean Sea • Jerusalem

When

0 Birth of Jesus — Paul — Spread of Christianity — 100 CE

Paul's vision and mission

Paul was one of the greatest travellers in the early Church. He travelled with a group of friends. He always proclaimed that Jesus was the Messiah, in the synagogues and among the Gentiles of the Roman empire, in order to establish new Christian communities. And he founded many, maintaining a close correspondence with them in Asia and Europe, part of which is found in the letters in the Bible addressed to Christians in Rome, Corinth, Galatia, Philippi and Thessalonica as well as to Philemon, a friend of his and to other Christian communities. Paul never tired of writing that he had seen the risen Christ and he had also spoken to him.

Christ had given him the task of being the apostle to the Gentiles. Paul's whole mission – his three missionary journeys, his exhaustion and worries, the dangers he encountered, his arrests and the long periods in prison – was based on the certainty that Jesus Christ was alive and that he had called him to work in his service in his mission to the Gentiles. Peter, on the other hand, had been given the job of apostle to the Jews. Paul was convinced that the risen Christ himself guided his missionary ventures, opening some doors for him and closing others.

Paul's death

We do not have accurate information about Paul's death. The book of Acts ends with the account of Paul at Rome, where he was under house arrest and awaiting trial. According to Clement of Rome, writing at the end of the first century, Peter and Paul died as martyrs in Rome, in uncertain circumstances: 'through jealousy and quarrelling'.

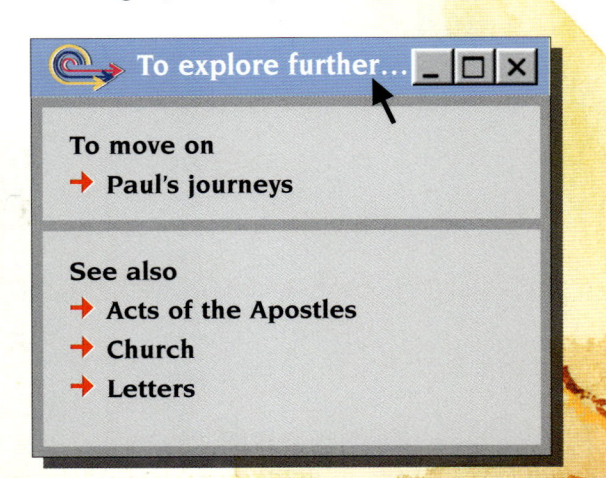

In the Bible

➡ In Paul's letters, the chief passages referring to his life are found in: Galatians 1:13-24; 2:1-10; 1 Corinthians 15:1-10; Philippians 3:5-12.

➡ In the Acts of the Apostles Paul is mentioned in: 8:1-3; 9:1-31; 11:19-30; 13:1-31.

To explore further...

To move on
➡ Paul's journeys

See also
➡ Acts of the Apostles
➡ Church
➡ Letters

PAUL'S JOURNEYS
A tremendous undertaking

The Romans had built a network of roads throughout the entire empire, known as consular roads, for travel by horse, with a cart or on foot. People could not walk more than fifty kilometres a day, however. The other means of transport was by ship. That involved great effort and was to be faced only by young and tough people. The book of Acts tells of a terrible voyage of Paul's where they were shipwrecked *(Acts 27:1-28:16)*.

Paul, a great traveller

The three long journeys of Paul always had a missionary aim. Paul never journeyed alone but always in a group. In about ten years (48-57 CE) of exhausting journeys, Paul and his group visited cities and countries in Asia Minor (Turkey) and Greece, establishing various Christian communities. His strategy was simple: Paul and his companions, as Jews, went first of all to the many synagogues spread around the vast Jewish Diaspora of the Roman Empire. In the synagogues they proclaimed Jesus as Christ, the Messiah of the Jews. The reactions varied. Rarely was the message accepted. Sometimes there was interest and a debate began on the biblical foundation of the proclamation. More often there was scepticism or a negative reaction. In the latter case, Paul and his group changed their strategy and went straight to the Gentiles. When direct persecution broke out, Paul and his companions ended up in prison or had a brush with death.

Read *Acts 16:16-40*.

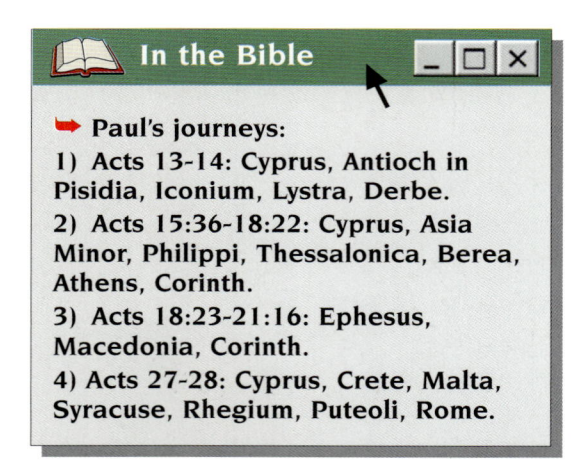

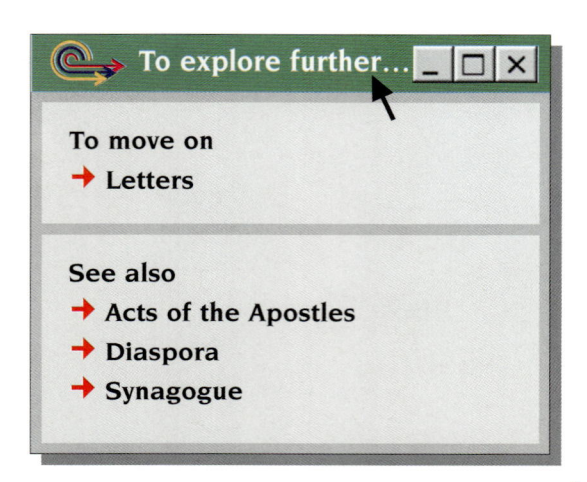

In the Bible

➡ Paul's journeys:
1) Acts 13-14: Cyprus, Antioch in Pisidia, Iconium, Lystra, Derbe.
2) Acts 15:36-18:22: Cyprus, Asia Minor, Philippi, Thessalonica, Berea, Athens, Corinth.
3) Acts 18:23-21:16: Ephesus, Macedonia, Corinth.
4) Acts 27-28: Cyprus, Crete, Malta, Syracuse, Rhegium, Puteoli, Rome.

To explore further...

To move on
➡ Letters

See also
➡ Acts of the Apostles
➡ Diaspora
➡ Synagogue

➡ 1st journey
➡ 2nd journey
➡ 3rd journey
➡ 4th journey

A big problem in the background

As the mission developed, two groups of Christians were formed: Christians of Jewish origin and those from Gentile backgrounds. The problem was one of circumcision. Did a Gentile who believed in Jesus Christ have to be circumcised, have to first become a Jew? Or could he become a Christian without circumcision, through faith only and by means of baptism?

The Christians in Jerusalem, with the apostles, decided that the Gentiles who believed in Christ were not obliged to be circumcised *(Acts 15:1-31)*. In spite of that, in the background of all Paul's journeys, the problem of the circumcision of Gentiles would remain unresolved and Paul was accused of encouraging Gentile Christians to abandon the Law of Moses. Paul describes some of the dangers and misfortunes that he encountered on his travels.

Read *2 Corinthians 11:23-33*.

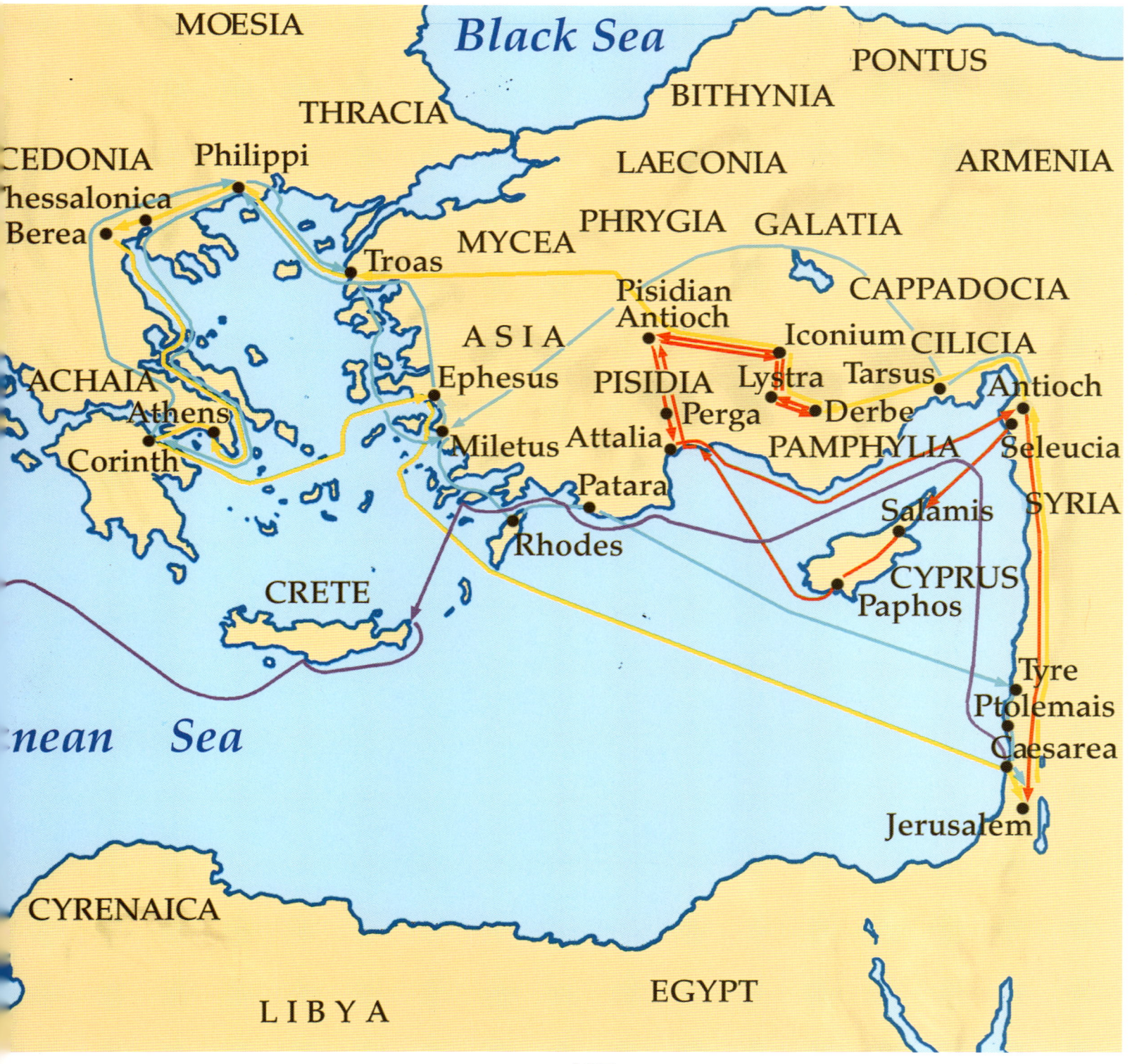

PEACE
Shalom

Peace, *'shalom'* in Hebrew, was the greatest gift that God associated with the Covenant established with Israel. Keeping God's Law, the Torah, meant that the people led a life interwoven with justice, which brought with it peace: not only the absence of war but the possibility of a prosperous existence, rich in meaning, in the land that God gave them. That is why the Hebrew word *'shalom'* is sometimes translated as 'prosperity' and the like.

> Read *Isaiah 32:15-20.*

The commandments of God were therefore a source of 'shalom'. In contrast, disobedience brought violence with it: just as, after the sin of Adam and Eve, murderous rage was unleashed, so, in the history of Israel, contempt for God's commandments destroyed peace. The Jewish Scriptures interpreted wars and especially Israel's military defeats, from Joshua up to the exile, as the consequences of the people's disobedience. God never broke for good the covenant of peace; even if *'shalom'* was temporarily withheld, this was to lead the people to change their ways. The true prophet knew that and declared it, even if it was an uncomfortable message; the false prophet, on the other hand, continued to announce *'shalom, shalom'*, even when there was neither peace nor justice. The Israelites were thirsty for 'shalom': in joyful and difficult times, they did not give up waiting in faith for God's 'shalom' which flowed like a river and brought blessing to Jerusalem *(Isaiah 66:12).*

Christ is peace

According to the New Testament's gospel message the richness of life which the Jewish Scriptures called 'shalom' had its source in Jesus Christ, the bringer of a different peace from that of the world: by means of his death, through love, he made it possible for people to be put right with God, that is, to receive the 'peace of God'. 'The peace of God, which is greater than anyone can imagine' *(Philippians 4:7)*, was not a vague inner peacefulness, but the joyful awareness that God kept his promise and, in spite of people's sins, he did not cease to call people to his service. If Christ made peace between the Creator and human beings, people also had to be at peace among themselves: God desired that the Church was a place of peace.

Read *1 Corinthians 14:33*.

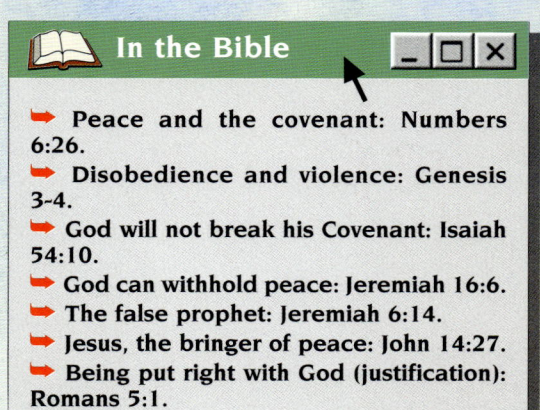

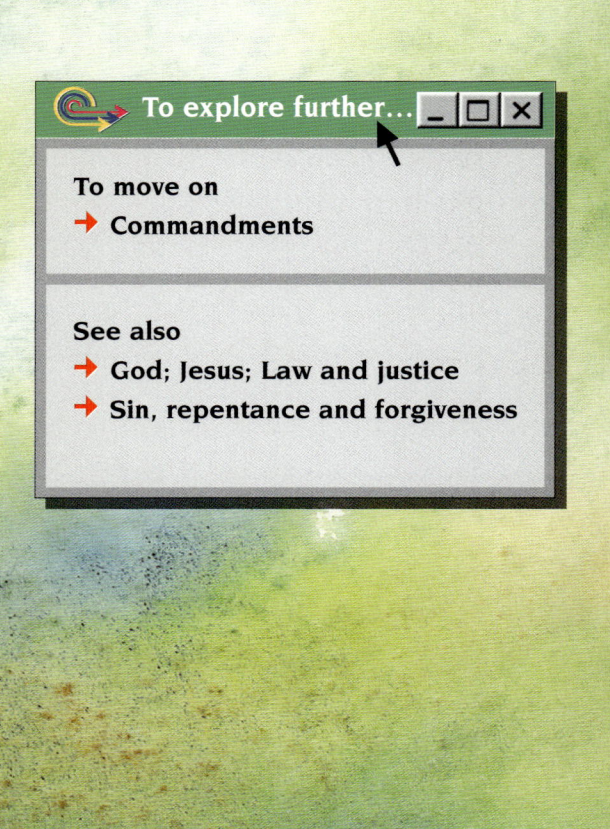

In the Bible

➡ Peace and the covenant: Numbers 6:26.
➡ Disobedience and violence: Genesis 3-4.
➡ God will not break his Covenant: Isaiah 54:10.
➡ God can withhold peace: Jeremiah 16:6.
➡ The false prophet: Jeremiah 6:14.
➡ Jesus, the bringer of peace: John 14:27.
➡ Being put right with God (justification): Romans 5:1.

To explore further…

To move on
➡ Commandments

See also
➡ God; Jesus; Law and justice
➡ Sin, repentance and forgiveness

PENTECOST (WHITSUNDAY)
The gifts of God

In Israel

Pentecost, or the Feast of Weeks ('*Shavuot*' in Hebrew) or harvest, was celebrated at the end of the reaping of the wheat, seven weeks after Passover, that is on the fiftieth day, from which the Greek name 'Pentecost' is derived. After the exile, as part of the festival, the gift of the tablets of the Law through Moses on Sinai was also celebrated. At the time of Jesus, therefore, the Jewish Pentecost was not only an agricultural festival of thanksgiving, but played an important role in Israel's religious calendar.

Read *Deuteronomy 16:9-12*.

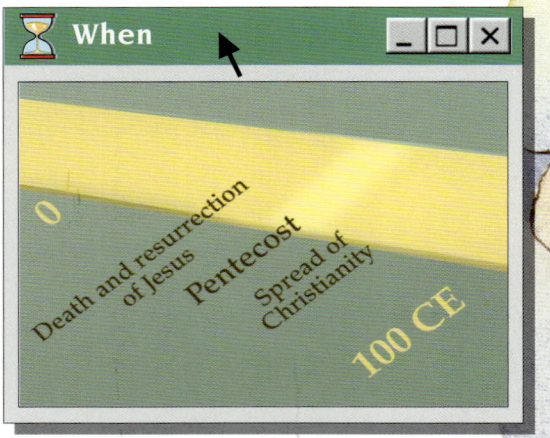

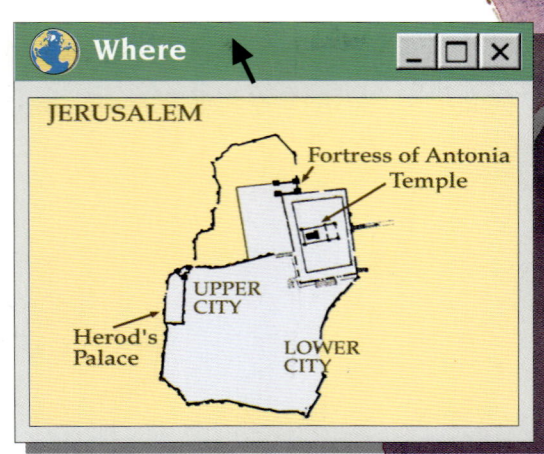

When

0 — Death and resurrection of Jesus — Pentecost — Spread of Christianity — 100 CE

Where

JERUSALEM
Fortress of Antonia
Temple
Herod's Palace
UPPER CITY
LOWER CITY

The descent of the Holy Spirit

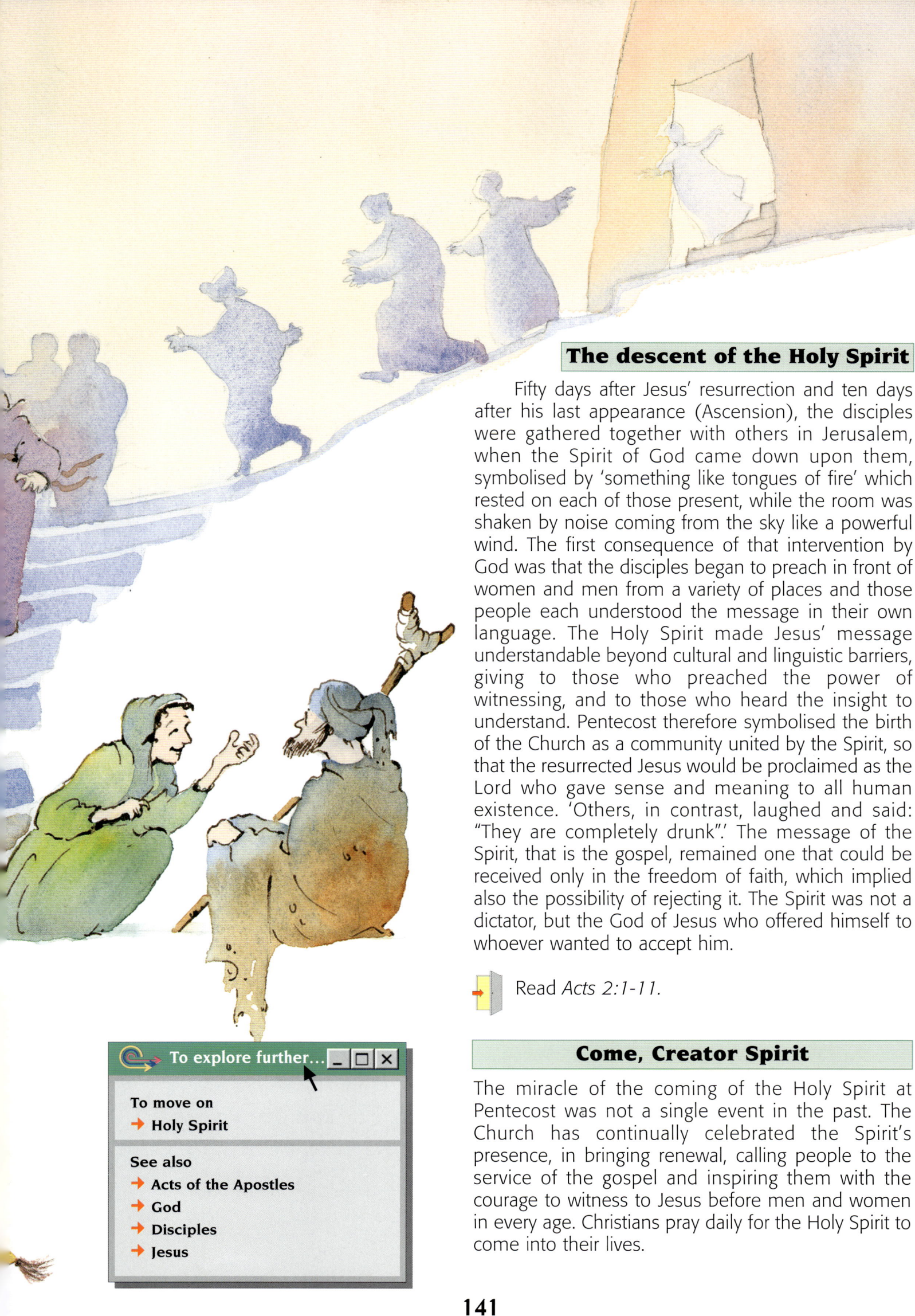

Fifty days after Jesus' resurrection and ten days after his last appearance (Ascension), the disciples were gathered together with others in Jerusalem, when the Spirit of God came down upon them, symbolised by 'something like tongues of fire' which rested on each of those present, while the room was shaken by noise coming from the sky like a powerful wind. The first consequence of that intervention by God was that the disciples began to preach in front of women and men from a variety of places and those people each understood the message in their own language. The Holy Spirit made Jesus' message understandable beyond cultural and linguistic barriers, giving to those who preached the power of witnessing, and to those who heard the insight to understand. Pentecost therefore symbolised the birth of the Church as a community united by the Spirit, so that the resurrected Jesus would be proclaimed as the Lord who gave sense and meaning to all human existence. 'Others, in contrast, laughed and said: "They are completely drunk".' The message of the Spirit, that is the gospel, remained one that could be received only in the freedom of faith, which implied also the possibility of rejecting it. The Spirit was not a dictator, but the God of Jesus who offered himself to whoever wanted to accept him.

Read *Acts 2:1-11*.

Come, Creator Spirit

The miracle of the coming of the Holy Spirit at Pentecost was not a single event in the past. The Church has continually celebrated the Spirit's presence, in bringing renewal, calling people to the service of the gospel and inspiring them with the courage to witness to Jesus before men and women in every age. Christians pray daily for the Holy Spirit to come into their lives.

To explore further...

To move on
→ Holy Spirit

See also
→ Acts of the Apostles
→ God
→ Disciples
→ Jesus

PETER
A tough witness

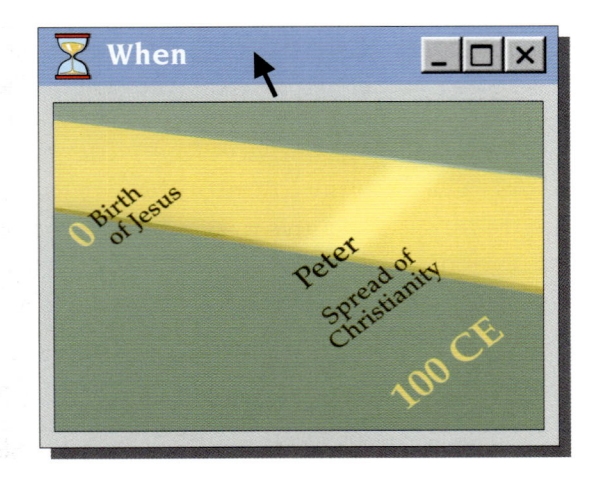

Simon

Peter's real name was Simon. He was a fisherman by trade and he owned a boat. Peter was married and his mother-in-law and his brother, Andrew, shared his home. At the time when he met Jesus he lived at Capernaum in Galilee.

Impulsive and full of enthusiasm

In discussions with Jesus, Simon was often the spokesperson for the eleven apostles, asking for explanations or giving his opinion before everyone else. He was full of courage and was enthusiastic and impulsive as when, at the invitation of Jesus, he got out of a boat onto the water of the lake to walk to him, but then became panic-stricken!

Read *Matthew 14:28-32*.

When Jesus was arrested, he drew out a sword and cut off the ear of one of the people who had come for the arrest. *(John 18:10)*
But he was severely told off at times, like when he shouted at Jesus for having spoken of the suffering that he would face. Jesus said to him: 'Get away from me, Satan. Your thoughts don't come from God but from human nature!' *(Mark 8:33)*

You are a rock

Jesus gave Simon the nickname Cephas, which meant 'rock' in Aramaic, perhaps because of his declaration of faith in Jesus as the Messiah or because of his character. Rock and stone meant the same thing and from then on Simon was called Peter, meaning 'stone' in Greek or Simon Peter. *(Matthew 16:15-18)*

In the Bible

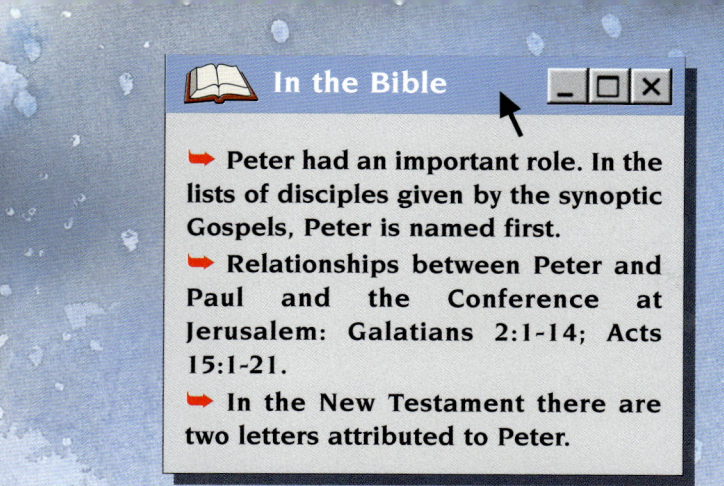

➡ Peter had an important role. In the lists of disciples given by the synoptic Gospels, Peter is named first.

➡ Relationships between Peter and Paul and the Conference at Jerusalem: Galatians 2:1-14; Acts 15:1-21.

➡ In the New Testament there are two letters attributed to Peter.

I will never deny knowing you

Jesus was about to be tried and he knew that everyone would abandon him. Peter said to him, 'No! Never! I will never deny that I know you.' And Jesus said to him: 'I tell you that before the cock crows twice tonight, you will say three times that you do not know me.'

Read *Mark 14:66-72*.

A leader of the Church in Jerusalem

The book of Acts described the early Christian community in Jerusalem where Peter had an important role. Peter explained to the crowd the significance of Pentecost and he healed some sick people. Peter gave witness to his faith in Jesus to a Roman official, Cornelius, which resulted in the first Gentile being accepted into the Christian Church.

An ecumenical conference

Differences of opinion between Peter and Paul were evident in Paul's letter to the Galatians and the book of Acts. The early Church risked serious division. But at a conference in Jerusalem, which could be called ecumenical (that is, representing all branches of the Church), the two apostles agreed to divide up their fields of work: Peter would be the apostle of the Jewish Christians and Paul would become the apostle to the Gentiles.

To explore further...

To move on
➡ Paul

See also
➡ Acts of the Apostles
➡ Disciples

143

PRAYER
Faith in God

In Israel

The God of Israel intervened in the history of his people and in the events of individual women and men. He spoke to them personally and so human beings could respond to him. That was what prayer was. Whoever prayed had faith that God listened and responded according to his will, but also in his love and his faithfulness. Prayer formed the sap of Israel's faith, the daily expression of a living relationship with the God of freedom. For the practising Jew, prayer marked the rhythm of the day, from morning *(Psalm 5)* to evening *(Psalm 4)*, and the rhythm of the week, above all through the Sabbath prayers. Many forms of prayer are found in the Bible, often interwoven one with the other. Prayers of intercession should be specially mentioned: here believers ask God to give them what they need or want. One type of intercession is from those who have committed sin or on behalf of someone else who has sinned, asking God for forgiveness. Prayers of thanksgiving and the singing of praise express acknowledgement of God's merciful intervention. But their faith embraced also the sorrowful pouring out of the lament. Further, prayer could be a real wrestling with God, and the Scriptures include cases where the person praying did not give in until they had compelled God to hear his prayer.

Read *Exodus 32:7-14*.

Israel's experience of prayer was concentrated in the book of Psalms, where every form of dialogue with God and every aspect of the human spirit were represented. That formed a fundamental school of prayer for Israel as well as for the Church. The faith of Israel was condensed into the prayer known as the Shema, meaning 'Hear, O Israel: the Lord is our God, the Lord is one!' *(Deuteronomy 6:4)*

Jesus the man of prayer

The faith of Jesus was that of Israel and the same was true of his praying. As a Jew of his time, Jesus prayed using the Psalms and the *Shema*. His daily spiritual nourishment came from his conversations with God. It was the space in which he sought and found the strength to live out his vocation. Jesus demonstrated an awareness of a special relationship with God, which was expressed by the Aramaic word *'abba'* ('daddy', 'father'). The Father of Jesus was certainly the thrice holy God, but was also a parent, full of affection, caring and concern for his daughters and sons. Jesus invited people who prayed to persevere, not give up and not to doubt God's willingness to grant whatever they needed.

Read *Matthew 7:7-11*.

Such deep faith did not abandon Jesus even in his most difficult moment, just before his arrest when he turned to his Father in a dramatic prayer, which at the same time was full of enduring hope, making it all the more authentic *(Mark 14:32-42)*.

PRAYER

The Lord's Prayer

The prayer that Jesus taught his disciples reflected Jesus' relationship with his heavenly Father and was made up of a series of requests. The first ones: 'hallowed be your name', 'may your kingdom come', 'may your will be done', referred to the manifestation of God's glory. Jesus invited people to pray like that so that God might reveal himself, that his will might become the centre of everyone's life so that the day would soon come when every tear would be dried and until then, that all believers would obey his words. The second part of the prayer: 'give us today our daily bread', 'forgive our sins as we also forgive those who sin against us', 'do not expose us to temptation,' asked God to intervene especially in people's favour, giving them as much as their material and spiritual needs required.

Read *Matthew 6:5-13*.

The prayer of the Church

The Psalms and the Lord's Prayer formed the guidelines for the prayers of the Christian community: that did not mean that people could not pray with other words or still less that it was the only effective method of learning how to pray but those words were the model and the combined elements of every prayer. Reciting the Lord's Prayer and some Psalms daily, taught people also how to turn to God with their own words. The church prayed in the name of Jesus *(John 14:13)*: its certainty that God would hear its prayers lay in God's faithfulness, exactly as the life and death of the man from Nazareth had demonstrated.

In the Bible

- **Prayers of request: 1Kings 18:36-37; Psalm 51.**
- **Prayer of intercession: Genesis 18:23-33.**
- **Prayer of thanksgiving: Exodus 15:1-18.**
- **Prayer of sorrow: Jeremiah 15:10-18.**

To explore further...

To move on
- **Passion**

See also
- **God**
- **Jesus**
- **Psalms**
- **Gospels**

PROPHECY
Inspired people

When prophecy is mentioned, there come to mind the inspired personalities of the prophets who spoke to people in the name of God. The phenomenon of prophecy was widespread in the ancient Near East and not limited to Israel. Yet, between 1000 and 160 BCE, prophecy developed so much in Israel that it formed a fundamental element of its religious history.

The prophets of Israel

Towards the year 1000 BCE, at the end of the period of the Judges, the prophets formed groups or classes inspired by a strong religious enthusiasm. Under the influence of the Spirit of God the prophets entered into a type of religious exaltation and spoke in the name of God *(1 Kings 22:6-28)*. With the passing of time, the prophets increasingly became the defenders of the pure religion of God, in order to free Israel from idols.

A prophet, like Nathan, could accuse King David publicly of murder and adultery *(2 Samuel 12:1-12)*. Around the greatest prophetic personalities, groups or schools of prophets were established, which were also interested in the politics of the king and nation.

Where

Mediterranean Sea
Gath-Hepher — Jonah — Sea of Galilee
ISRAEL — Tishbe of Gilead
Abel-Meholah — Elisha — Elijah
Samaria
Anathoth — Jeremiah
Jerusalem — Isaiah
Tekoa — Ezekiel
Amos
Dead Sea
JUDAH

Prophets and politics

With the rising of the great empires of Assyria and Babylonia between 700 and 600 BCE, the great personalities of the prophets whose prophecies have been preserved in the books carrying their names also appeared: Amos, Hosea, Isaiah, Jeremiah and Ezekiel.

These people had a universal vision of new events and they made known the voice of God, which spoke to king and people. On the other hand, those prophets who confined themselves to defending traditional institutions like the monarchy and the Temple, without understanding God's message for the king and the people, are called false prophets in the Bible.

In the Bible

➡ The prophetic texts are made up of very brief sentences introduced by the expression: 'Thus says the Lord' (Amos 1).

➡ Almost all the prophets whose prophecies have been preserved in the books carrying their names told the story of their own calling by God to the prophetic task: Amos 7:10-17; Hosea 1; Isaiah 6; Jeremiah 1:4-19; Ezekiel 3:1-15.

The false prophets

The prophet Jeremiah encouraged the exiles deported into Babylonia (598 BCE) by writing a letter to them. He asked the deported Jews urgently to work to build a future for themselves, and to have lots of children and to pray for the well-being of the city: 'Because if they are prosperous, you will be prosperous too.' *(Jeremiah 29:4-10)* Jeremiah also wrote to the deported Jews saying that their exile would last for at least two generations. For this reason he fiercely attacked the lies of the false prophets. They reassured the deported people with optimistic messages of a return to their homeland within the next two years. But Jeremiah knew the false prophets well! In fact, a short time before in Jerusalem…

➡ Read *Jeremiah 28:1-15*.

To explore further…

To move on
➡ Samuel

See also
➡ David
➡ Jeremiah
➡ Isaiah

149

PSALMS
Let us sing to the Lord

What are the Psalms?

The word 'psalm' is derived from the Greek and refers to a sung poem accompanied by a stringed musical instrument called a psaltery. There are one hundred and fifty psalms in the Bible. They are, for the most part, prayers written as poetry.

The psalms were closely linked to Israel's worship. They were written in a period between the time of King David, several centuries before the deportation to Babylonia, and some centuries after the return to the homeland. The whole history of Israel's faith was contained in the Psalms.

The poetry of the Psalms

Many familiar poems rhyme. This does not happen in Hebrew poetry, which is expressed by parallel verses. This means the two verses may be similar in that they express the same concept but in different words. Or the parallel verses might use similar words, which express concepts of opposite meaning. Here are two examples:

'Praise the Lord, my soul!
All my being, praise his holy name!' *(Psalm 103:1-2)*

'Such people will stumble and fall,
but we will rise and stand firm.' *(Psalm 20:8)*

In the first example the same concept is expressed in this way:

Praise	=	Praise
the Lord	=	his holy name
my soul	=	all my being

In the second example concepts with opposite meanings are expressed like this:

| Such people | = | we |
| Stumble and fall | = | rise and stand firm. |

So, poetic parallels are also used to compare the meaning of the words.

Where

The contents and use of the Psalms

The Psalms are used by both Jews and Christians in public worship. They have been translated from the original Hebrew into rhyming poetry in different languages. Among the most famous translations is the Huguenot Psalter, used to this day in the reformed Church of Holland. The Psalms express in prayer, that is, in conversation with God, many different human feelings and human situations: gratitude for God's goodness *(Psalms 8, 24, 30, 33, 34, 73, 100, 104, 105 etc.)*; communal laments for national misfortune or individual laments for personal crises *(Psalms 44, 74 79 and 7, 13, 51 etc.)*; there are also royal psalms, which refer to the kings from the two kingdoms of Israel and Judah *(Psalms 2, 18, 20, 21, 45, 72, 110)*. A typical Psalm might include a cry for help of a believer in difficulty, then, after reflection, their confession of faith in God, and finally the priest's or community's support and encouragement.

➡ Read *Psalm 121*.

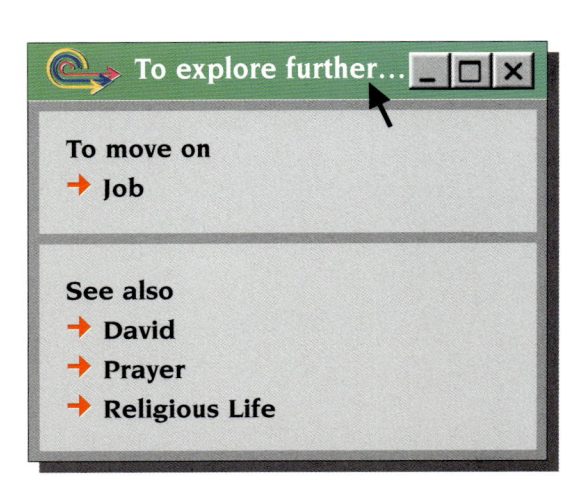

In the Bible

➡ 1 Chronicles 16:1-4, 8-43, gives information on the use of some Psalms in Temple worship, by the chorus, while the community replied with 'amen' and 'alleluia'. The Psalms partly sung and partly recited are 105:1-15; 96:1-13; 106:47-48. The book of Psalms is one of the most read books in the Bible. Many people today are familiar with Psalms 1, 23, 24, 27, 103, 121, 127.

To explore further…

To move on
➡ Job

See also
➡ David
➡ Prayer
➡ Religious Life

RELIGIOUS LIFE
Worshipping God

In the distant past it was thought that high places were nearest to the gods who lived in the sky. That explains why many peoples of the earth built impressive temples with steps to the top, as if people wanted to climb heavenwards. The Bible tells of the failed attempt at building a similar construction in the narrative of the Tower of Babel *(Genesis 11:1-9)*.

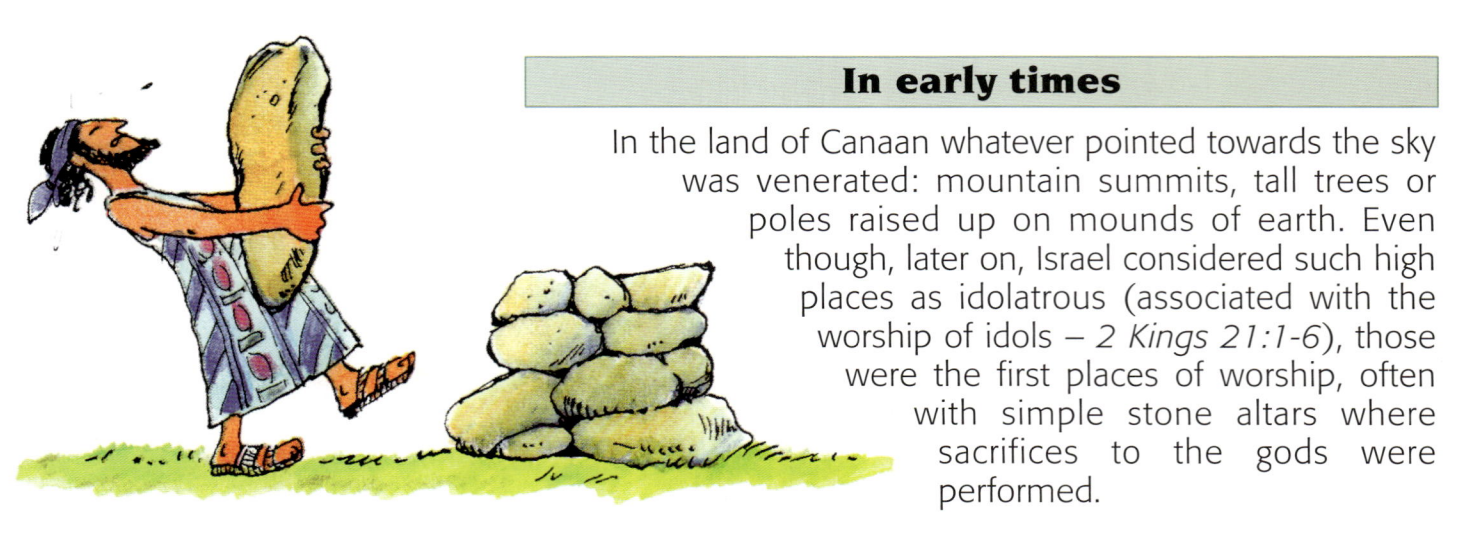

In early times

In the land of Canaan whatever pointed towards the sky was venerated: mountain summits, tall trees or poles raised up on mounds of earth. Even though, later on, Israel considered such high places as idolatrous (associated with the worship of idols – *2 Kings 21:1-6*), those were the first places of worship, often with simple stone altars where sacrifices to the gods were performed.

Abraham and his descendants, the Bible says, erected altars or consecrated existing ones to their God.
At that time, some of those locations had great importance, becoming places of worship and destinations for pilgrimages: Shechem, Bethel, the oaks of Mamre, Beersheba. Besides those, in later times, Israel had sanctuaries at Gilgal, Shiloh, Mizpah, Gibeah, Ophrah, Dan.

Sacrifices

In ancient times, in order to gain the favour of the gods, the produce of the fields and especially cattle were offered in sacrifice. When the offering in its entirety was burnt it was known as a 'burnt offering'. However, often most of the animal was eaten by the priests and by those who made the offering. Human sacrifice was not unknown either, but in Israel it was always considered outrageous *(Jeremiah 7:31)*.

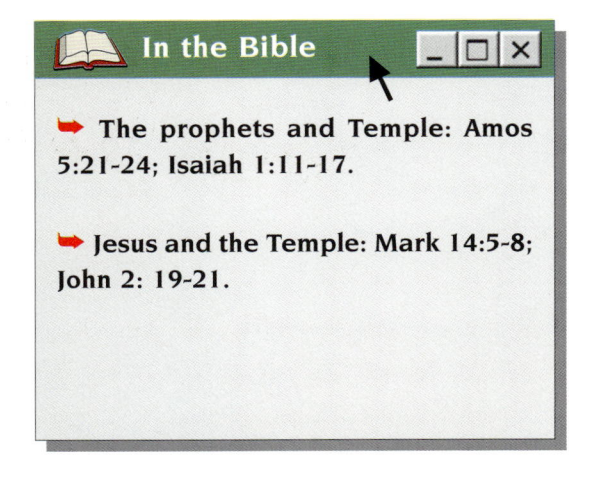

In the Bible

➡ The prophets and Temple: Amos 5:21-24; Isaiah 1:11-17.

➡ Jesus and the Temple: Mark 14:5-8; John 2: 19-21.

To explore further…

To move on
➡ Law and justice

See also
➡ Church
➡ Commandments
➡ Idolatry

RELIGIOUS LIFE

The tent of meeting

Real organised worship began for the Israelites during the time in the desert, after their liberation from Egypt. On Mount Sinai God gave Moses the tablets of the Law and a whole series of directions for civil and religious life (which at one time were considered to be one and the same). Yet God was not tied to a fixed place, and so even worship was celebrated in a 'movable' way, according to the needs of a people who were still nomadic. A special tent, the tabernacle, was a mobile temple: inside, what was needed for the sacrifices was kept and the symbol of the presence of God, the ark. It was a type of throne where God could be seated even though remaining invisible. Israel, unlike other peoples, did not have statues or representations of God. The temptation to be like the others, however, was very strong and idolatry was a recurring sin in the history of God's people.

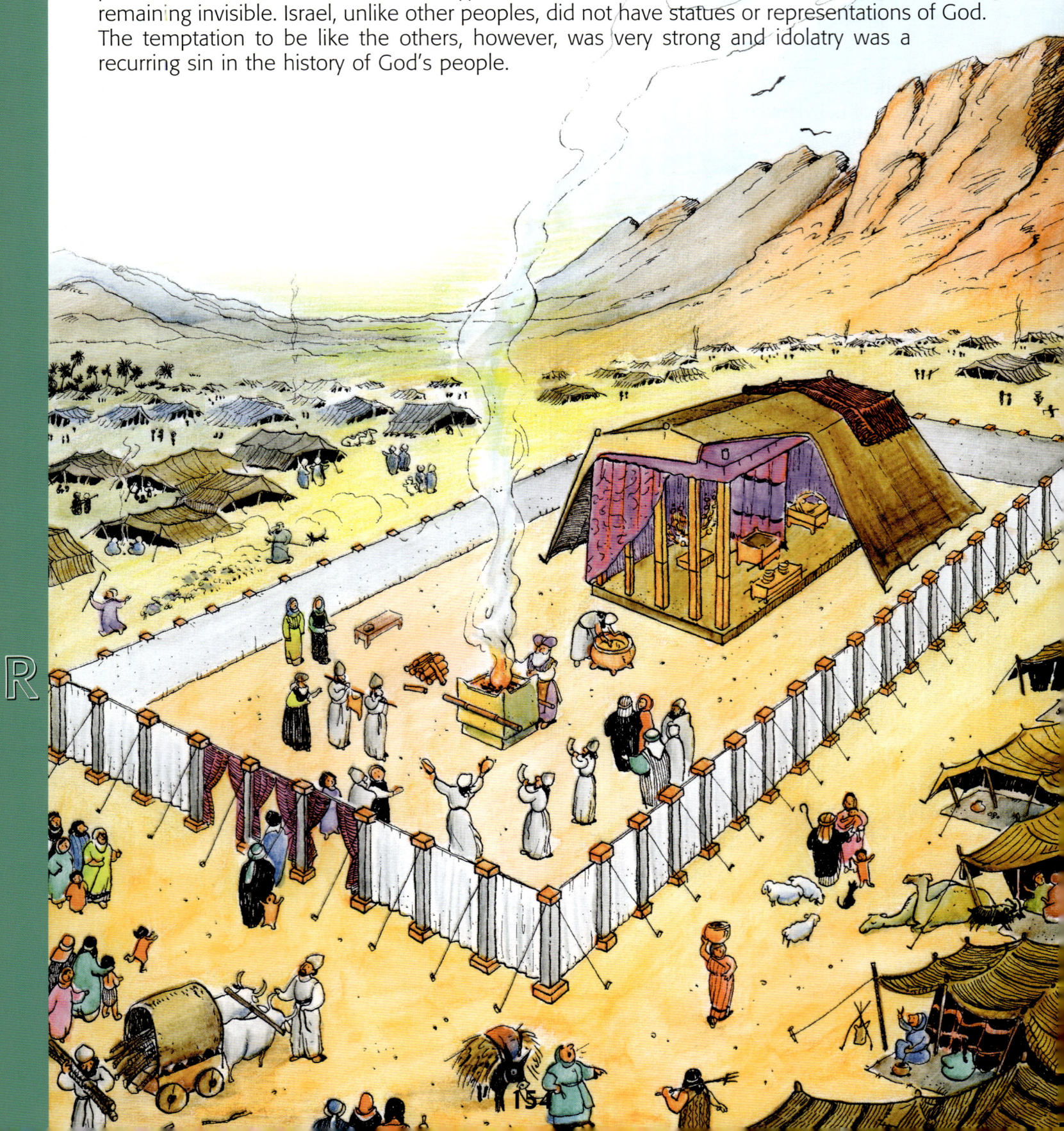

The Temple of Solomon

The organisation of the worship required people who were dedicated to it. So the priesthood, assigned especially to offering the sacrifices, began. Also the Levites, called that because they were the descendants of the tribe of Levi, were formed for more general religious duties. They carried out all the organisational tasks in the Temple constructed at Jerusalem at Solomon's wish. That majestic building was not God's dwelling, but the place where he manifested his presence *(1 Kings 8:27-30)*. With the Temple, which rose up near the royal palace, worship and political power were centralised in one place.

Following on

The 'high places', however, did not disappear – on the contrary, cults of other gods were welcomed in the Temple itself. Only the religious reform of King Josiah finally got rid of the contamination of idolatry *(2 Kings 23:1-15)*. But that happened much later: by then the power of Babylonia was at the door and Jerusalem, which had not wanted to surrender, was destroyed and with it the Temple. The period of deportation and exile began. Israel no longer had a place of worship but two aspects of her own faith held her together: circumcision and the observance of the Sabbath.

Herod's Temple

The Temple was rebuilt only very much later, after the return of part of the population to their homeland *(Ezra 6:13-18)*. That building was less majestic and rich than the first Temple, but in the time of Herod it was greatly enlarged, giving it new splendour. A little later, the Temple was destroyed once and for all by the Romans at the end of the Jewish revolt in 70 CE.

The prophets and Jesus

The Temple was the centre of the religious and economic life of Israel. But the prophets warned Israel: it was more important to do God's will rather than perform sacrifices; it was wrong to think they were safe just because they had the Temple.

Read *Jeremiah 7:3-11*.

Even Jesus harshly condemned the use made of the Temple, which should have been a house of worship for all the peoples of the earth.

Read *Mark 11:15-17*.

Jesus was accused of wanting to destroy the Temple, but in fact he wanted to emphasise that the worship of God could not be tied to a holy place, but had to be based on God himself and it must be carried out 'in spirit and in truth' *(John 4:23)*. The apostle Paul confirmed that the worship that pleased God was for people to offer themselves to God, and let God transform them, rather than to go along with current standards *(Romans 12:1-2)*.

RESURRECTION APPEARANCES
Encounters with the risen Christ

Paul's witness

The oldest account of the appearances of the risen Christ is in the first letter to the Corinthians, chapter 15: Paul speaks about what the Christian community had declared for some time, that the crucified Jesus had risen and had appeared first of all to Peter, then to the Twelve, then to five hundred people at one time (perhaps this refers to a large gathering of people come together for worship). After that Jesus appeared to his brother James, then to all the apostles and finally also to Paul. All these encounters confirmed the truth of the Easter announcement: 'The Lord has risen indeed'. Paul, however, did not say how the resurrected Christ had appeared and how the witnesses had reacted.

Fear

The Gospel accounts are more specific. The details help explain to those who have not seen the risen Christ that even the first Christians experienced difficulties. The women who went to the tomb found it empty. But they met a messenger who announced the resurrection of Jesus to them and they were frightened *(Mark 16:1-8)*.

The reason for their fear is found in various other biblical passages. When God revealed himself in power, human beings, including believers, were always unprepared and perplexed.

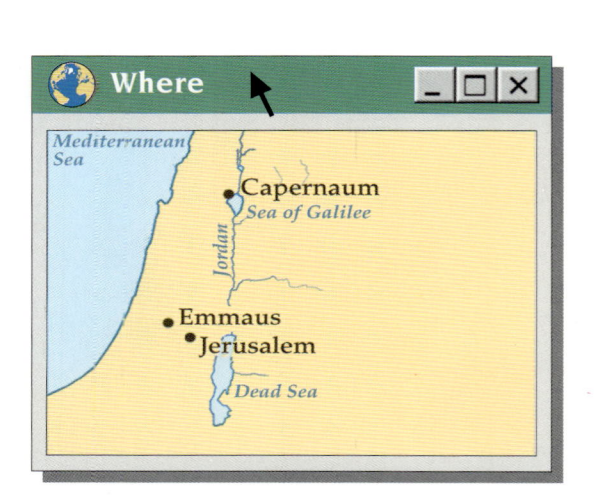

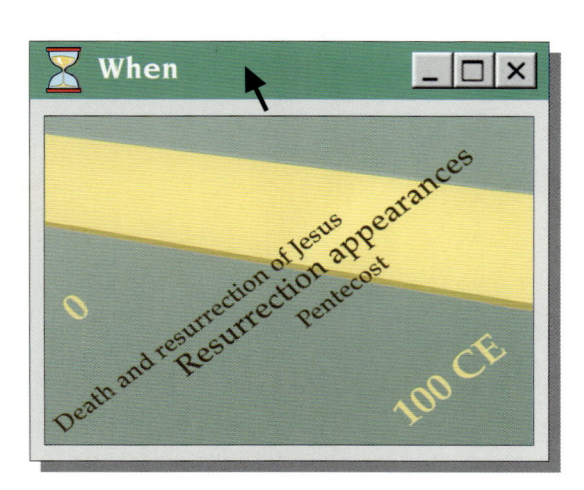

Where
- Mediterranean Sea
- Capernaum
- Sea of Galilee
- Jordan
- Emmaus
- Jerusalem
- Dead Sea

When
- 0
- Death and resurrection of Jesus
- Resurrection appearances
- Pentecost
- 100 CE

'In that moment ... they would recognise him'

Often, in the Gospel narratives, the risen Christ was not immediately recognised. Mary Magdalene mistook him for the man who looked after the garden where she met him *(John 20:11-18)*. The disciples on the Sea of Galilee did not know it was Jesus even though it was his third appearance *(John 21:1-14)*. The disciples going to Emmaus had a lively discussion with Jesus without suspecting anything.

The resurrection of Jesus was such wonderful news that it did not seem true. Just as eyes have to get used to the light, so a bigger heart or greater spiritual understanding was needed to make room for the greatness of the gospel.

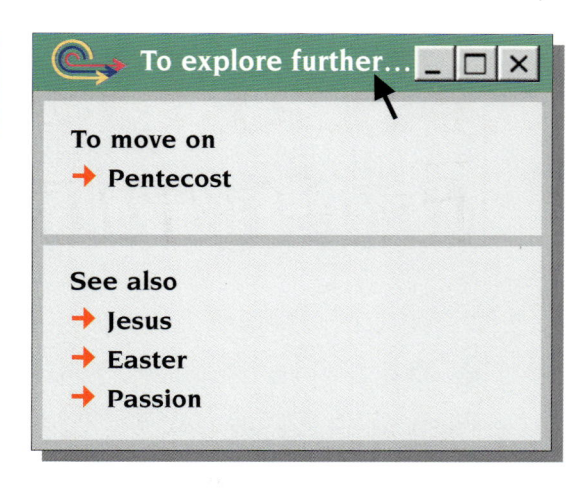

To explore further...

To move on
→ Pentecost

See also
→ Jesus
→ Easter
→ Passion

In the Word and the breaking of bread

The disciples on the road to Emmaus were sad and disillusioned because of the death of Jesus. Their hope for the liberation of Israel had died with him. Jesus showed them the meaning of the Scriptures but they did not seem to understand. Only later, at the table, did they recognise him, while he broke the bread and then indeed the Scriptures were understood. But what happened at Emmaus takes place in all Christian worship. In the words of the Bible and in the Eucharist, Mass or Lord's Supper, all believing women and men can meet the risen Christ.

→ Read *Luke 24:13-35*.

RETURN *and rebuilding*

In 539 BCE the Persians occupied Babylonia and absorbed it into their empire, which stretched from India to the Mediterranean. This event was of great importance for the future of the Jews, because the Persians allowed all the people deported by the Babylonians to return to their homeland. So the Jews too were free to return to Judah.

A difficult return

Only some of the many Jews then present in Babylonia returned to their old homes. Why, in fact, should they leave the good living conditions they had acquired over so many years? Why leave the land where by then, most of the Jews had been born? Those were their questions, without taking into account that, in Judah, their fathers' houses had new owners and the Jews who had remained behind did not practise their faith in God in such a strict way as their deported brothers and sisters. Too many things had changed in fifty years of exile.

The rebuilding of the Temple

In spite of these doubts, some Jews returned to Judah. Guided first by Sheshbazzar then by Zerubbabel, descendants of David, they undertook the rebuilding of the Temple (or rather, its restructuring, since in spite of severe damage, the Temple had continued to function after a fashion). That renovation of the Temple lasted, with successive enlargements, until the Romans destroyed it in 70 CE.

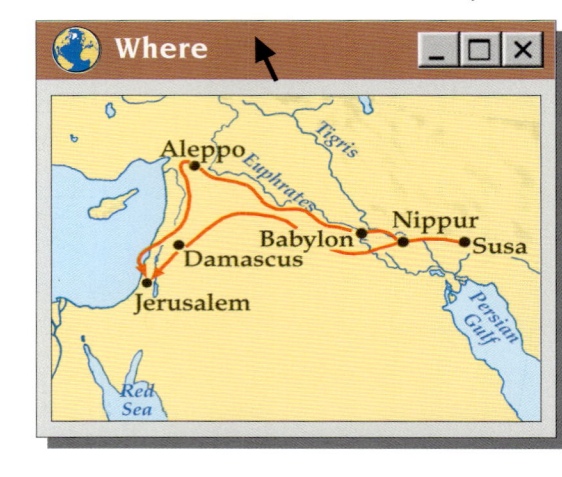

The reconstruction of the Jewish nation

Two charismatic figures took control of the reconstruction of the Jews in the Persian period: Nehemiah and Ezra.

Having both grown up in the Babylonian Diaspora (among the Jews 'scattered' in Babylonia), they reorganised the Jews around the strict observance of the Law of Moses (as it had been defined amongst the exiles in Babylonia), laying down the final foundations of what would become the Judaism of the following centuries.

Their task was not easy because they were met by the fierce opposition of many of those who had remained, who did not accept either the rigid rules of separation from pagans or the narrow declaration of monotheism, which made up the heart of the exiles' beliefs about God during the Babylonian Diaspora. In the end, however, those beliefs were affirmed at the price of separation from the Samaritans. These were the Jews from the ex-Northern kingdom of Israel who had not been deported but amalgamated with other populations brought in by the Assyrians after the fall of Samaria in 722 BCE.

When

Cyrus' decree (538 BCE)
500
400
Return and rebuilding
Alexander the Great's conquest (332 BCE)

In the Bible

➡ The books of Ezra and Nehemiah tell of the reconstruction.
➡ The prophets Haggai and Zechariah record phases of the Temple's reconstruction.
➡ Psalm 126 reflects the state of mind of those years.

To explore further...

To move on
➡ Ruth

To learn more
➡ Diaspora
➡ Synagogue

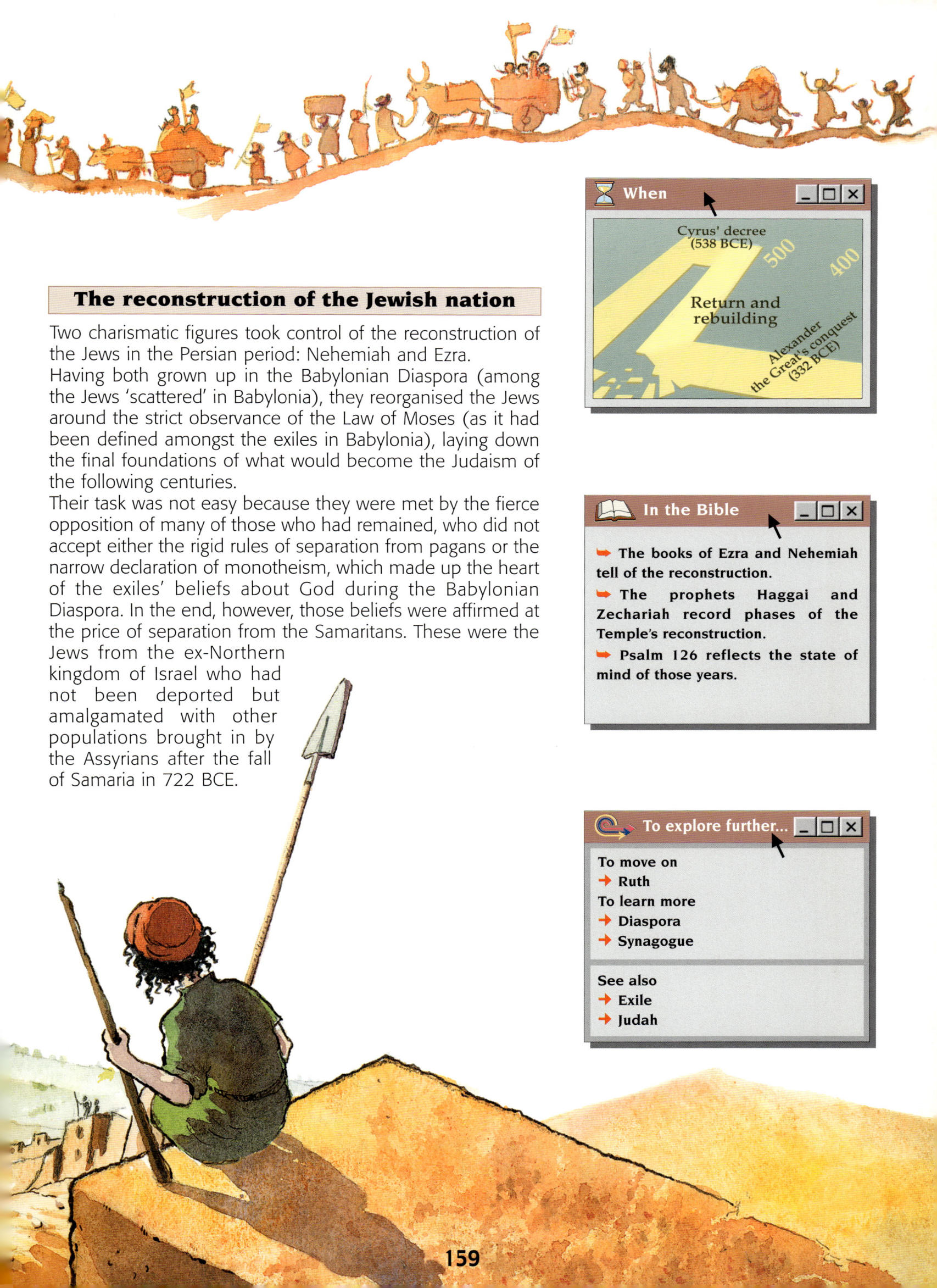

See also
➡ Exile
➡ Judah

REVELATION
A coded language

Persecution of Christians

The first real persecution against Christians occurred under the Emperor Domitian. He officially introduced the worship of the current emperor into the Roman Empire. When Domitian gave orders to his officials, he wrote, referring to himself: 'Our Lord and God orders the following to be done….' These orders could not be questioned since they were given by a god. Christians, however, declared: 'Jesus Christ is the Lord' *(Philippians 2:9-11)*. They obeyed the emperor's laws but knew that their Lord Jesus Christ was above the emperor. So persecution against the Christians was inevitable.

Where

ASIA MINOR
Pergamum
Thyatira
Smyrna
Sardis
Ephesus
Philadelphia
Laodicea
Patmos
Mediterranean Sea

The word 'revelation' or 'apocalypse'

'Apocalypse' comes from the Greek word meaning 'revelation'. In the Bible there are various apocalyptic writings, for example the books of Daniel and Ezekiel. The book of Revelation, with 'apocalypse' in its opening sentence, revealed to the persecuted Christians God's plans for them and the future of the world. The purpose of the book was to encourage the persecuted believers.

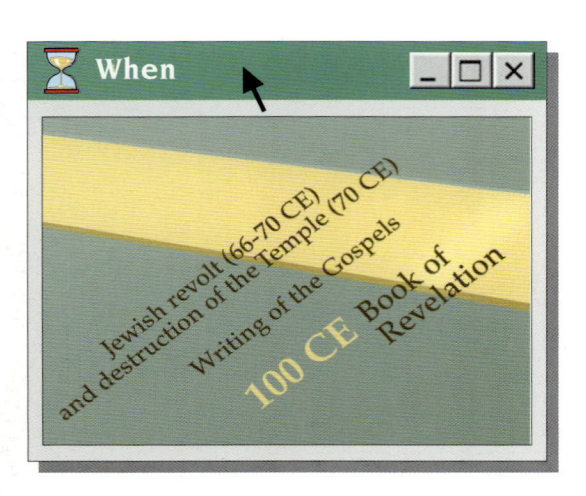

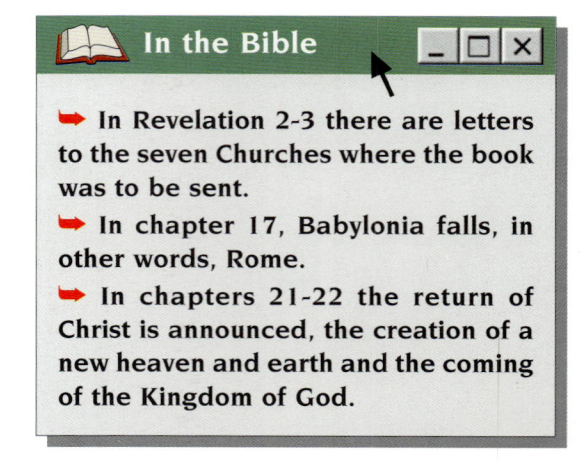

When

Jewish revolt (66-70 CE) and destruction of the Temple (70 CE)
Writing of the Gospels
100 CE Book of Revelation

In the Bible

➡ In Revelation 2-3 there are letters to the seven Churches where the book was to be sent.
➡ In chapter 17, Babylonia falls, in other words, Rome.
➡ In chapters 21-22 the return of Christ is announced, the creation of a new heaven and earth and the coming of the Kingdom of God.

Outline of Revelation

At the beginning the author introduces himself. He is called John and he has been deported by the authorities to the island of Patmos, in the Aegean Sea. John saw the persecution but he also had a vision of God's reality, which was about to clash with the present-day reality.
In the first part, John saw the difficult situation of the seven Christian Churches of Asia Minor, for each of which Christ dictated a letter.
In the second part, John saw many images that described God's plan to counter the brutal powers of persecution and death. He saw Jesus, the Lamb, who opened the book of the seven seals; the seven trumpets of judgement sounded; he saw the Roman legions rise from the sea as a beast, but in the end he saw the 'Great Babylonia' (Rome) fall: God created a new heaven and a new earth. Jesus would return and every tear would be dried and death would be no more.

The language of Revelation

It is a coded language, full of images. The persecuted Christians understood that language well and they drew great courage from it because they got to know even the name of the beast who inspired those who persecuted them. But the Roman authorities, on the other hand, would not be able to understand it. *Revelation 13:18* appeared to be a puzzle: 'Whoever is intelligent can work out the meaning of the number of the beast, because the number stands for a human name. Its number is 666'. The Jews wrote their numbers beginning with the first letter of the alphabet, for example: A = 1, B = 2 up to 10, then 20 up to 100 and so on. The number 666 could be the total value of the following Hebrew letters:

N	= 50	R	= 200	O	= 5
N	= 50	Q	= 100	S	= 60
A	= 1	R	= 200		

Total = 666:   NERO CAESAR

Read *Revelation 13,1-18*.

To explore further...

To move on
→ God

See also
→ Daniel
→ Rome

ROME
The great enemy

From city state to empire: an unprecedented story

The Romans dated the foundation of their city as 753 BCE.
At that time Rome was a small settlement whose importance was due to its control of the shallow water at the island of Tiberina; but within about five hundred years it was able to build an empire, which controlled all the countries of the Mediterranean. What was surprising and fascinating was the long duration of its power: in the west it survived until 476 CE, in the east until 1453 CE.

From ally to ferocious enemy

Relations between the Jews and the Romans began in the second century BCE with an alliance against Syrian attack; but it was a brief friendship because in 63 BCE Pompey occupied Jerusalem, torn to pieces by civil war. The land of Israel would not be really independent again until 1948!

Jesus and Rome

Jesus grew up in a period in which the Romans decided to take direct control of Judaea, which up until then had been entrusted to the vassal king Herod and his sons (6 CE). That decision immediately created serious tension because the Romans were pagans and the nationalistic Jews could not possibly accept them as their masters. A long series of major and minor revolts began which the Romans always put down with bloodshed. Jesus himself was killed because he was considered a dangerous agitator and a potential rebel leader.

Where

The Jewish wars

The Jews twice tried to free Israel from that foreign yoke through a major rebellion. The first time was in 66 CE and only in 70 CE did the Romans retake Jerusalem, destroying the Temple. The second time was in 132 CE, and the war lasted until 135 CE. At the end of that war the Romans destroyed Jerusalem for good and rebuilt it as a pagan city, forbidding access to the Jews.

The famous prostitute

In the Revelation of John, Rome was identified as the instrument of extreme evil. It warned that at the end of time her power would be demolished by God's armies.

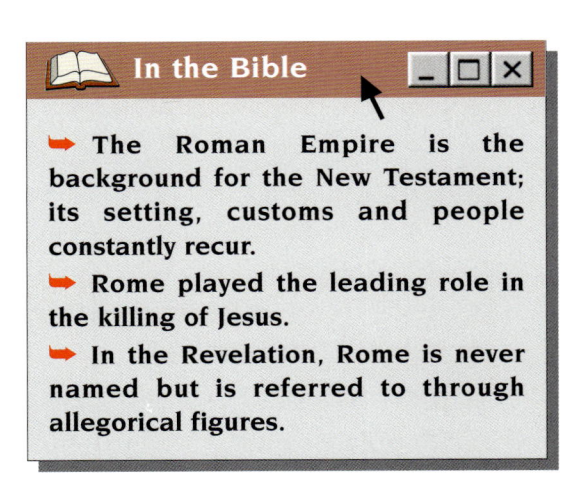

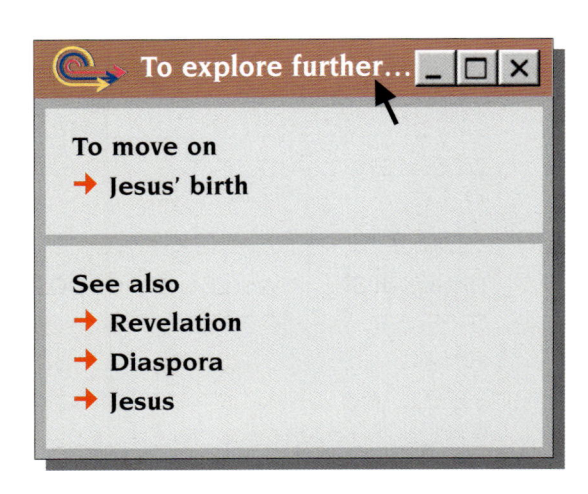

In the Bible

➡ The Roman Empire is the background for the New Testament; its setting, customs and people constantly recur.
➡ Rome played the leading role in the killing of Jesus.
➡ In the Revelation, Rome is never named but is referred to through allegorical figures.

To explore further…

To move on
➡ Jesus' birth

See also
➡ Revelation
➡ Diaspora
➡ Jesus

RUTH
The great-grandmother of King David

Even though it is set in the turbulent period of the judges, the book of Ruth does not tell a war story of violence and rejection. On the contrary, it is a story of love and faithfulness, of trust and acceptance. A foreign woman went to Israel and became one of them. She was able to understand instinctively Israel's way of life and to have faith in its God.

A way of life

In Moab, her homeland, Ruth became a member of a family from Judah. Their different traditions did not prevent the young wife from becoming attached to her mother-in-law Naomi, and when Ruth's husband died, the prospect of their separating showed just how strong and important the relationship between mother-in-law and daughter-in-law was.

Read *Ruth 1:16-18*.

In Naomi's country, Ruth was well received: she decided to go and glean in the fields and found herself in the estate of a generous and sympathetic relative who invited her to share the midday meal with the harvesters.

Love produced love

The words of a local person showed the general opinion of the people: 'We know what you have done for your mother-in-law. You have left your father, mother and homeland to live with a people who were unknown to you. God will reward you for what you have done. May the God of Israel, in whom you believe, give you the reward your generosity deserves.' It was true that Ruth had had faith and had taken a new path towards a new way of life, and instead of being rejected, she had been accepted. In the story of Ruth it seemed true that love produced love. Was this story over-optimistic or was it a story from which something could be learned? Israel was invited to welcome foreigners, not to cut itself off, not to look suspiciously at new arrivals.

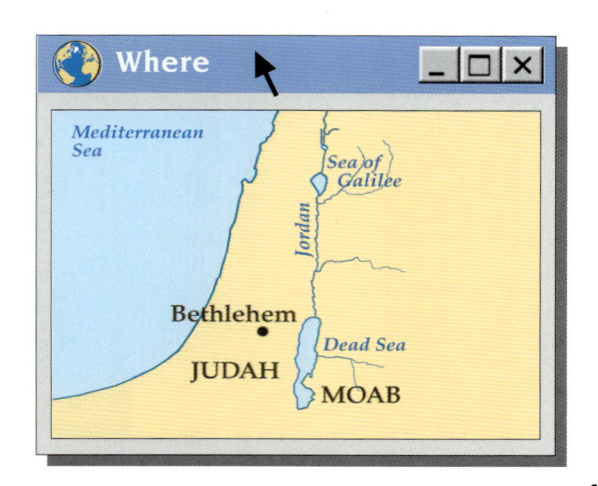

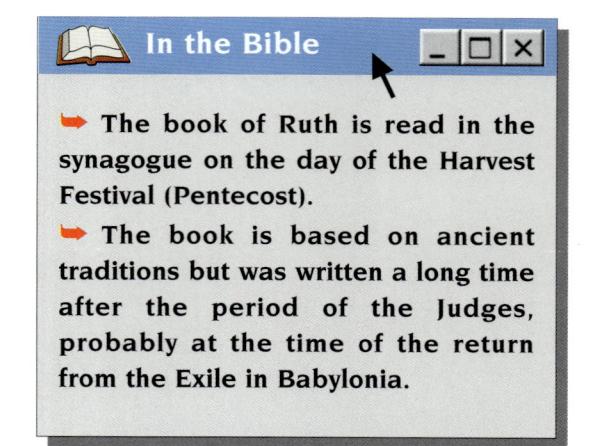

Where

In the Bible

- The book of Ruth is read in the synagogue on the day of the Harvest Festival (Pentecost).
- The book is based on ancient traditions but was written a long time after the period of the Judges, probably at the time of the return from the Exile in Babylonia.

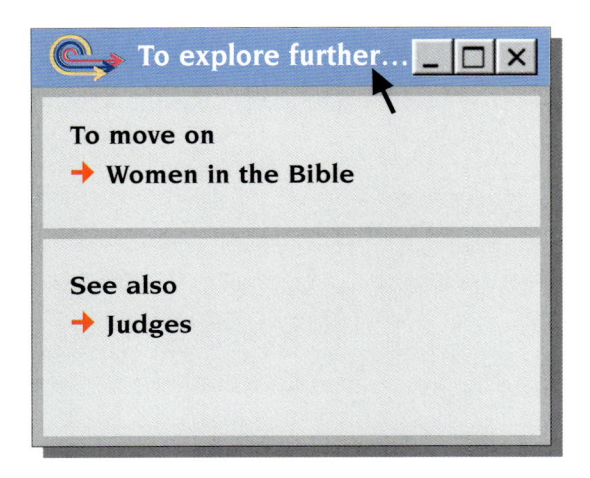

The line of descent

At Bethlehem Ruth found a husband amongst her husband's relatives and gave birth to a son. The baby boy was called Obed. Obed would be the father of Jesse, David's father. Ruth was the great-grandmother of the most loved King of Israel. She would also have a place in Jesus' genealogy (family tree).

Read *Matthew 1:5-6.*

To explore further…

To move on
→ Women in the Bible

See also
→ Judges

SABBATH
The Lord's Day

The seventh day

In the Bible no day of the week has a name except the seventh, which in Hebrew is called 'Shabbat', Sabbath, meaning 'rest'. The Sabbath begins on the evening of the sixth day at the moment when the first stars appear. It ends at the same time on the evening of the seventh day. In Jewish families, at the beginning of the Sabbath, candles are lit, prayers are said, everyone sings together and there is a special meal, which is different from the usual one. During the day of Sabbath, they go to synagogue.

A day of joy

The Sabbath is a day of joy. There is rejoicing in remembering that God led Israel out of Egypt, the land of slavery, 'with great and extraordinary power'. The list of the commandments found in the book of Deuteronomy says that it is necessary to remember the Sabbath, the day of rest, precisely because it recalls freedom from Egypt *(Deuteronomy 5:15)*.

A day of rest

The Sabbath is consecrated to God. During this day Jews rest, having toiled, worked or studied for six consecutive days. Even God, as the narrative of creation says, having toiled for six days creating the whole world, rested on the seventh day *(Genesis 2:2-3)*. The list of the commandments found in Exodus, records that the Sabbath should be observed because even God rested on the seventh day. It is a day that belongs to God *(Exodus 20:11)*. If you work on the Sabbath day strange things can even happen, as in the story of the manna.

Read *Exodus 16:1-30.*

The sabbatical, the seventh year

Seven years make a week of years and the seventh year in the Bible was called a sabbatical year. That was a year in which the fields were not cultivated and whatever grew of its own accord had to be left for the poor and foreigners who lived in the country. Israelite slaves had to be freed *(Exodus 21:2)* and debts cancelled *(Deuteronomy 15:1)*.

Jubilee, the year of freedom

After seven sabbatical years, there was a year that was utterly special, the fiftieth year, which was called 'Jubilee'. It was announced by the blowing of the ram's horn: the 'Yobhel', which means 'ram' in Hebrew (perhaps the word 'jubilee' comes from that).

In that year the freedom of all the inhabitants of the country was proclaimed *(Leviticus 25:10)*. Whoever had been forced to sell his land could reacquire it.

In the Bible

➡ It is very important to respect the Sabbath: **Exodus 20:8-11** and **Deuteronomy 5:12-15.**

➡ The non-observance of the Sabbath is harshly punished and sometimes linked to idolatry: **Ezekiel 20:23-24.**

SABBATH

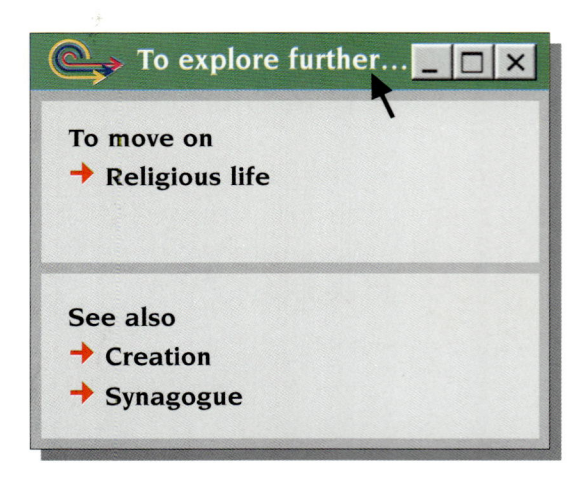

To explore further...

To move on
→ Religious life

See also
→ Creation
→ Synagogue

The Sabbath during the exile

The exiled Jews in Babylonia understood very clearly the importance of the Sabbath. They were far from their country. The Temple had been destroyed. They risked losing their faith itself.
The Sabbath became a special sign, which showed they belonged to God. 'The seventh day, the Sabbath, is a day of rest. On that day do not work, but gather for worship. The Sabbath belongs to the Lord, no matter where you live.' *(Leviticus 23:3)*

The prophets warned: beware of misusing the Sabbath

The Sabbath could also be misused, for example, by having great religious celebrations on that day but then, in daily living, doing evil things against God's law.
So, God communicated with the people, through the prophets, that he hated solemn feasts, including the Sabbath. He preferred them to do good *(Isaiah 1:13-17)*.

168

Jesus confirmed: take care not to misuse the Sabbath

Jesus, when preaching in the synagogue at Nazareth, mentioned the Jubilee, a favoured year of freedom and grace, and he associated it with his arrival *(Luke 4:19)*. In the time of Jesus, observance of the Sabbath was very important. The Pharisees had established rigid rules, which had to be observed on that day, for example, you were not allowed to light a fire or walk more than a kilometre. You were not even allowed to heal someone.

Jesus took offence at that strict observance because it took joyfulness away from the Sabbath. He underlined the positive side of the Sabbath. It was a day in which you should do good to others *(Mark 3:4)*. He also said: 'The Sabbath was made for the good of human beings; they were not made for the Sabbath.' *(Mark 2:27)*

Those declarations of Jesus were harshly criticised by some of the Pharisees who were looking for a way to kill him *(Mark 3:6)*. But the Gospel of Luke, after having recorded a debate of that kind because of a healing on the Sabbath, commented: 'The people rejoiced over all the wonderful things that he did.' *(Luke 13:17)*

The first day of the week

The Gospels recorded that some women went to Jesus' tomb on 'the first day of the week' *(Matthew 28:1; Luke 24:1)* and they found that Jesus was no longer in the tomb. The Christian community assembled with the apostle Paul: 'On Saturday evening we gathered together for the fellowship meal.' *(Acts 20:7)*

The first day of the week was a day of rejoicing because it was the day of Jesus' resurrection. So, Sunday became the special day of the week for Christians.

SAMUEL
The first prophet

The call

From the beginning it was clear that Samuel was destined to perform a great service among his people. His mother, Hannah, could not have children and that was a great sorrow for her. God, however, granted her prayers and so Samuel was born. Hannah was happy, thanking God with a very beautiful song and consecrating her son to him. The young child grew under the guidance of the priest Eli in the sanctuary of Shiloh where at that time the ark of the covenant was kept. One night Samuel heard someone calling.

▶ Read *1 Samuel 3*.

Prophet, priest, judge

Very soon everyone recognised that Samuel had been chosen by God as his spokesperson. He would be the first to be called a prophet instead of simply a seer.

Samuel would become also priest and judge of Israel. Once a year, setting out from his home town of Ramah, he travelled through the country, stopping at various sanctuaries – Bethel, Gilgal and Mizpah – and administering justice. Samuel was at the head of the people even in battle. He would be the last of the judges because he found himself as the key person in the delicate phase of transition towards the monarchy.

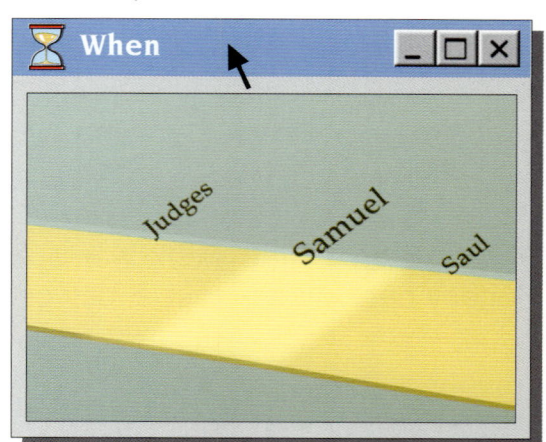

170

The birth of the monarchy

The Israelites wanted to be like all the other nations and they also looked for greater political stability as they were faced with the threatening armies of their neighbours. That change to monarchy would mean that in time there would be a permanent army made up of professionals instead of an army that was formed occasionally by mobilising the people. A state system would be created with government officials, offices and a court. The people would pay a high price to maintain all that and they would have to contribute with a type of forced labour, to the carrying out of great public building works.

Who commanded in Israel?

Was the demand for a king an act of distrust towards Samuel or God? God himself thought it was more likely the latter and even though he alerted the people to the risks of monarchy, he accepted their request and gave Samuel the task of anointing, that is consecrating, a king. Saul, therefore, the person selected by God, became the first king of Israel. Samuel's religious role did not diminish. On the contrary, when Saul himself offered a sacrifice before a battle without waiting for the arrival of Samuel, he was told that he could not count on God's favour any more. It would be God himself who would identify in David the new king and Samuel would consecrate him while Saul was still officially the legitimate king. On account of that, both Samuel and David would have to flee from the anger of Saul. A hard struggle began, but Samuel would not play a part in that for long. He would die shortly after among all his mourning people.

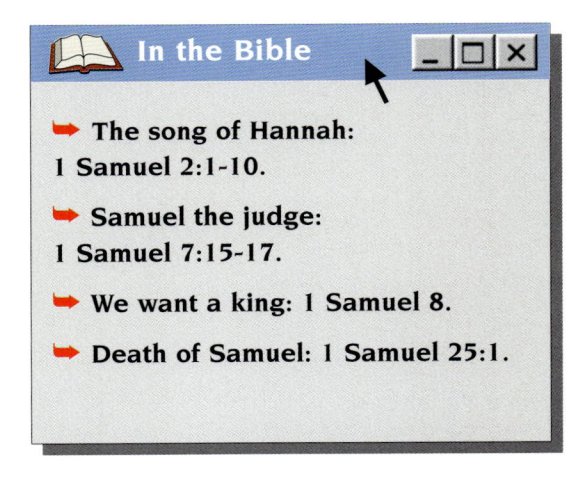

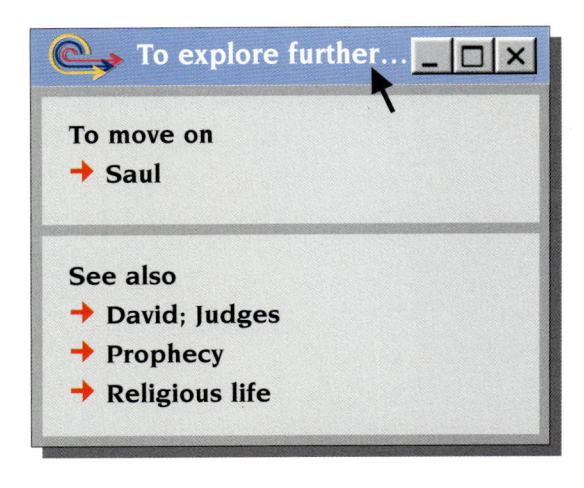

In the Bible

→ The song of Hannah: 1 Samuel 2:1-10.

→ Samuel the judge: 1 Samuel 7:15-17.

→ We want a king: 1 Samuel 8.

→ Death of Samuel: 1 Samuel 25:1.

To explore further...

To move on
→ Saul

See also
→ David; Judges
→ Prophecy
→ Religious life

SARAH
The fellow-traveller

Sarah, the wife of Abraham, was ready for their departure *(Genesis 12:4)*. She felt calm. Abraham had explained to her why they were setting out on a journey to an unknown land and he had repeated to her the words God had addressed to him: 'I will give you many descendants.' While the camel made slow progress, Sarah thought over those words. For so many years she had hoped to have a son, but she had almost given up hope, yet now, perhaps....

Having arrived in the land of Canaan, the caravan did not stop, but crossed the whole area and when they finally pitched camp, the place they had selected was parched and mountainous.

They stayed there only a short time because a serious famine hit the country, so they started travelling again towards Egypt. The narrative never hints at Sarah's complaining or protesting. She said nothing, remaining silent.

Sarah had an idea

By now, Abraham and Sarah had lived in the land of Canaan for some time, but they had not had any children. What about the promise? Sarah owned a slave-girl called Hagar. Why didn't Abraham take Hagar so that she could give him a child in Sarah's place? In those times, that was the custom and Abraham accepted. Hagar became pregnant. Would her child be the promised son?

Sarah's idea was the source of pain. In fact, Hagar was proud of her pregnancy and despised her mistress. Sarah was deeply humiliated and became hard and cruel. Abraham did not interfere. Sarah ill-treated her slave-girl, who fled into the desert.

God, taking pity on Hagar, intervened and saved her. The slave-girl returned to her mistress and Ishmael was born.

Read *Genesis 16:7-16*.

The birth of Isaac

As has been said, God favoured Sarah. He did what he had promised her *(Genesis 18:1-15)*. Sarah became pregnant and at the time that God had stated, she gave birth to a son. Abraham called him Isaac.

Isaac and Ishmael: two sons, two nations

Isaac grew and, on the day of his weaning, Abraham organised a great feast. It should have been a joyful occasion for everyone, but Sarah spoilt everything by saying to Abraham: 'Send this slave and her son away. The son of this woman must not get any part of your wealth, which my son Isaac should inherit.'

Abraham was distressed, but God said to him: 'Do whatever Sarah tells you, because it is through Isaac that you will have the descendants I have promised. I will also give many children to the son of the slave-woman, so that they will become a nation. He too is your son.'

Hagar and Ishmael went out by themselves towards the desert. God protected them as he had said to Abraham that he would.

Read *Genesis 21:14-21*.

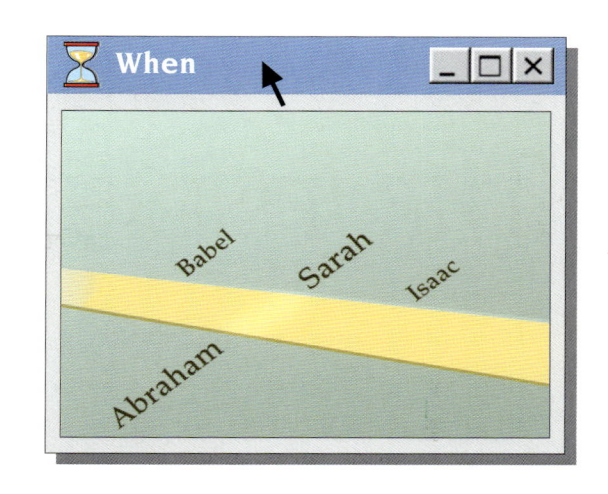

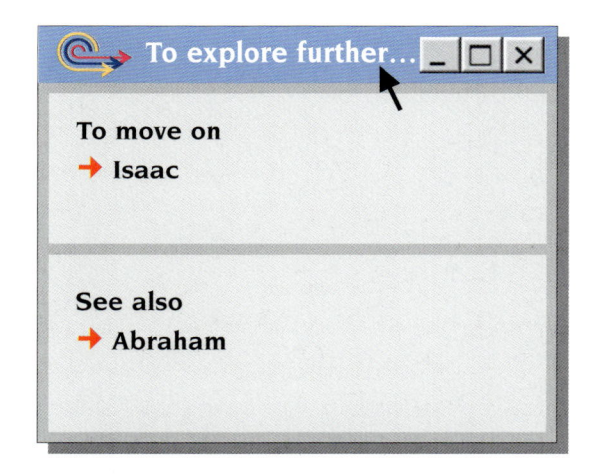

When

Babel — Sarah — Isaac
Abraham

To explore further…

To move on
→ Isaac

See also
→ Abraham

SAUL
The first king

Saul belonged to an important family, even if it was the smallest of the tribe of Benjamin, which in its turn was the smallest tribe of Israel. Yet God chose him as the first king of his people: it was not important to have a large following or a lot of relatives to hold that office. There were other qualities that God saw in Saul. In fact it would be he who would free Israel from her oppressors. Saul was described as a handsome young man, tall and strong, a head taller than everyone else. He was very skilled in battle where he knew how to surround himself with courageous fighters.

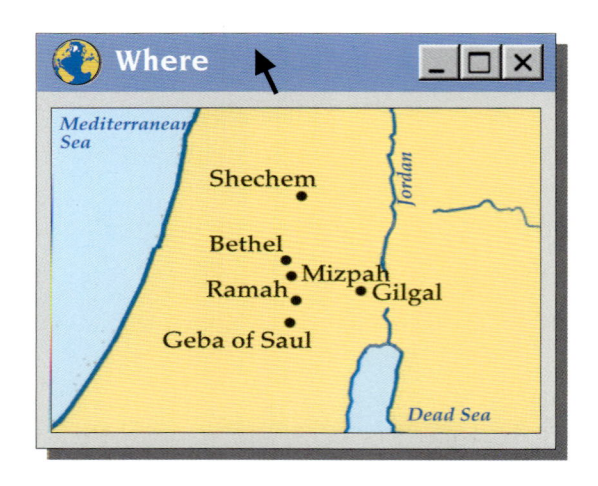

Where

Mediterranean Sea, Shechem, Bethel, Mizpah, Ramah, Gilgal, Geba of Saul, Jordan, Dead Sea

Victorious but disobedient

Saul was consecrated king by Samuel at the sanctuary of Mizpah, in front of all the people, after God's will had been expressed through the casting of lots.

He was not at first accepted by everyone, but even the most sceptic had to change their minds when faced with his first military victories. However, Saul on more than one occasion disobeyed the orders God gave him through the mouth of the prophet Samuel. That was the cause of his own and his family's ruin. While Saul was still alive, God chose David as the new king. David would be the one to reign after the death of Saul.

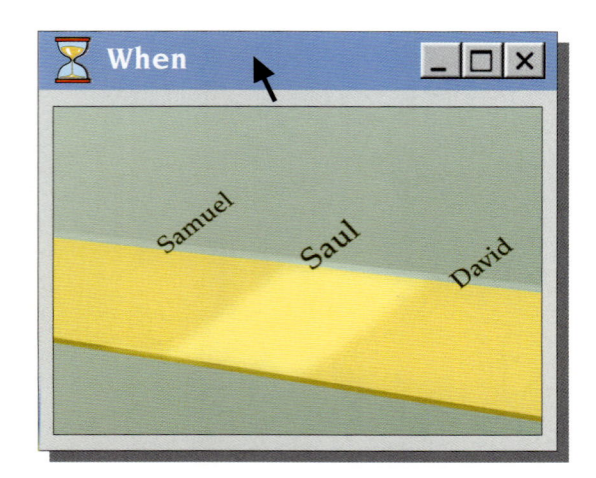

When

Samuel, Saul, David

In the Bible

➡ Saul's appearance: 1 Samuel 9:2.

➡ Saul consecrated king: 1 Samuel 10:17-27.

➡ Saul and David: 1 Samuel 16:18-23; 1 Samuel 18:9-16.

Saul and David

Saul is remembered more for his struggle against David than for his military victories and for having been the first king of Israel, governing over all the tribes. Right from the beginning, Saul proved to be jealous of the successes that David had in war and more than once he tried to kill the young man, already secretly anointed king by Samuel. But thanks also to the help of two of Saul's children, Jonathan who was very close friends with David, and Michal whom he would marry, David was able to save himself. However, he had to flee and he even made himself head of an armed band to ensure he stayed alive. Nevertheless, David always remained loyal to Saul. Even though he had the chance to kill the king twice, he did not do it.

Read *1 Samuel 24*.

A tormented king

The Bible describes Saul, especially in the second part of his life, as obsessed by the presence of David: it was as if an evil spirit had entered into him. He did not hesitate to kill a great number of priests because he suspected that they were on David's side. At the same time, he demonstrated contradictory attitudes. He felt that David was like a son and blessed him *(1 Samuel 26:25)*, but then he went back to attempting to take his life. The tormented life of Saul ended in battle when he was overpowered and in order not to fall into the hands of the enemy alive, he threw himself on his own sword.

Read *1 Samuel 31:1-6*.

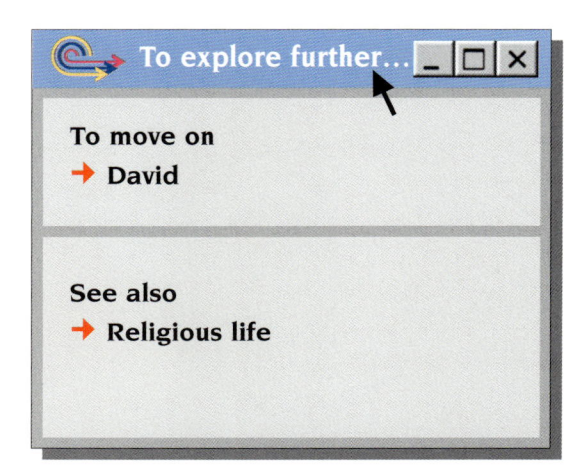

To explore further…

To move on
→ David

See also
→ Religious life

175

SIN
Repentance and forgiveness

A story of unfaithfulness and forgiveness

The covenant between God and Israel brought with it the gift of the Law, which expressed God's will. If Israel lived obediently, blessings would accompany her: otherwise, when Israel 'sinned' she distanced herself from God, which did not damage God, but damaged the people. Sin, therefore, was not a simple breaching of the Covenant, but a way of life that was different from God's. The narrative in *Exodus 32* summarises the biblical vision of collective sin. Naturally, individuals also sinned, practising violence and fraud. *(2 Samuel 11-12)*

The Bible maintains that everyone sinned, but does not recognise a real doctrine of original sin and of corrupt humankind. Even the origin of sin is not made clear. What was important was to know that humankind was responsible for sin and they were called on to repent and say sorry.

Often it was the consequences of sin that determined the repentance and the request for pardon from God: God did not refuse his forgiveness, even if the people could not generally make good use of it.

Read *Psalm 51*.

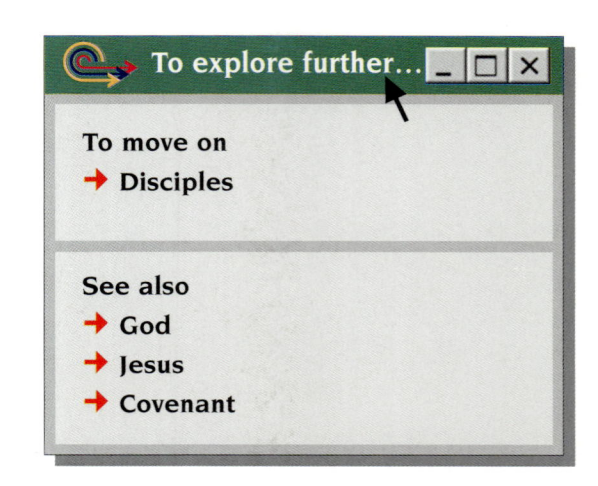

To explore further...

To move on
→ Disciples

See also
→ God
→ Jesus
→ Covenant

He who takes away the sins of the world

Jesus was the one who would save his people and individuals from their sins *(Matthew 1:21)*, in so far as he was sent by God who chose to pardon through grace alone, or as Paul expressed it, to 'justify' sinners. In particular, Jesus was friendly and sympathetic towards those who were regarded, rightly or wrongly as more sinful than others, like the tax collectors and the prostitutes, thus stirring up scandal amongst respectable people. *(Matthew 9:10; Mark 2:15 Luke 15:1-3)*

According to Paul, sin was something more than the sum of individual shortcomings: it was a type of illness, which afflicted human beings starting with Adam *(Romans 5:12)* and it pushed them to distance themselves from God and to try to live not with but against others. Jesus was the 'new Adam' who broke the vicious circle of sin, bringing the pardon of God into history. And that made new life possible – conversion. Without the grace of God no one could get out of the tunnel of sin: only God's willingness to love, in spite of everything, gave people that new and unexpected energy, that enabled them to hear and obey the exhortation: 'Go and sin no more'.

Read *John 8:1-11.*

SOLOMON
A powerful king

Solomon did not become king after David without opposition: other brothers aspired to the throne. Nevertheless, he managed to strengthen his power, ridding himself of his adversaries and replacing the chief of the army and the chief priest. Then he carried on with the work undertaken by his father: the construction of the Temple to centralise the political and religious power at Jerusalem. It was a modest building but in those times it was considered a wonder because of its structure and its rich decoration.

The Bible supplies numerous details about its construction. Also its inauguration was particularly solemn. Solomon prayed to God in front of all the assembled people.

➡ Read *1 Kings 8:27-30.*

His wisdom

Solomon has passed into history on account of his wisdom: people rushed from the farthest places to hear him, as happened with the Queen of Sheba. His wisdom was a gift from God, which Solomon had expressly asked for in prayer. Thanks to that, he was able to administer justice even in the most difficult cases. One day two women appeared before him and they explained their case.

➡ Read *1 Kings 3:16-28.*

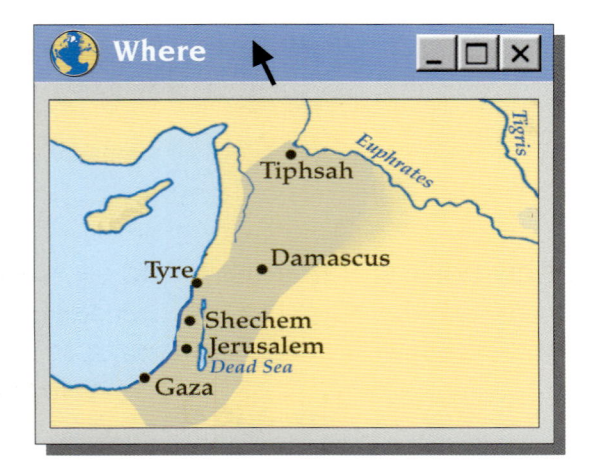

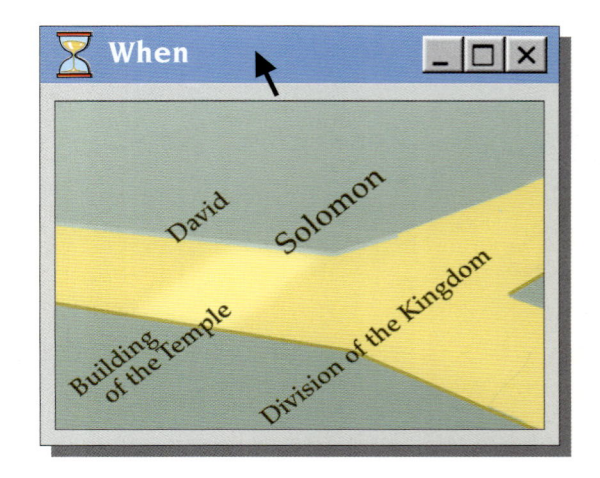

Where: Tiphsah, Euphrates, Tigris, Tyre, Damascus, Shechem, Jerusalem, Dead Sea, Gaza

When: David — Building of the Temple — Solomon — Division of the Kingdom

His greatness

Solomon was also famous for his wealth. The political stability of his reign, the absence of strong foreign enemies and a vast network of alliances had allowed small Israel to enlarge its territory and to operate in a new sector, that of commerce.

To increase trade, Solomon married different foreign women, the first being the daughter of the pharaoh of Egypt. It was said that he had seven hundred princesses as wives and three hundred concubines. Those foreign women led Solomon to accept a great many cults and gods into his kingdom. That naturally did not please God who announced to him that at his death, a great part of his kingdom would pass to others who were not his descendants.

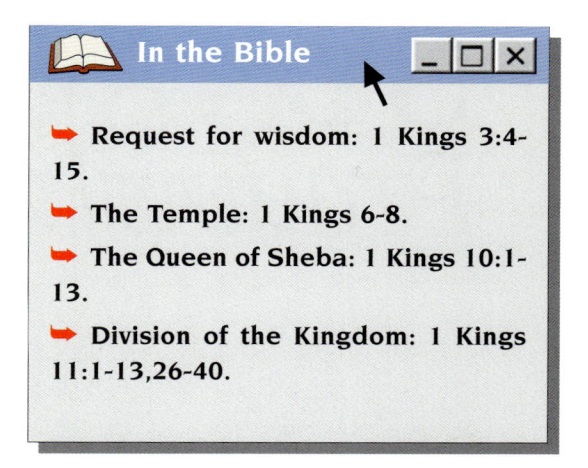

In the Bible

- Request for wisdom: 1 Kings 3:4-15.
- The Temple: 1 Kings 6-8.
- The Queen of Sheba: 1 Kings 10:1-13.
- Division of the Kingdom: 1 Kings 11:1-13, 26-40.

To explore further...

To move on
→ Judah

To learn more
→ Temple

See also
→ Idolatry

The divided kingdom

At the death of Solomon, his son Rehoboam, all ready to be crowned king at the gathering at Shechem, did not accept the requests of his oppressed people to lighten the heavy taxes and the forced labour, which Solomon had imposed on them in order to carry out his politics of grandeur. And so the tribes of the North chose Jeroboam as their king, already identified by God through the prophet Ahijah. Only the two tribes of Judah and Benjamin remained loyal to the house of David. So the kingdom divided into two: to the North was Israel and to the South was Judah, much smaller, but with Jerusalem as its capital city.

SYNAGOGUE
Praying together

The term 'synagogue' comes from Greek and refers both to the place in which the Jews gathered together every Sabbath and the assembly of people itself.

From the beginning, the synagogue was the place where the Scriptures were read and explained.

At the time of the New Testament there were many synagogues in Palestine and in the whole of the Diaspora (the Jewish communities outside Palestine).

During the exile

In the Old Testament the term 'synagogue' does not occur. But the need to come together to pray, to teach the youngest children and to pass the faith of Israel on to them, probably arose during the exile in Babylonia.

Where

ITALY, MACEDONIA, GREECE, Black Sea, PONTUS, PHRYGIA, MESOPOTAMIA, PAMPHYLIA, SYRIA, Mediterranean Sea, JUDAEA, EGYPT

• Synagogues

When

Jewish revolt (66-70 CE) and destruction of the Temple (70 CE)

Diaspora

100 CE

What was the synagogue building like?

In the New Testament the word 'synagogue' appears at least forty times and so it is possible to reconstruct what the building was like and how worship was conducted. Generally there was a fairly large room. There, the sacred container for the scrolls of the Law and Prophets was always found; there was also a platform or pulpit from which the Scriptures were read and some seats for the teachers of the law or the scribes. People sat on stone benches along the walls or on mats on the floor.

Synagogue worship

This was directed by a council of elders who elected the president of the synagogue. The president organised the procedures of the Sabbath meeting and sometimes invited someone from those present to preach *(Acts 13:15)*. A server presented the scrolls of the Scriptures.

The worship generally began with the prayer and confession of faith, the so-called *'Shema Israel' (Deuteronomy 6:4-9)*, which the congregation listened to standing up, facing Jerusalem.

The reading from the Bible was made up of passages from the Law (the first five books of the Bible) and the Prophets. An explanation of the text was given by any one of the male adults present.

A place for debate

The New Testament gives a very lively picture of the synagogue meetings: for example, the bitter disputes that occurred when Jesus healed the sick on the Sabbath, or some very lively discussions, found in the book of Acts, which developed into quarrels and the separation between Jews and all who had accepted Jesus as Messiah. Once, when Jesus spoke in the synagogue at Nazareth, his home town, it caused great disorder and Jesus was pushed to the top of a hill.

Read *Luke 4:16-30*.

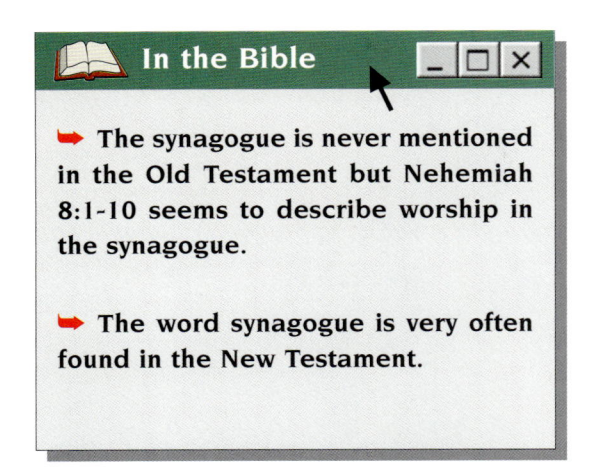

In the Bible

➡ The synagogue is never mentioned in the Old Testament but Nehemiah 8:1-10 seems to describe worship in the synagogue.

➡ The word synagogue is very often found in the New Testament.

To explore further...

To move on
➡ Ruth

To learn more
➡ Diaspora

See also
➡ Acts of the Apostles
➡ Sabbath
➡ Paul's journeys

TEMPLE
O Lord, listen and forgive!

Solomon's Temple

Solomon began to build the Temple on a piece of land acquired years before by his father David. Good Phoenician architects were sent for, to direct the work. The famous tree trunks of the cedars of Lebanon were brought from Tyre to Jerusalem first on rafts by sea, then dragged over land. The stones came from quarries in the Judaean hills. The panels of carved wood that lined the inside were decorated with gold. A great deal of copper was also used to give the Temple its spectacular appearance. According to the Bible, about a hundred thousand men worked on it for seven years. The Temple remained the vital centre of Israel until its destruction by the Babylonians in 587 BCE. Later on, after the return of the exiles in 539 BCE, the Temple returned to being the centre of Israel's religious and civil life.

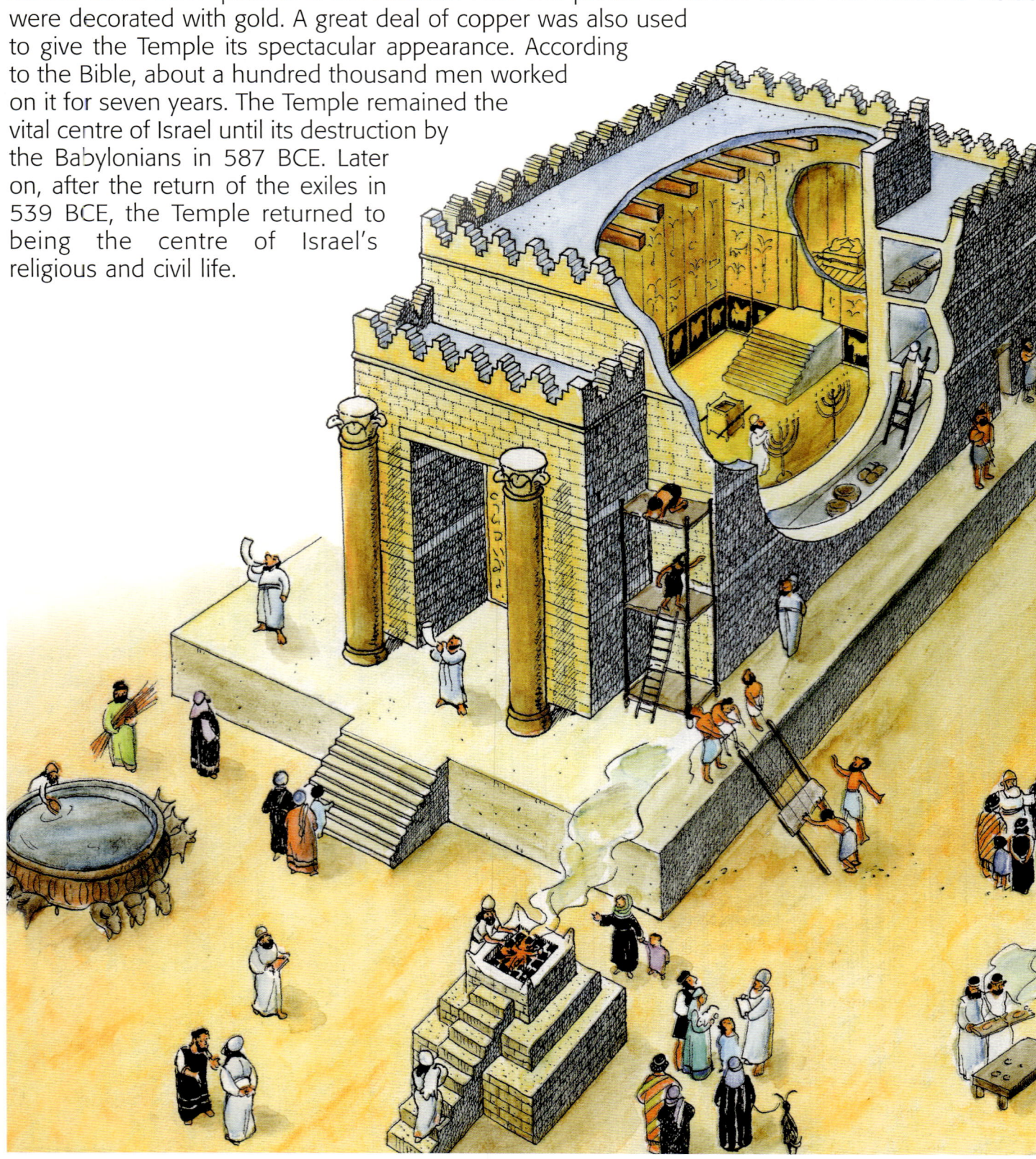

182

Herod's Temple

Jerusalem was dominated by the magnificent structure of the Temple, with its glittering walls and rich gold and copper decorations.

The Temple was at the centre of the city's life and about eighty per cent of the inhabitants lived off its activities – priests, Levites, craftsmen, traders and workers.

Its wealth was considerable, coming both from the offerings, which poured in even from distant countries, as well as from the taxes demanded by law. The expenses for the building work, maintenance and for the running of the Temple itself were enormous too.

Herod the Great was responsible for a huge enlargement of the Temple. The work was begun in 19 BCE and finished just six years before the Romans destroyed it in 70 CE.

All that remained of the Temple was the large terrace. The western side of that became known as the 'wailing wall' because there, still today, the Jews weep for the destruction of their Temple, never again rebuilt.

To explore further...

To move on
→ Judah

See also
→ Exile; Jerusalem
→ Return and rebuilding
→ Religious life

WOMEN in the Bible
A continuous presence

The Bible is an ancient book, which reflects the culture of those who wrote it. The role of women in ancient Near Eastern society was certainly secondary to that of men. In spite of this, there were lots of women in the Bible who were active characters in the story of salvation. Those women, who are often forgotten, are presented here. The other more famous women are referred to in other entries in this dictionary: Eve, Sarah, Hagar, Rebekah, Rachel, Ruth, Deborah, Abigail, Bathsheba, Mary.

The heroines

In Genesis the story of Tamar is told. She was the daughter-in-law of Judah, one of Jacob's sons. Having been widowed, she took the law into her own hands. At the beginning of the book of Exodus, the story of Shiprah and Puah is found. They are two midwives who, by disobeying the Pharaoh's order to kill the Israelite male babies, saved the lives of many newborn boys. They, like Daniel, preferred to obey God rather than the king and risking their own lives, performed a real act of civil disobedience. Also, Moses owed his life to three women: his mother, who in order to save him entrusted him to the waters of the river; the Pharaoh's daughter, who took in and raised the infant; and Miriam, his sister, who kept watch over the journey of the basket until the baby was safe. Later on, Miriam became a priestess and led the people during religious celebrations.

Read *Exodus 15:20-21*.

Esther, to whom a whole book in the Scriptures was dedicated, was remembered as one who turned the fate of her people upside down, by exposing Haman's wicked plans to exterminate the Jews. The book of Judith is found in the Apocrypha. After having killed cruel Holofernes, she forced the invading Assyrians to flee.

Foreigners

There was Rahab, a foreign woman who lodged and saved the lives of three spies who were sent by Joshua to Jericho. Delilah, on the other hand, is remembered for the opposite reason. She defeated the invincible Samson by craftiness, making him disclose the secret of his strength.
The rich and fascinating Queen of Sheba arrived from distant lands to meet King Solomon and acknowledge his wisdom. She blessed God and the people of Israel. (1Kings 10:1-13)

The victims

There are some tragic stories about women. Jephthah's daughter was killed by her father because of a foolish vow made to God. And then there was the story of the wife of a Levite, tortured and killed by wicked men, then cut into pieces by her husband to ask the tribes of Israel for justice. There are other young women who were remembered for the violence they suffered: Dinah *(Genesis 34)*, used by her brothers as an excuse to provoke a war against the Shechemites, and another Tamar, the sad daughter of David *(2 Samuel 13)*.

Barren mothers

Barren women who became fertile by God's intervention are a recurrent theme in the Scriptures. Those women were often chosen by God for a particular mission.

The mother of Samson, for example, was called to bring up her son according to the Nazirite rules, which was a form of consecration to God.

Hannah, the mother of Samuel, because she was childless called on God's name and she bore witness to the fact that God had heard her, in a beautiful song.

→ Read *1 Samuel 1:1-28; 2:1-11,19-21*.

The woman of Shunem gave hospitality to the prophet Elisha and received from him the promise of a son. The story, however, became complicated. *(2 Kings 4:18-37)*

In the New Testament, Elizabeth, a relation of Mary's, was old when she received the gift of a son from God, John (who would be nicknamed the 'Baptist'). She accepted that act of God with joy and faith. Further, she was able to recognise the Messiah, before he was even born, in Mary's womb.

→ Read *Luke 1:39-45*.

The prophetesses

They are often mentioned only in passing for their vocation, like the wife of the prophet Isaiah and Miriam, the sister of Moses. The story of Huldah is fascinating. King Josiah went to consult her. Also in the early Church, women were recognised as messengers of God.

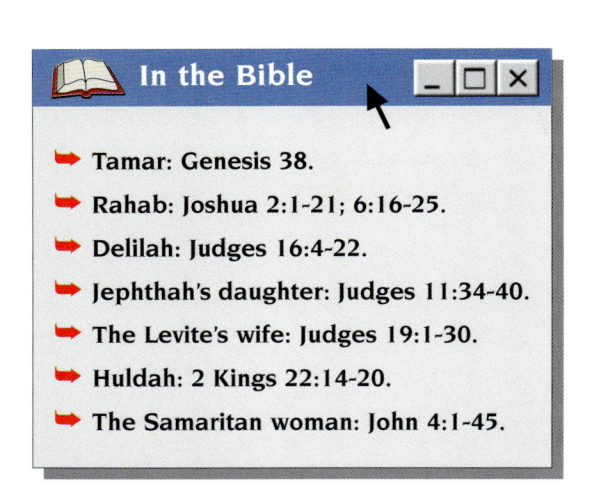

📖 In the Bible

- → Tamar: Genesis 38.
- → Rahab: Joshua 2:1-21; 6:16-25.
- → Delilah: Judges 16:4-22.
- → Jephthah's daughter: Judges 11:34-40.
- → The Levite's wife: Judges 19:1-30.
- → Huldah: 2 Kings 22:14-20.
- → The Samaritan woman: John 4:1-45.

WOMEN in the Bible

The women around Jesus

During his life, Jesus met many women whom he helped, listened to and to whom he explained the Scriptures, in spite of the mistrust of men of his time. Some would become faithful disciples and occupy important roles in the early Church. Amongst those Mary Magdalene, or Mary of Magdala, is remembered in particular: she is mentioned in all four Gospels. It was to her that the risen Christ appeared, entrusting her with the task of announcing the resurrection to the apostles. Because of that, later on she came to be called 'the apostle of the apostles'. In women, Jesus would find generous friends, courageous disciples and sharp debaters. A prostitute, in the home of a Pharisee, bathed Jesus' feet with her tears, dried them with her hair, kissed them and sprinkled perfume over them *(Luke 7:36-50)*.

At Bethany, another woman poured very precious perfumed oil on Jesus' head. Jesus said to the disciples, who were shocked by this waste: 'Wherever the gospel is preached all over the world, what she has done will be told in memory of her.' *(Matthew 26:6-13)*

Mary and Martha, two sisters who were close friends of Jesus, lived at Bethany together with their brother Lazarus. Jesus often found refuge and refreshment in the home of these friends. Mary loved to stay at Jesus' feet to listen to his stories, while Martha preferred to express her personal faith by devoting herself to serving the guests.

Read *Luke 10:38-42*.

Some women met Jesus at extremely difficult moments, like the adulteress who was about to be stoned or the woman who sought his help from amongst a crowd, because she continuously menstruated, so her illness made her impure. That frightened woman, after she had received her healing without the others noticing, found the strength to witness publicly to her faith in Jesus. And there was Jairus' daughter who had died at twelve years old, whom Jesus took by the hand and brought back to life. The Gospels record other women who were helped by Jesus: Peter's mother-in-law, the widow of Nain and the woman with the bent back who was cured on the Sabbath.

Some women helped Jesus to clarify his mission. There was the case of the foreign Syrophoenician woman, who cleverly overturned Jesus' objections and led him to realise that the Gentiles also were included in God's plan for salvation *(Mark 7:24-30)*. A Samaritan woman is remembered as the one who, having received the water of life from Jesus, became a missionary and spread the news of the gospel in her town in Samaria.

Women in the early Church

In the Church of equality, where neither social class nor gender (being male or female) was important, the women worked actively together in order to spread the gospel and occupied important positions. Often they organised home Churches like Lydia of Philippi. She was the first woman to receive the gospel in Europe through Paul's preaching. Then there was Priscilla who, together with her husband Aquila, gave Paul hospitality for a long period and prepared believers for baptism. Tabitha was the generous disciple from Joppa, brought back to life by Peter. The daughters of Philip prophesied at Caesarea. Other women prophesied at Corinth, while Eunice, Timothy's mother and Lois, his grandmother, are remembered for their faith.

To explore further...

To move on
➜ Gospels

See also
➜ David; Isaac
➜ Jacob; Mary
➜ Ruth; Sarah

INDEX

Aaron	69, 80, 125
Abel	45
Abigail	49
Abraham	**16**, 41, 61, 70, 82, 118, 119, 172
Absalom	51
Acts of the Apostles	**18**, 31, 33, 77, 134, 136
Adam	44, 126, 138, 177
Ahab	62, 65
Ahaziah	65
Ahijah	179
Alexandria	54
Amaziah	21
Amos	**20**, 149
Andrew	57, 101, 142
Antioches Epiphanes IV	47
Apocalypse: see Revelation (Book of)	
Apocrypha	30, 33
Apostles	57
Aquila	117, 187
Ark of the Covenant	50, 106, 154
Asherah	35, 62, 80, 109
Assyria	**22**
Assyrians	108
Augustus	97
Azariah	46

Baal	35, 62, 63, 80, 109
Babel	**24**, 26
Babylonia	**26**, 54
Babylonians	23, 48, 66, 74, 108, 109
Baptism	100
Barabbas	133
Bartholomew	57
Baruch	89
Bathsheba	51
Beersheba	152
Benjamin	104, 105, 111, 174
Bethel	20, 21, 152, 170
Bethlehem	48, 97, 165
Betrayal (of Jesus)	132
Bible	**28**
Bishops	37
Burnt offerings	153

Cain	45
Cana	121
Canaan	**34**, 60, 152
Canaanites	16, 34
Capernaum	142
Carchemish	89
Cephas	148
Chronicles 1 and 2	33
Church	**36**, 18, 141, 187
Circumcision	67, 155
Claudius	117
Clement of Rome	135
Colossians (Letter to the)	117
Commandments	**38**, 53, 69, 138, 166
Cornelius	143
Corinthians (Letter to the)	117, 156
Covenant	**40**, 127, 138, 176
Creation	**42**
Cross: see Passion	
Crucifixion: see Passion	
Cyrus' decree	91

Damascus	134
Dan	113, 152
Daniel	**46**, 33, 160
David	**48**, 90, 108, 110, 150, 158, 165, 171, 174, 175
Deacons	19, 37
Deborah	112
Decalogue: see Commandments	
Delilah	184
Desert	**52**, 69
Deuteronomy	32
Diaspora	**54**, 18, 67, 159, 180
Dinah	185
Disciples	**56**
Domitian	160

Easter	**58**
Ecclesiastes (or the Preacher)	33
Egypt	**60**, 122, 123, 124, 125
Elephantine	54
Eli	170
Elijah	**62**, 64, 100

188

Elisha	**64**, 185
Elizabeth	120, 185
Emmaus	157
Ephesians (Letter to the)	117
Ephesus	54
Epistles: see Letters	
Esau	86, 87
Esther	33, 184
Eucharist	132, 157
Eunice	187
Eve	44, 126, 138
Exile	**66,** 54, 74, 168
Exodus	**68**, 32
Ezekiel	32, 67, 149, 160
Ezra	33, 159

Faith **70**
Flood 126
Forgiveness: see Sin

Galatians (Letter to the) 143, 117
Gallio 117
Gamaliel 18, 134
Garden of Eden 44
Genesis 32
Gethsemane 132
Gibeah 152
Gideon 78, 113
Gilgal 152, 170
God **72**
Gods 24, 27, 35, 61, 80, 152
Golden calf 69, 70, 80
Goliath 48
Gomorrah 118
Goshen 105
Gospels **76**, 31, 33

Hagar 172, 173
Haman 184
Hammurabi 26
Hananiah 46
Hannah 170, 185
Haran 16, 83, 87
Hebrews (Letter to the) 31, 116, 117
Hebron 49
Herod 91, 97, 129, 162
Hezekiah 108, 111
Holofernes 184
Holy Spirit **78**, 36, 121, 141

Horeb	63, 124
Hosea	65, 111, 149
Hulda	109, 185

Idolatry **80**, 108, 109, 155
Isaac **82**, 86, 173
Isaiah **84**, 22, 32, 108, 111, 149
Ishmael 172, 173

Jabin 112
Jacob **86**, 61, 104, 110
Jairus' daughter 186
James 57, 116, 156
James son of Alphaeus 57
Jehoiakim 88, 109
Jehoram 65
Jehu 65
Jephthah 78, 185
Jeremiah **88**, 32, 109, 149
Jericho 106
Jeroboam 21, 179
Jerome 31
Jerusalem **90**, 50, 130, 178, 179, 182
Jesse 48, 165
Jesus **92**, 58, 75, 96, 130, 156
Jesus' birth **96**
Jezebel 62, 65
Jezreel 65
Job **98**, 33
Joel 22
John: see Disciples, Gospels, John the Baptist, Letters, Revelation
John the Baptist **100**, 56, 92, 185
Jonah **102**
Jonathan 175
Jordan 106
Joseph **104**, 87
Joseph (father of Jesus) 48, 96
Joshua **106**, 32
Josiah **108**, 61, 88, 111, 155, 185
Jubilee 167, 169
Judah (a land, a tribe, a kingdom) **110**, 49, 184
Judas 57, 93, 132
Jude 31, 116
Judges **112**, 32, 78
Judith 184
Justice: see Law

Kingdom of God 59, 100, 121, 128
Kings 32

Laban	87
Lamentations	33
Last Supper	41, 132
Law and justice	**114**, 41
Law (God's): see Torah	
Lazarus	59, 186
Leah	87
Lebanon	182
Letters	**116**, 31, 33
Levi	111
Leviticus	32
Lois	187
Lord's Prayer	146, 147
Lot	**118**
Luke	18, 33, 76, 77, 100, 120, 132
Luther, Martin	31
Lydia of Philippi	187
Manasseh	108
Marduk	26, 27, 109
Mark	33, 76, 77, 130, 132, 133
Martha	186
Mary (mother of Jesus)	**120**, 79, 96
Mary (sister of Martha and Lazarus)	186
Mary Magdalene	157, 186
Matthew	33, 57, 76, 77, 132
Matthias	57
Megiddo	88
Mesopotamia	26
Messiah	48, 53, 76, 95, 97, 110, 115, 121, 142, 185
Michal	50, 175
Midian	113, 123
Miriam	184, 185
Mishael	46
Mizpah	152, 170, 174
Moab	164
Monarchy	171
Moses	**122**, 38, 69, 72, 140, 184
Nabal	49
Nahum	23
Naomi	164
Nathan	51, 148
Nathanael	101
Nazareth	92, 96, 169
Nebuchadnezzar II	27, 66, 89
Necho	88
Nehemiah	33, 159

New Testament	30, 31, 33
Nineveh	23, 102, 103
Nisan	58
Noah	**126**, 41
Numbers	32
Nun	106
Oaks of Mamre	152
Obed	165
Old Testament	30, 32
Ophrah	152
Palestine	52, 54
Papyrus	29
Parables	**128**, 103
Parchment	29
Passion	**130**
Passover	58, 109, 125, 130, 131
Paul	**134**, 19, 31, 37, 57, 71, 116, 143, 156, 177, 187
Paul's journeys	**136**
Peace	**138**
Pentateuch	30, 39
Pentecost	**140**, 36, 79, 143
Persians	158
Pesah: see Passover	
Peter	**142**, 31, 57, 101, 116, 117, 135, 156
Pharisees	77, 129, 134, 169
Philemon	117, 135
Philip	57, 101, 187
Philippians (Letter to the)	117
Philistines	48, 49, 113
Phoenicians	34, 62, 182
Plagues of Egypt	125
Pompey	162
Prayer	**144**
Preacher: see Ecclesiastes	
Presbyters	37
Priscilla	32, 117, 187
Promised Land	16, 34, 52, 69, 106
Prophecy	**148**
Prophets	30, 32
Proverbs	33
Psalms	**150**, 33, 48, 66, 144, 147
Puah	184
Purim	33
Qumran	29, 100
Queen of Sheba	178, 184

Rachel	87, 104
Rahab	106, 184
Rainbow	127
Ramah	170
Rebekah	83, 86
Rehoboam	179
Religious life	**152**
Repentance: see Sin	
Resurrection	59
Resurrection appearances	**156**
Return	**158**
Revelation (Book of)	**160**, 27, 31, 33
Romans (Letter to the)	117
Rome	**162**, 54
Ruth	**164**, 33
Sabbath	**166**, 42, 67, 155, 181
Sadducees	133
Saints	37
Salvation	21
Samaria	23, 54, 110, 159, 187
Samson	78, 113, 184
Samuel	**170**, 48, 174
Samuel 1 and 2	32
Sanhedrin	18
Sarah	**172**, 16, 17, 82
Saul	**174**, 48, 49, 171
Saul of Tarsus: see Paul	
Septuagint	30, 31, 33
Shabbat: see Sabbath	
Shavuot	33, 140
Shechem	107, 152, 179, 185
Shema	80, 144, 145, 181
Sheshbazzar	158
Shiloh	152, 170
Shiprah	184
Shunem	185
Simon (called Peter): see Peter	
Simon the Zealot	57
Sin	**176**
Sinai	32, 38, 40, 69, 140, 154
Sodom	118, 119
Solomon	**178**, 90, 155, 182
Song of Songs	33
Stephen	19
Synagogue	**180**
Synoptic Gospels: see Gospels	

Tabernacle	154
Tabitha	187
Talmud	54
Tamar	184, 185
Tarsus	54, 134
Tekoa	20
Temple (in Jerusalem)	**182**, 35, 36, 47, 84, 90, 108, 109, 121, 131, 155, 158, 163, 178
Ten Commandments: see Commandments	
Thessalonians (Letter to the)	117
Thessalonica	54
Thomas	57
Timothy	117
Tishbe	62
Titus (Emperor)	29
Titus (Letter to)	117
Torah	30, 32, 39, 46, 55, 67, 93, 118, 138
Tower of Babel: see Babel	
Translation	31
Tyre	182
Unleavened bread	58, 125
Ur	16
Uriah	51
Uzziah	84
Vulgate	30, 31
Wailing Wall	183
Whitsun: see Pentecost	
Wine	41
Women in the Bible	**184**, 43, 56, 156
Word (of God)	28, 70, 78
Writings	30, 33
YHWH (Tetragram)	72, 73, 74
Yobhel	167
Zechariah	130
Zerubbabel	158
Ziggurat	26
Zipporah	123